"Torie Osborn has written a vivid and passionate account of one of the great contemporary liberation movements, as well as a guide to an effective political strategy. Her vision of a new style of leadership should be used as a blueprint by all groups who suffer from 'oppression sickness.' Finally, she manages to teach straight America a crucial lesson by describing the gifts of wisdom and of difference that gay America brings to the national table."

—NAOMI WOLF,
author of The Beauty Myth *and* Fire with Fire

"Civil rights has a new heroine in Torie Osborn, and a new platform in her historic call for America's invisible gay and lesbian communities to come out of hiding and teach America the meaning and joy of justice. In a brilliantly conceived, deeply ethical memoir, Osborn has crafted an appeal for all Americans—gay and straight alike—to embrace hope. When a story is told this well, it demands to be read. And when the truth is told this lovingly, it is irresistible."

—MARY FISHER,
AIDS activist and author of My Name Is Mary

"Torie Osborn's *Coming Home to America* brings us all home—out of ignorance, fear, and isolation to understanding, compassion, and community. It is crucial reading for those who are straight and believe that love is a country club with membership restricted to folks just like them."

—BARBARA LAZEAR ASCHER,
author of Landscape with Gravity

"Torie Osborn has given us a gem. This book glows with the positive energy and tough thinking that lesbians and gay men in all our diversity need to realize our potential to be forces for transformation in U.S. society."

—CHARLOTTE BUNCH,
director, Center for Women's Global Leadership, Rutgers University

"Torie Osborn, one of America's most experienced gay leaders, has given us a lively, provocative, and passionate vision of what gays and lesbians have the power to achieve, to shape a better future for themselves and the country."

—MITZI HENDERSON, *president of P-FLAG*

"Torie Osborn is a masterful storyteller who weaves the true-to-life tales of lesbian women and gay men and their friends and families, as well as her own, to give us a book that is must-reading for anyone who wishes to work for the freedom of all citizens."
—REV. TROY D. PERRY, *founder of the Universal Fellowship of Metropolitan Community Churches*

"*Coming Home to America* is a warm and readable book, invaluable for all those who want to help shepherd a progressive movement in the next millennium."
—PHILL WILSON,
founder of the National Black Gay and Lesbian Leadership Forum

"*Coming Home to America* illuminates the bold face of gay and lesbian courage. Moving testimony by dozens of Americans amplifies the voice of a movement that continues to change the world."
—HOLLY NEAR,
singer and songwriter

"Osborn has a gift for igniting passion and political action in others. With *Coming Home to America*, she will affect a whole generation of gay Americans."
—ELIZABETH BIRCH,
executive director, Human Rights Campaign

"Brimming with human interest, verve, and humor, delicious difference and surprise, this is a book to cherish and to share with lovers and families, friends and enemies. Torie Osborn's visionary work is a compelling reminder of how much we Americans have in common despite our diversity, and it shows us how to stake our claims on the promise and hope of American democracy."
—ROBERT DAWIDOFF,
co-author of Created Equal

"In gripping fashion, Torie Osborn makes many points clearly and persuasively about the power of coming out and of active involvement in the organized gay community. This book holds the reader's rapt attention from beginning to end, while teaching invaluable lessons."
—FRANKLIN E. KAMENY,
longtime gay activist

COMING HOME
TO AMERICA

COMING HOME TO AMERICA

A Roadmap to

Gay & Lesbian

Empowerment

Torie Osborn

St. Martin's Press ★ New York

Lyrics from the songs "Simply Love" (Hereford Music, © 1986), "Wrap the Sun Around You" (Hereford Music, © 1981), and "The Rock Will Wear Away" (music by Meg Christian; Hereford Music, © 1977), reprinted by permission of Holly Near.

Design by Richard Oriolo

Library of Congress Cataloging-in-Publication Data

Osborn, Torie.
    Coming home to America : a roadmap to gay and lesbian empowerment / by Torie Osborn. — 1st ed.
        p.   cm.
    ISBN 0-312-14572-1
    1. Gay men—United States—Social conditions.   2. Gay men—United States—Political activity.   3. Lesbians—United States—Social conditions.   4. Lesbians—United States—Political activity.   5. Coming out (Sexual orientation)—United States.   6. Social action—United States.   7. Social change—United States.   I. Title.
HQ76.3.U5082   1996
306.76´6´0973—dc20   96-20378
                                                                                              CIP

First Edition: October 1996

10   9   8   7   6   5   4   3   2   1

For Sheila Kuehl:

Always in my heart

ACKNOWLEDGMENTS

This book has traveled a long distance. I want to gratefully acknowledge the fine craft and warm encouragement (and great wit) of my wonderful editor at St. Martin's Press, Keith Kahla. His belief in this book and supreme expertise guided it home.

The amazing Jed Mattes, good friend and literary agent, helped me through the roughest stretches and gave the book some important shaping at critical junctures.

Lauren Jardine and her laser mind served this project brilliantly as friend, reader, editor, organization maven, and great believer in its worth. *Coming Home to America* would not exist without her.

Nor would it exist without Sheila James Kuehl, my dearest friend and family in the world, who gave unstintingly of her time and attention, reading and rereading the manuscript during the past two years, even in the middle of two campaigns for the California Assembly. This book and I owe her an infinite debt.

Ellen Malcolm gave me friendship and love during the year I spent birthing this book. It meant more to me than words can express.

My mother, Michelle Osborn, a beautiful writer and excellent editor, lent me the great gift of her creative mind and helped this work immeasurably. My father, O'Neill Osborn, was a strong cheerleader for my work, as always, and a sharp and insightful reader, raising tough questions I needed to hear.

The rest of my family of origin gave much-appreciated support: Hugh Osborn and Claudia Wallis, Madeleine, Nat, and Alice; Ann Osborn; Julie Osborn and Paul Randall, and Leah.

The Los Angeles Gay and Lesbian Community Services Center was the source, the inspiration, the seedbed of much of the thinking and work reflected in this book; I will always be grateful for the five years during which I had the honor of working there.

The whole team at St. Martin's Press was a joy to work with: Mikel Wadewitz, editorial assistant; Evan Gaffney, jacket designer; Charles Rue Woods, creative director; John Karle, publicist; John Murphy, publicity director; and Robert Cloud, production editor. A special thanks to the awesome Jolanta Benal, copy editor, as well as to my media and marketing mavens Bob Witeck and Wes Combs, and tour-booker-extraordinaire, Michele Karlsberg.

My wonderful readers saw early or late versions of some or all of the manuscript and gave me much-needed guidance: Mario Cooper, Ellen Malcolm, Linda Garnets, Luke Adams, John D'Emilio, Mary Fisher, Marj Plumb, Emily Blake, Patricia Bostleman, JoLynne Worley, Lorri Jean, Jim Heynan, Joanie Parker, David Smith, Michael Kearns, Donna Jenson, Susan Kennedy, and Robert Dawidoff.

The genius of Pacy Markman, political and creative consultant, gave me the metaphor that shaped my 1993 March on Washington speech and then this book: "We're coming home, America."

Two writer-mentors deeply believed in me and this book; both died of AIDS too soon to see the full manuscript: my beloved friend Paul Monette, who told me the last time we spoke, "Follow your passions and everything will be perfect," and Randy Shilts, who drummed into me the vital importance of the outline.

Special thanks to the hundreds of people whose stories are the heart and soul of this book. Those stories have been my inspiration over the course of two and a half decades of advocacy and organizing work around the country as an "out" lesbian. Some of you have no idea that I mentally filed away your touching or sad or empowering anecdote after a quick, serendipitous chat at a party, a conference, or a lecture, or perhaps during a conversation about something else entirely. Unfortunately, not knowing I would be writing about you, I have forgotten too many of your names, and sometimes the exact city where we met. I have tried to be as accurate as memory allows, but details are bound to be wrong. For these failings, please forgive me. In particular, I thank the people who inspired some of the more detailed stories in the book, or who gave me important background information: Meg Biddle, Marcia Perry, and

Celia Perry; Holly Gunner; Tim Sweeney; Tina Podlodowski; Sheila Kuehl; Rob Roberts; Michael Kearns; Robin Gagos Dengá and Tracie Warden Dengá and Tracie's mom, Linda Warden; Charlene Orchard; Linda Garnets; and Connie Norman. You are all, named and unnamed, my heroes and heroines.

My mentors and teachers so far in this life have each given me something that lives in this work: Dorothy Healey, Steve Early, Ken Dawson, Holly Near, Anne and Russell Near, Charlotte Bunch, John D'Emilio, Sheila Kuehl, Sally Fisher, Ann Osborn, Deborah Johnson, David Mixner, Sean Strub, Karen Siteman, Phill Wilson, Robin Tyler, Richard Rouilard, Niles Merton and David Russell, Patricia Pynchon, Michael Kearns, Margie Adam, and friends of Bill W.

Finally, I must acknowledge with deep gratitude the incomparable genius of Gabe Kruks (1950–1992), brilliant national advocate for gay and lesbian youth, AIDS and social-services planner, lobbyist, poet, carpenter, architect, engineer, filmmaker, electrician, gourmet cook, helicopter pilot, and about a zillion other things. Gabe was one of my closest friends, and he spent years pushing me to write a book. He died of AIDS before this one was born, but he has guided it, for the following reason: at a rough, very early stage of this book's development, when I was having trouble pulling the outline together, I was using a creative-visualization technique for inspiration. In the middle of a meditation, Gabe (who had died a year earlier) suddenly appeared to me, luminous and utterly himself: chunky, short, and strong; dressed as he always loved best, in an old white T-shirt with his belly hanging over ragged blue jean cutoffs; curly brown hair too long and a bit messy; that crooked, warm smile filled with irony; those deep brown eyes, with love. He walked out of some woods, came right up close to me, and said, clear as a bell: "Torie, you must build your book like a youth shelter—practical *and* visionary." I have tried my absolute best to honor his direction, although Gabe himself was always the practical and visionary one, I'm afraid.

If this book succeeds in any way, it is because of all the people mentioned above, but most of all it is because Gabe's spirit was watching over its creation.

CONTENTS

INTRODUCTION

April 25, 1993. The crowd was an endless, shimmering sea of people and rainbow flags that stretched out beyond the horizon. That sunny day, under a brilliant azure sky, 850,000 gay men and lesbians, along with friends, families, and allies, marched, chanted, and danced together, shouting themselves hoarse and feeling alive with a passionate sense of possibility. Our moment in history had arrived. The crowd's energy pulsated across the stage as I stood waiting for my turn to speak; hope was palpable in the air.

Standing on that stage, I flashed back to the two earlier gay rights marches. Seventy-five thousand of us rallied in October 1979, but it was a stealth gathering that few others were even aware of. In October 1987, a phenomenal 600,000 of us came together. Thousands were arrested in militant AIDS protests across Washington; a mass wedding celebrated hundreds of our committed relationships. Following the 1987 march, chapters of ACT UP (AIDS

Coalition to Unleash Power), P-FLAG (Parents, Families and Friends of Lesbians and Gays), and GLAAD (Gay and Lesbian Alliance Against Defamation) sprang to life in cities all across the nation. But there was almost no coverage of the march in the mainstream media, so most of the world never heard about one of the largest, most energetic civil rights demonstrations in American history.

This day was different. By any measure this march was a triumph; not only were we nearly a million strong, but the mainstream media were omnipresent. The 1993 gay and lesbian March on Washington was beamed into American living rooms everywhere. This was *our* year, it seemed—as if gays and lesbians had suddenly emerged from society's shadows, our lives and our issues bursting forth into the dazzling sunlight of public attention. As I took my place at the podium that day, I felt a part of a new and promise-filled moment in history. America's outcasts were finally coming home, from the margins to the mainstream.

But that optimism and buoyancy were not to last.

The crushing defeat on the gays-in-the-military issue a few months later quickly eclipsed our moment in the bright April sun. The political pessimism that followed spread through the gay and lesbian community like a dense, dark rain cloud. We had mobilized for Bill Clinton with an outpouring of grassroots enthusiasm never before seen in our community, and now our loss left us mired in confusion and deep discouragement that have dominated the mood of the gay community ever since. Even the 1996 Supreme Court victory—the historic 6–3 pro-gay-rights decision striking down Colorado's Amendment 2—was overshadowed by the ugly storm of homophobia generated that political season by allies and enemies alike about the gay marriage issue.

The 1993 failure on the military issue also set in glaring relief other weaknesses of the gay and lesbian community that remain core challenges today: we being outspent and outspun by a powerful radical right, whose influence on policymakers was strengthened by the widespread ignorance about gay and lesbian people. (*Newsweek* wrote in 1993 that only 43 percent of Americans reported even *knowing* someone gay.) It was also painfully clear that, as a movement, we were severely underdeveloped, with little capacity to mobilize large numbers of our own people, let alone others beyond the confines of the gay world. Worst of all, we lacked any coherent strategy or vision. There was little connection between local communities and national groups, and bitter infighting between and among key groups and individuals was sapping whatever constructive energy we had.

This book grew out of that sunny April day and its dark aftermath. I wanted to help counteract the confusion that has set in, because I see within the gay and lesbian community a wealth of talent and determination that, called forth, can truly change the world. I also believe that we have had too little opportunity to see ourselves clearly, with vision unblurred by homophobia and fear from within and without. Until we can grasp the full spectrum of our strengths, we will not be able to seize our potential power.

This is not an academic tome, but rather an informal weaving together of one longtime organizer's experiences. It is unabashedly a gay and lesbian movement cheerleader's attempt to inspire optimism during tough times. This book is not intended just for the longtime activists out there, but also for those who never *dreamed* of being activists, those who are newly out and those who are grappling with their closets or trying to find their place within the gay and lesbian community and the world at large. And it is written, with great love, for the many nongay family members and friends of the lesbian and gay community.

I have had the honor of being an activist for thirty years, and much of this book springs from the journey of my own life. In particular, it has grown out of thousands of conversations over those years with hundreds of people I've worked with, watched, listened to with awe, and learned from. Their stories populate this work because they animated my own life and my thinking. They are my heroes and heroines, and the themes of this book emerged from observing and admiring their real-life struggles and experiences.

I felt the need to write *Coming Home to America* partly because we live in a country with very little sense of history and continuity, particularly within and between social-change movements. Mostly, though, I wrote it because I believe we have been so busy these past couple of decades just fighting to survive in a world that still fears and hates us that we have not had sufficient chance to sense, to feel, to grasp, and to learn from the full weight of our collective successes and failures. Ours is a young movement for equality, and in order to travel forward most effectively, we must capture and understand the living, breathing energies and lessons of our own amazing lives. When we do, hope and empowerment will grow in great abundance.

We have traveled roads we never dreamed of to get to this place. We have faced agonizing abandonment by our families, unspeakable violence and bigotry, the horrors of our own closets, and far too much death and dying. But our odyssey has given rise to new strengths. We have found love and intimacy in greater measure than we ever imagined. We have even rewoven the fabric of spirituality, family, and community, and generated a new political potential for this country that is becoming our true home at last.

Once we take the time to honestly reflect on where we've been and where our experience has brought us, our movement for freedom will be powered with a startling and profound new vibrancy and direction. We will have to take some collective responsibility for our own failings, too, but, for the most part, this will be an inspiring and positive process of recognizing and naming our own tremendous vital strengths. In that which we have already built lies the blueprint of our future success; in the stuff of our daily lives, we can trace the best map to a brighter future.

My greatest hope for this book is that it will serve to hold up a mirror to a group of people I think are awe-inspiring. I hope that this mirror shines back some of the many ways that the ordinary lives of gay, lesbian, bisexual, and transgendered Americans—and their family and friends—have made them extraordinary. We are all on a journey, individually and collectively, and it is a journey that, I believe, has enormous significance. We who have been exiles from our families of birth and from mainstream society, are, at last, coming home from the outside—and the world will never be the same again. Our homecoming will, I believe, reveal the truth that the ultra-right most fears: that the people it demonizes in fact represent the very best of what America can be. Far from being immoral people, we are a highly ethical, thoughtful, caring, and extraordinarily talented people who quietly embody some of the very values that this country desperately needs to tap more vigorously: personal courage and honesty at all costs, self-reliance, community concern, love of family, spiritual depth, and a desire to help leave the world a better place.

On the morning after the 1993 March on Washington, I went for breakfast at a coffee shop near Dupont Circle. A group of young people sitting at the next table recognized me and called me over to join them, excited and bursting with talk. Eight high school juniors and seniors from Seattle, they were part of a contingent of thirty who had chartered a bus to come across the country to the march. They were four girls and four boys, white, black, Latino, and Asian, and I'll never forget their shining faces, bright eyes, and impassioned words. Their stories—and their diversity—reminded me of just how far we'd come: these eight kids (and most of the rest of the busload) had engaged in a communal coming-out rite in advance of their trip east, all telling their parents they were gay, lesbian, or bisexual on the same night, only three days before the bus was to leave. They giggled while telling me of the many interwoven phone calls to calm last-minute jitters that night; they sadly shared the story of two boys in their crowd who were immediately grounded and prevented from making the trek (several others were also grounded but decided to sneak out anyway). They all expressed no small amount of anxiety about returning home to Seattle and facing their parents. They threw a million questions at me and, during the two hours we talked back and forth, I came to see them as a kind of microcosm for our community: their diversity, their strong bonds with one another, their gutsiness and humor, their inherent power to change the circumstances of their own lives and to shape the world around them. Meeting them was one of the best moments of the 1993 March for me and I deeply regret losing the piece of paper on which they wrote their names. But their faces and their stories are unforgettable and many of their questions burned into my brain:

- What is the role of the individual's coming out in our big-picture political strategy?

- How do we move our activism from cynicism—or rage—to hope, and sustain it over the long term? How do we counteract our internal divisions?

- What exactly is the art of building community? And how do we translate that spirit into creating permanent institutions for future generations?

- What are the values that drive us, consciously and unconsciously, as we craft our culture, our communities, our movement? Do those values have relevance in the broader, nongay world?

Their questions are some of the central ones for the gay and lesbian movement, and *Coming Home to America* is my attempt to address them. I hope this book reaches those young people, wherever they are today, because in their fearless asking of the right questions lies our future. With their passion and determination, America will some day soon become a real home—a place of belonging and replenishment, of safety and empowerment—for *all* of its people.

Our journey home to America, like every other journey, both great and small, begins with a single first step. For us, that first step is coming out.

Coming Out: Coming Home to Ourselves

1. Coming Out Is Coming Home to Ourselves

Coming out of the closet is the first giant step to freedom. By consciously acknowledging that we are gay, lesbian, or bisexual, we share a fundamental truth about ourselves. For each of us, coming out is a complex and evolving story of self-discovery and acceptance that, over time, touches the lives of many people. But first, we must come out to ourselves.

It was a freezing cold January night in 1973. I was twenty-two years old, attending a women's conference in Vermont that I'd helped organize, and this was the final event at the huge old Victorian inn—a Saturday night dance featuring the feisty New England feminist rock band the Deadly Nightshade. Pushing open the door to the packed ballroom, I felt a rush of erotic energy generated by hundreds of women dancing together—an exhilarating energy that seemed to bounce off the walls. I suddenly felt embraced by that room, totally at home in that open lesbian environment.

That night I knew I couldn't pretend any longer. Despite several years of heterosexual dating (punctuated by some surreptitious lesbian affairs), I knew that I could no longer maintain the denial and internal conflict of passing as straight. Driving away from the dance on that icy night, alone in my car, I said out loud, for the first time, "I'm a lesbian." I remember that as I spoke those fateful words, I could see my breath swirling like white smoke in the cold air, and my voice seemed gigantic and booming. All of a sudden, I began to laugh wildly, with release and joy. Even today, I chuckle at the memory; that night is still utterly vivid, caught forever in time.

For me, walking into that lesbian dance meant finally stepping out of my own closet; it meant waking up inside, coming alive in some fundamental way, and connecting with something deeply, instinctively comfortable. For me, coming out meant setting off down a new path that altered the course of my life.

Coming Out Takes Personal Courage

Coming out is a journey. If we have begun that journey, we have experienced personal growth and satisfaction. We know the startling strength gained by telling others the truth about our lives, our desires, our love, and our pain. We know the struggle and the joy of triumphing over the invisibility, isolation, and exile that remain facts of life for too many gay people. We know the joy of friendships and family founded on real love and on the truth, not on hiding and hoped-for intimacy.

Society force-feeds us the poison of shame, and we grow our own closets, develop our own internalized homophobia. Coming out is the only antidote, the way to claim, or reclaim, our true selves and develop pride and confidence. Coming out to ourselves is the first step in our journey out of lonely exile; it frees our voices, our energies, and ultimately our most creative and empowered selves. Coming out is coming home to ourselves.

Coming out *always* takes a measure of personal courage. Every single time. In stark contrast to the lie that we are weak and immoral—the lie perpetrated by those who despise and fear us—the real daily lives of gay men and lesbians brim over with strength of character, responsibility-taking, and personal courage. As my friend the lesbian rabbi Denise Eger says: "What is the first foundation of true morality, of ethical conviction, if not personal honesty and courage?"

Coming out demands those strengths. I often think of Paul, a young man whose story seems a paradigm of the everyday bravery exhibited by gay men and lesbians in taking the critical, bold first step in coming out.

———

For over an hour Paul sat motionless in his father's battered old blue Buick, hands tensed on the steering wheel. For the third Friday in a row, he had borrowed the car to "go study at the library" and instead had driven fifty miles to Los Angeles from his suburban home, only to sit here in the car, frozen with fear. His eyes remained fixed on the sign at the front of the building before him: "The Los Angeles Gay and Lesbian Community Services Center" were words he was too afraid to say out loud.

A seventeen-year-old high-school senior in Calabasas, a conservative Southern California bedroom community, Paul read in a local alternative paper about the gay youth support group meeting Friday nights at the Center. This Friday he was determined to finally make it inside. Noting some laughing young people walking in the door who looked very much like kids at his own school, he found the strength to pry his hands from the wheel and get out of the car. He walked slowly toward the front door, heart drumming wildly. The Center's door felt heavy, leaden, but as he pulled it open and entered the warmly lit lobby, Paul felt a rush of relief. Then, with an unexpected surge of pride, he felt like Rocky, triumphant on top of those museum steps.

———

His soft green eyes flickering with remembered pride, Paul told me that story when I was the newly appointed director of the

Center. By then he was a twenty-four-year-old high-school math teacher, a confident and proudly open gay man. His story illustrates the kind of real-life triumph over fear demanded of every gay person who makes the decision to open the closet door and walk out.

Given the current level of social intolerance and ignorance of gay and lesbian life, coming out is still an incredibly brave act. In the course of the coming-out journey, gay people quell self-loathing to discover self-love, and face down contempt to find community and group affirmation against monumental odds. Even in our own community, we do not seem to name correctly, or honor sufficiently, this daily life bravery. Perhaps the marginalization of the gay world and the intensely individual nature of the coming-out experience have combined to block adequate recognition of the colossal courage displayed by lesbian and gay Americans every day. Are we too close to the struggle and the old pain to see how amazing we are? It's not an exaggeration to say that so-called average gay men and lesbians are unsung contemporary heroes and heroines in their own lives, and in a world where true personal courage and honesty are all too rare.

Our Coming-Out Stories: Queer Cultural Ritual

Most of us are somewhere along the journey of coming out. We know, to the marrow of our souls, that coming out is probably the experience most central to our lives because it is about our core identity. To acknowledge who we are, it is imperative for us to come out, because we are born invisible even to ourselves. We are born with a hidden identity and then raised and nurtured by people who deny—and sometimes express hostility to—our very existence. In no other minority do the members have this particular and peculiar experience of invisibility within their own birth families. When we discover and reveal who we are, these families may even reject us. The greatest punishment a culture can inflict on its members—the punishment of ostracism, of banishment from the tribe—is reserved for us alone. When we come out of the closet and acknowledge who we are, we risk becoming exiles from our own homes, banished in our own homeland.

Carrying with it both the exhilaration of newfound freedom and the fear of ostracism, the coming-out experience is weighted with enormous meaning to gay people. It is, in fact, a central and unifying event that bridges even great differences among us. Telling our coming-out stories—the funny stories of sudden and amazed self-recognition, the stories of apprehension and tough decisions, the joys of finding intimacy and love beyond words, the sweet and sour reactions of those we care about—is a unique bonding experience, a cultural folk ritual that transcends class, culture, age, race, and gender differences. The following happens every day in a hundred cities: two gay people of whatever cultural background run into each other at the laundry, the library, or the post office. One recognizes that the other is gay and strikes up a conversation. The first most likely question? "When did you come out?" The subsequent conversation, told in brief, coded paragraphs, may extend to coffee or lunch, creating a unique connection, often a memorable moment, and sometimes even a lifelong friendship.

On a first date, at dinner parties, in college dorm rooms, at rap groups, in virtually every social situation where gay people find each other or get to know each other, our coming-out story is the icebreaker, the common experience that unites us. We even celebrate National Coming Out Day every October 11 (commemorating our second March on Washington, in 1987) as an annual grassroots event, a ritualized remembrance of this most central aspect of our lives. On NCOD, I have attended "coming-out speak-outs" at which I was mesmerized for hours by the coming-out stories of gays and lesbians from every corner of life.

A trip to a gay bookstore anywhere in America will attest to the centrality of the coming-out experience. The shelves are lined with handbooks and how-tos galore on coming out to ourselves, our friends, our families, along with multiple volumes of first-person testimonies. My local gay and lesbian bookstore, Lambda Rising, in Washington, D.C., carries a line of greeting cards to congratulate friends on the occasion of their coming out to parents or co-workers. We seem never to tire of the staggering varieties on this common theme; it is a staple of our growing body of fiction, film, and art. There is even an unauthorized but commonly used Anglican ceremonial blessing specifically designed to celebrate coming out.

Coming out, however, is not a single fixed act. It is a dynamic, recurrent and complex process: a personal, psychological, and, inevitably, political process that continues throughout our lifetimes. There may be months or years between steps, but once we begin the process by coming out to ourselves, we begin a brave journey of continuous unfoldings. And none of us is ever alone in the process. New generations are constantly coming out to themselves and to others for the first time. Others are moving on to their next steps in the process.

And it all begins with each individual's brave first step of self-awareness and self-acknowledgment.

2. COMING OUT TO ONESELF: THE COMING-OUT "CLICK"

The building block for gay and lesbian freedom is the individual act of coming out to oneself. Although there are as many stories as there are gay people, and although the process is often difficult and slow, it usually involves discovery, whether instantaneous or slow. Many gays and lesbians report a full-color epiphany freeze-framed in time—an "aha" experience or experiences marking the inescapable realization that they are gay or lesbian. I call these moments coming-out clicks.

Sometimes the coming-out click involves specific verbal self-acknowledgment, the use of words: "I'm a lesbian" (or "I'm gay," or "I'm homosexual," or "I'm bisexual," or "I'm queer"). Sometimes the click is a deep feeling, without specific language, of being different in sexual identity or affectional preference. It can be joyful and liberating, or it can be an ambivalent experience—simultaneously freeing and shame-filled.

———

José remembers the first time he felt attracted to an older boy at school, while in second grade. The boy walked across the basketball court and José was flooded with attraction for him. With a flash of clarity and a rush of shame, he knew instinctively that his desire was taboo. He looked around quickly to see if anyone somehow had noticed the intensity of his feelings. He recalls wondering if, at that moment, he had suddenly physically changed, perhaps marked with a giant "HOMO" emblazoned on his forehead for all to see. He also recalls that there was plenty of surreptitious homosexual sex among school chums in locker rooms and elsewhere over the next few years, but he stayed far away because he was so afraid. "I can recall that one moment in vivid slow motion today. I suddenly knew I was gay. The other boys weren't, and their boyhood sex play wouldn't get them in trouble—but I knew mine would. It was experimental for them, but for me it was all too real."

Lauren's ten-year marriage was stalled—nothing dramatic, just a sad, slow drifting apart. By the time she was thirty, only the couple's two young girls were keeping the marriage together. Living in suburban Phoenix, Arizona, back in school working on her Ph.D. in women's studies, Lauren was normally a disciplined, efficient, and rapid researcher. However, she had inexplicably spent a whole three months of her dissertation research on what was to be a minor (eleven-page) section on lesbians. For those three months, her life felt oddly out of synch; she felt weird, as if drugged. One day, she walked out of the library after a ten-hour immersion in reading and photocopying and note-taking. The sunlit campus world seemed to be in Technicolor. Suddenly, feeling breathtakingly alive and inexplicably happy, she felt sexually drawn to every woman she saw, old or young. "Oh, my God, I'm a lesbian," she said out loud, startling herself even more than the group of students a few feet away.

Marty was an athletic, masculine farm boy from southern Indiana. He recalls one Thanksgiving Day when, as on every other holiday in his farming community, lots of friends and neighbors gathered together at his folks' house. In the hours before and after the big meal, the custom was strict gender separation—the men in the living room, watching football games on TV; the women in the kitchen, chatting and cooking and cleaning up. Marty vividly remembers the Thanksgiving when he was nine years old, and a sudden flash of panic and confusion enveloped him. He suddenly realized that he didn't want to be in the living room, yelling and backslapping and watching TV football with the beer-drinking men and boys; instead, his heart pulled him in the direction of the kitchen. There, the women were gossiping and telling stories about people in a homey environment of turkey and apple pie smells. "I'll never forget that moment. My boy's script took me in one direction; my true nature took me in another. I didn't have the word for it for a few years, but from that moment on I knew I was homosexual. I knew I looked and acted exactly like the other boys on the football field, but I knew inside I was totally different."

Jane was twenty-six years old, a graduate student in psychology at a major midwestern university. She had recently broken off a relationship with a man, and had begun to date a woman. One night, they went to the only bar in town that had one night a week for gay men and lesbians. Jane was on the dance floor with her date, and had what seemed like a "sudden jolt of lightning. I realized at that moment that I was bisexual, and it was okay. I know it sounds weird, to be at a gay bar and suddenly own being bisexual, but that was the turning point for me. After that, I got steadily more and more comfortable with my identity, and even with the somewhat awkward sense of not quite fitting into either the straight or gay worlds."

Jennifer and Diana were suburban Texas housewives and neighbors, best friends whose six kids played together and whose husbands were climbing the corporate ladder together at a major firm. For years the families shared vacations, hiking trips, holidays. One night on a camping trip, after a long moonlit walk, Diana and Jennifer looked into each other's eyes and found love beyond friendship. "I don't know why we didn't see it before, but that one night, in that one moment, our lives were permanently changed. We just 'got it' that we were in love with each other, and committed ourselves to being together," says Diana. The rest of the story was not simple, but it was "absolutely the only natural path for both of us, the only honest road to fulfillment," says Jennifer. It involved difficult divorces and child custody fights, but they've now been together for twenty-two years, during which they raised their six kids together and have built a successful advertising partnership. They are now helping raise their grandchildren.

Terence ignored some adolescent gay dreams and crushes on other male choir members at his church, and got married right out of high school. He and Marla had a daughter, whom he adored. The marriage was a good friendship with little passion. After several years of working at different jobs, Terence went back to school at night, at age thirty-one, to get a business degree. The first week he struck up a friendship with Jerome, a fellow student, also African-American, who came out to him the first time they had a drink together. Although he felt no specific attraction to Jerome, that evening in that dim and smoky bar Terence experienced a sudden rush of recognition. "I'm gay, too," he said quietly. As it turned out, Marla was very understanding; they stayed married for five more years until their daughter was in high school, and have remained good friends and "family" to each other over the years.

———

I myself had a series of coming-out clicks. I remember being nine years old and falling madly in love with Bonnie, my neighbor of about the same age. All seemed totally normal—in fact, I was ecstatically happy. Then, one day while Bonnie and I were playing together, her mother pulled her aside, narrowed her eyes in a stern look, and sharply rebuked her about seeing too much of me and being "abnormally involved." Clearly the elevated passions we felt for each other frightened Bonnie's mother. That fear was then passed on to me. After that scolding, a veil of self-doubt and shame descended. I began to hide my feelings about Bonnie from my own parents, feeling guilty, feeling I had to sneak out to play with her. Even worse, a few months later when her family moved away and she suddenly, without notice, left my life, I felt I had nowhere to turn to talk about my heartbreak. I can still feel that ache of loneliness today.

Years later, I had my second click. At age fifteen, after sharing a drunken sexual evening, a schoolmate and I fell asleep in each other's arms. I will never forget the look in her eyes the instant we woke up. The panic, the shame, and the guilt that flashed across her face bored right into my soul. It was the most intense moment of my life to that point. For months afterward I couldn't look directly at her. And, not coincidentally, the following weekend I determined to go out and get a boyfriend (which I did, at a coed pickup football game I regularly played on Saturdays).

My final and culminating coming-out click was on that fateful icy January night in Vermont, after I spent several confused years trying painfully hard to make it as a heterosexual. I liked men well enough, and had one serious relationship, but knew all along that something was missing in my life. Finally, within the context of a lesbian-positive feminist counterculture in the early seventies, that self-acknowledgment at twenty-two felt joyfully liberating.

For me those three "click" moments marked a full circle: natural lesbian childhood joy smashed into caution and secrecy and hiding; the growing terror of sexual shame; and, finally, the return of joy with the adult freedom of self-acknowledgment.

3. HOMOPHOBIA'S WEAPON: THE POWERFUL CLOSET

As it was for me, coming out to oneself is often a dual experience: liberation from lies and denial is compounded with a sense of shame or fear. A flash of clarity is often followed immediately by the crash of reality—of knowing intuitively that the truth must inexorably bring with it fear or guilt or shame that society has bequeathed us. Gays and lesbians are socialized like everyone else. We internalize heterosexism—the presumption of heterosexuality's dominance and superiority—in addition to homophobia—fear and hatred of homosexuality—just as nongay people do. Lesbians in particular also play out the potent social script of "compulsory heterosexuality" (the lesbian poet Adrienne Rich's term), which pushes women automatically toward their roles as heterosexual wife and mother.

Just as I jumped right into a reflexive hunt for a boyfriend after my first sexual lesbian experience, gays and lesbians often thwart their true desires and stifle their true selves and their relationships to others. I spent years trying hard to be happy as a heterosexual before my final coming-out click. I desperately didn't want to be a lesbian and tried incredibly hard to find the right boyfriend, someone who could "fix" me. I had one serious relationship with a man who remains a friend, but I can still recall my bitter nighttime tears of disappointment at the lack of sexual satisfaction, my anger and disillusionment at the lack of emotional fulfillment, the purposeful trying and trying and trying—and always failing—to truly connect. I remember convincing my boyfriend to sleep with a housemate, a woman *I* secretly desired, and taking guilty, vicarious pleasure out of it.

I remember the awkwardness and loneliness of not fitting in to the straight dating world—the now-embarrassing things I did, such as coming on to men with whom I really wanted only to be buddies. I spent six long years trying hard to feel right as a heterosexual, hating myself, hiding my dreams and fantasies from friends, stealing drunken same-sex kisses and caresses, and parading boyfriends home for Thanksgiving while suffering unrequited crushes on women friends. A young life in the closet is a life of self-doubt, in which deep yearnings are never fulfilled.

The knowledge of our potential social ostracism and exile from society's mainstream is imprinted early on our souls, and gives rise to the all-powerful closet. Every gay person believes that defying heterosexual norms will lead to pain, rejection, loss of family and friends, and limitations on career and social status. In the past, this internalization of negative social attitudes—and our subsequent closeted lives—led many of us to suicide and drug and alcohol abuse, low self-esteem, difficulty with intimacy, sabotage of long-term relationships, and all too many fragmented and stunted lives at the margins of society. Thanks to the twin transformative forces of gay liberation and a new wave of feminism over the past thirty years, those once common stories are finally changing.

Although the closet's stranglehold on our lives is steadily loosening, it remains homophobia's basic weapon. What is this powerful force that has ruled so many gay lives, that still throttles too many of us, psychologically and spiritually?

The closet is unique. This institution dominating millions of people's real daily lives is, in fact, a metaphor—a metaphor for denial and hiding. Although traditionally associated to some extent with the notion of privacy, the closet is a fascinating and extraordinarily potent force that is, quite simply, a structured lie. Coming out of the closet, then, shatters the lie—breaks silence—and begins the truth-telling that leads to the possibility of a sane and happy life.

Permanent Closets

For some people, particularly those who are now in their sixties and older and grew up before the rise of the modern gay movement (let alone this contemporary era of vastly increased visibility), the closet seems to be a permanent, immutable fixture. Internalized shame about being gay rules their daily life. They simply cannot come out and be comfortable. They've spent decades carefully constructing compartmentalized lives of secrecy, limiting openness to gay bars or a small friendship circle. The closet is a compulsive and habitual part of their reality, like a permanent addiction, and leaving it would be unimaginably disruptive. Theirs are stunted lives led in silence.

I had a gay uncle, very typical of his generation, who died last year at age eighty. During his entire career he worked for the Navy in a civilian desk job, retiring at fifty-five. Needless to say, he was in the closet at work. He made no formal pretense of heterosexuality; his life was simply never talked about in our family. Once, after I came out of my own closet, he opened up privately to me, and I discovered he actually had a certain pride about his friends who were more "out" than he—successful gallery owners and artists in the Honolulu and San Francisco gay men's communities of the 1970s. I discovered that he had carefully put together quite a collection of photographs and letters documenting his (and my) family's gay history, as exemplified by his first cousin, who had died of cancer in her forties, and who had engaged in a happy, twenty-year-long lesbian relationship.

His attitude toward the hidden nature of his own life, however, was a stark contrast. He was totally rigid and unquestioning about his closet. He knew coming out meant he would lose his job with the Navy. Most of his friends were straight. He was matter-of-fact and accepting about his fate, once telling me curtly: "I was born in the closet and I'll die in the closet." From my uncle I learned that there is a vast limbo between "passing" as heterosexual and openly acknowledging you're gay—a land occupied by thousands of lesbians and gay men before today's greater freedom was possible. Many lesbians and gay men don't actually marry or try to pass as heterosexual but never breathe a word about their often fascinating gay lives. Men and women like Uncle Harold, whose silence cloaks a secret life, were the forerunners of the "Don't ask, don't tell" military policy. From Uncle Harold's example, I learned about the concept of the "glass closet." It was clear to me that many people could guess about Uncle Harold's sexuality: his occasional campiness coupled with his solitary and secretive life would have clued in anyone who paid attention. There are lots of gay people like him who think others don't know they're gay or lesbian. In truth, their personal style, or their transgression of traditional gender roles, or their long-term same-sex partner clearly reveals their sexual orientation to coworkers or neighbors. This is especially true today, now that the gay and lesbian issue has come out of *its* closet. Still, closeted gay people maintain the fiction to themselves that no one knows.

The cost of Uncle Harold's closet, however deep his own denial, was painfully obvious to those who knew him: he was a lonely, scared, sad man. He never had a relationship that lasted longer than a few months; in his later years, he was preyed upon by a young man who showed up periodically to salve my uncle's loneliness in return for several thousand dollars of his modest savings. He lived his whole life as a guilty, self-loathing Catholic, confessing his "sin" weekly. He was trapped by history in a closet he would never leave.

Fortunately, many older gays and lesbians *are* able to break down that closet door late in life. One such heartwarming story was told at an open-microphone town hall speak-out on National Coming Out Day a few years ago in Los Angeles:

As she stepped to the microphone to tell her story, Sally proudly announced she was sixty-eight. Some fifty years before, she had fallen in love with her best girlfriend in high school in Topeka, Kansas. For two years they enjoyed a blissful but closeted sexual and emotional relationship, parting ways to go off to college, unusual as that was for women of modest means in those days. They stayed in touch for a few years through their respective college careers, got married, moved to separate cities, had kids, and eventually lost contact with each other. Sally became a nurse, raised her kids, went to work full-time, and got divorced a decade later. Barbara became a teacher and led a parallel life of kids, career, divorce. Then Sally found Barbara at a high school reunion, where they fell in love again, at age sixty-four, and have been together ever since. As Sally told this story, she choked up, relating the fulfillment of finding the "one great love of my life" again after a half-century of separation. She repeated her urgent message over and over: "Follow your heart," she said. "Don't do what we did. Don't deny yourself the life you really want. You can have kids. You can raise a family. It's tougher, but you can't have real meaning and true love in your life unless you come out."

Partial Closets: Living "Half In / Half Out"

Every gay man, lesbian, and bisexual knows all too well the contours of the closet. And we know that the closet can be a fluid and changeable thing. Even my Uncle Harold—who self-identified as totally closeted—eventually used the word "gay" about himself once at dinner at my parents' house. Over time many gay people negotiate different relationships with the closet in different spheres of their lives. They slice up daily life into compartments, choosing one area of their life in which to come out and get support while leaving the closet intact in other areas. I have a friend who is closeted at her new job in a dental office and to her parents, but totally out at her Episcopal church, where she is very active. Some folks are comfortably out to neighbors but not to brothers and sisters. Some share their lives with grandparents but stay closeted to parents and friends.

Richard, thirty-four, a successful child psychiatrist in Baltimore who was out to most of his professional colleagues, was convinced for fifteen years that his parents, divorced and living separately, couldn't possibly handle the fact of his homosexuality. "My weekly Sunday phone call home to Mom became harder and harder over the years, as if literally weighed down by the pack of lies I'd told over so long a time—the dates that didn't really happen, the girlfriends I hadn't had. And my conversations with my father, my greatest mentor and friend, were increasingly filled with awful awkward silences. I kept

my identity a secret from them while leading a flourishing professional and personal life out of the closet. In fact, I was convinced I'd
be responsible for my mother's death, literally—by heart attack or
stroke—if I came out. I made a sort of peace with that existence. I
simply saw no other way."

Roberta, forty-five, was out to her working-class Italian Indianapolis
family but closeted at work. "I actually felt fine, not conflicted at all,
being closeted at work for eighteen years climbing the corporate ladder. It's just the way it was. My family knew, and included Vicky in
holidays; our neighbors knew, but the line was drawn at the office
door. I learned how to survive my reputation as a solitary loner, who
never talked about what was in fact a rich and wonderful family life.
I carried precious pictures in my wallet of kids of lesbian friends I
godparented, but didn't feel I could share them on the job. For some
reason, I lived perfectly comfortably that way for a very long time,
much to the annoyance of my more out friends."

———

What's interesting is that this half-in / half-out existence often
changes over time. The closet is a shape-shifting phenomenon; the
"out" spheres broaden over time, the closet shrinks. Richard says,
"For years my partial closet remained in place. Then, at some point,
my own tolerance for it diminished. I realized I was afraid of ghosts,
and got over myself. So I came out to Dad—it was wonderful, tears
and laughter and mushy connection all the way—but I stayed closeted to Mom for another two years."

Roberta's closet also narrowed after nearly twenty years, as her
confidence and professional status grew: "I edged into it, I admit. I
remember slowly realizing the closet had become a bad habit I no
longer needed; in fact, it was working against me. I felt it diminished
my leadership capacities as a manager. So, I spent a busy month
coming out to everyone I worked with in my department. What
struck me the most was how a state of mind I'd accepted for literally decades suddenly seemed needless, even silly. I didn't, however,
come out to other department heads for another year. Like a large
moving cloud, my closet changed as I did."

Making our peace with our partial closets can seem utterly

functional and necessary at one time in our life, in order to keep jobs, family, friends. Then, at another time, it becomes superfluous, due to our own personal growth or new political or social openness. Our intuition will usually guide us to that moment of truth when personal courage finally can kick in, and we can narrow or entirely eliminate the closet from another section of our life.

Other Closets

The struggle to overcome the shame that has stunted gay lives for centuries is becoming a universal metaphor. The phrase "coming out of the closet" has now entered popular jargon and is used daily on television talk shows about overcoming private guilt or silence about a whole range of previously taboo or unpopular issues. People testify regularly about "coming out" as Buddhists, about having hidden tattoos or secret talents, about surviving domestic violence or sexual abuse, and more. "You're only as sick as your secrets" is a slogan of the huge addiction-recovery movement, and people who participate regularly in Twelve-Step meetings hear "coming out" stories of all kinds explicitly using that closet image.

In part, this reflects a broad social "click"—a recognition that silence and invisibility can, indeed, equal death, the death by smothering of one's own real self. For this reason, it is understandable that gay men and lesbians have been at the forefront of identifying and bringing forward many social issues previously hidden or considered shameful. In some measure, being locked behind one closet door sensitizes us to the existence of others. Once we break silence about our own lives and face our private truths squarely, many of us are drawn to work on other similarly taboo issues. I know several lesbian therapists, for example, who specialize in working with incest survivors. Gay men and lesbians continue to be the ground troops fighting AIDS, which remains stigmatized primarily because of its popular association with homosexuality.

For some, the doors open on these other issues first. Countless gay and lesbian advocates who are people of color cut their activist teeth fighting for civil rights in the 1960s. Many of the lesbians who helped build the battered women's movement were moved, after years of staying in the closet, to come out after working so long on ending the silence of battered women. Toiling to give voice to others who are voiceless often releases our own cries for freedom.

4. FEAR OF COMING OUT IS WORSE THAN THE REALITY: BUSTING THE BIG LIE

A few years ago, there was a TV ad that showed a car zooming toward a brick wall, gathering speed as it approached an inevitable crash. Just at the horrific moment of impact, the car burst through to the other side, and you realized that the "wall" was just painted paper.

I am often reminded of this image as I hear about people's fears of coming out. At the moment of approach, the unknown and terrifying consequences of coming out at work, to your parents, or to others form a daunting, seemingly real, impenetrable wall. Your worst fears take over, and you imagine you will be smashed by everyone's hatred and contempt. Strangely enough, you never for a moment imagine you will be happier, more whole, and more able to love, and that you'll have lots of new friends and a whole new community.

Some of the fears are certainly legitimate; we know all too well that murders of openly gay and lesbian people do occur, that one in four gay men experiences antigay harassment, as does one in seven lesbians, that jobs are lost, promotions forgone, housing denied. Lesbians in particular fear economic discrimination, and, if we have children, loss of our kids. Gay men in particular fear harassment. Yes, it is true that gay children are thrown out into the streets by raging parents; sometimes entire towns even rise up to drive out queers. The horror stories are real.

So contemplating coming out brings up frightening visions of genuine and imaginary risks. In addition, it appears that the most daunting fear of all is not that of overt discrimination or antigay violence. The greatest fear is the pervasive and agonizing fear of rejection, of ostracism, by family and friends—the loss of love and acceptance. The caring and the phone calls will cease. Where will we go for the holidays?

Coming out is always worth it. The truth is that—just like that "brick wall"—the fears of coming out are far worse than the reality. The collective wisdom of thousands of gay people who have come out over decades can be summed up in one phrase: *Coming out is always worth it.*

The Big Lie—one that gay people have believed for years—is that the closet protects us. There may be pain and rejection when we come out, but the price of the closet is invariably greater than the cost of coming out. Always. And the benefits—never imagined—are enormous. This is a critical and undersung truth that needs to be emphasized: **Nobody regrets coming out, no matter what the consequences.** I have talked with thousands of gay people during nearly twenty-five years of gay and lesbian advocacy and organizing work and never met one person who regretted coming out—not one, not at any stage of coming out. I've met lots of people who wish they had come out sooner, who say, "I wish I had come out to my parents in my twenties instead of my thirties," or "I wish I hadn't been so afraid of losing my job that I cowered in fear for so long and let so much life pass me by."

As Karen Thompson, lover of Sharon Kowalski and champion of gay family rights—one ordinary lesbian whom destiny made extraordinary—put it: "Nothing has happened to me out of the closet that was anywhere near as dangerous as being closeted."*

Craig, an Iowa college student, told me he thought he'd "signed his own death warrant" when he came out by buying ad space (for $37.50) in the college newspaper to print a letter on National Coming Out Day (the paper wouldn't print the letter except as an ad).

---

*After her lover, Sharon Kowalski, became paralyzed and unable to talk in a car accident in 1984, Karen Thompson sued for legal guardianship. It took nine years (during three and a half years of which they were prevented from seeing each other) and $225,000 in court costs, but an appeals court finally ruled in their favor, and Kowalski returned home to the wheelchair-accessible house Thompson had built for her. Thompson had been a closeted conservative who was transformed into an outspoken activist for the rights of people with disabilities and gays and lesbians—and against the closet.

"I feared the worst, but the opposite happened. It was wonderful—
the big football player down the hall in my dorm walked up to me
with a huge grin and said, 'I gotta shake your hand, man. You got a
lot of guts!' People applauded me the next day when I walked into
the cafeteria. I thought I'd be forced out of the residence halls, but
wound up instead becoming the university's first openly gay resident
assistant one year later. Much to my surprise, I became a hero, not
an exile."

Being in the closet adds tremendous anxiety to life. When we
live with that anxiety, we get used to its burden. When we throw
off that burden, life gets easier. "I didn't realize how much the
closet affected me," another college student, Rosalind of Memphis,
Tennessee, told me. "The regular issues college kids deal with—
choosing a major, working extra jobs, worrying about a career—were
enormously complicated by my anxiety about being gay and hidden. Coming out didn't take away those problems, but it freed me
up to focus better on solving them." As Ken, an elementary school
teacher in Sacramento, California, who has been coming out more
and more at work and in his neighborhood, told me recently: "I
sleep so much better at night. My life has an entirely different
quality to it, a peace, a sense of integrity I never thought possible."

Believe me, I have met people victimized by homophobic reactions to their coming out: lesbian moms who lost their children in
ugly custody disputes; kids thrown out of their homes by their parents; people who have been beaten up. I've met countless people
who lost jobs and homes, people who were shunned by everyone in
their life, from neighbors to sisters to childhood best friends, and
on and on and on. I've heard every conceivable story of rejection by
families. I've met people who grieved mightily the loss of heterosexual comfort and privilege. Who among us has not experienced
the ugly taunts hurled from cars or passing strangers? But despite
all this, I have also heard, like a whispered (sometimes shouted)
mantra, over and over and over again—from every single gay person
I have ever met—"I only wish I'd come out sooner."

The truth of our collective experience has finally broken the
mesmerism of the lie that it's safer to be in than out of the closet.
For far too long, nobody was telling us about all the good things that

happen when we come out. Fortunately, that is finally changing. The freedom of opening the closet door and walking into the sunlight of honesty is a gift much greater than social and parental approval. Aside from the comforting truth that most family members and friends eventually come around to some degree of tolerance, coming out is an unqualified act of liberation. As one Utah Mormon woman in her fifties said, with tears in her eyes, "I have an ex-husband and four beautiful kids who don't speak to me anymore. The pain is too deep for words, but do I regret it? No way—I'd never go back to that closet. My lover and I have a life brimming with love. And it's finally an honest life for me." One man who spoke to me from his hospital bed, bruised and broken after a gay-bashing by a bunch of kids in West Hollywood—a man who had just come out of the closet at work and at home both as a gay man and as HIV-positive—conveyed a spiritual quality of newfound inner strength now that his closet had been cast aside. "I'll heal this physical pain," he told me. "I couldn't heal the self-hatred inside with anything but being out."

None of these people is an extraordinary, larger-than-life superhero. They are regular people who have experienced some real pain, but who would never trade their newfound freedom for the soul-deadening life of a return to the closet. No one should be naïve about the consequences of coming out; there will be some. But nobody can ever take away our new strength of character, our hard-won sense of expanded potential. By coming out, we become more whole, more integrated, more capable of greatness in our life. We are able to love. These things happen only when we recognize the destructive power of the closet, and shed the cloak of lies about our deepest self. By coming out, we become ourselves.

Our Number One Goal: Obliterating the Closet

The importance of coming out was a great legacy of the contemporary gay liberation movement that exploded in 1969. Nearly thirty years later, as we approach the millennium, that call to action has greater depth and urgency. Today, we also have the accumulated wisdom of tens of thousands of us: the closet stands for prison, not privacy, not protection. For this reason, the single most important goal for our community is the obliteration of the institution of the closet.

We are crippled when we live a lie. As best-selling psychologist Harriet Lerner writes: "The closet precludes joy and diminishes energies. Failing to come out feeds back a sense of dishonesty, deceit, and self-doubt that erodes self-esteem and encourages self-hate. Failing to come out affects the very fabric of relationships and quality of day-to-day life. Neither intimacy nor self can flourish in an atmosphere of secrecy and silence."*

No matter what the closet's pervasiveness and control, its lure, its cunning changeability, it is ultimately a destructive force in our lives—psychologically, spiritually, politically. And no matter how traumatic it is for us to break through our own fear and internalized homophobia, it is essential to come out to ourselves, to name and claim our rightful sense of self, and to begin in earnest the lifelong journey of coming out. In the closet we eclipse our potential; by coming out, we find the capacity to bring our fullest best selves to all we do.

5. COMING OUT IS ABOUT COMMUNICATION: THE NEXT STEP IS TELLING OTHERS

Coming out to oneself is the huge and heroic first step toward embracing freedom in our daily lives, but the journey doesn't stop here. Both personal empowerment and political change depend on each of us coming out to others around us. In fact, let's face it: "Don't ask, don't tell" is not just the policy of the U.S. military, it's the unwritten social code that we must battle as we face the next century. Although there is increasing (and reluctant) recognition that gay men and lesbians actually exist, society regards homosexuality as permissible only if we keep it to ourselves. If America is ever to accept us as part of its diverse family, in fulfillment of the

*Harriet Lerner, *The Dance of Intimacy* (New York: HarperCollins, 1989), p. 141.

embracing American vision of a pluralist democracy, our ally needs to be the truth: "Do ask, do tell!"

Sharing the true stories of our lives, of whom we love and how we live, must be our basic personal strategy for achieving freedom. The act of communicating who we are to those we care about—in all its glory and ambivalence—is liberating to our souls and fundamental in our own personal empowerment. Coming out to others also enriches our relationships with them, for how can we have authentic ties to anyone who doesn't know the basic truth about us? Coming out to others provides a wonderful opportunity to find commonality across our differences, to teach and learn more fully, to share life more richly with those around us.

Although the steps may take several years, and occur in a different order for different people, we gay people need to come out to our parents and family, to all of our friends, and in our workplaces. While a mass migration out of America's closets has been occurring, especially in recent years, many gay men and lesbians are still only partially out. We have a circle of friends, and perhaps some family members who know we are gay, but we are closeted at work. Or, we're out to some folks at work, but our parents don't yet know because we've moved two thousand miles away from our hometown. It's time for this state of eclipse to end, for these half-lives to become whole—not only for our own freedom, but for the freedom of the young lesbians and gay men coming out in our wake. Coming out to all those people who are significant in our lives is the only viable strategy for real change for gay people. Our honesty bridges differences, builds bonds, busts stereotypes, and changes public opinion. Most of all, it feels *great*.

Coming Out to Friends

For many of us, the first step after coming out to ourselves is coming out to friends, people we already trust and confide in. Our gay friends, of course, are often our first "real" family: those who provide some unconditional caring when we most need it. Gay and lesbian friendship circles are one of the richest sources of meaning for most of us throughout our lives.

Our straight friends can be equally important. The fear we'll lose them as friends can sometimes be a daunting disincentive not to share the truth about our sexual orientation, but the collective queer wisdom on coming out shows that statistical probabilities are solidly with us. Anecdotal evidence indicates that 90 percent of the time our straight friends stick by us after we come out to them.

Ellen remembers coming out at age twenty-six to her lifelong best friend, Connie, during a trip to her suburban New Jersey hometown. Heart hammering and voice stammering, she told her she was in love with a woman. Connie narrowed her eyes and asked her: "How long have you known you are a lesbian?" "Oh, probably five years or more," Ellen replied. Her friend's next reaction completely jarred Ellen: she actually got angry. "I'm supposed to be your best friend— how come you never told me? How can I be your best friend if you don't tell me everything important going on in your life?" Twenty-three years later Connie and Ellen are still great friends.

Holly was a high-level corporate management consultant, a Harvard M.B.A. who had been with her lover, Eileen, for fifteen years. "We were very closeted. We picked who we socialized with very carefully. For the most part, I'd come home from work and pull the shades." Suddenly, all this changed. Eileen, struck down by an aneurysm, died at forty-eight. "I totally fell apart," Holly says, her eyes still filling at the memory. "We were an isolated, closeted lesbian couple. In my time of desperation, I came out to a circle of old women friends from my Barnard College days, and it was those women who moved into my life and took care of me—they called me every day, fed me, literally made me get out and walk. During the week of sitting *shivah* [the traditional Jewish week of formal mourning] they took charge of my life. Because of this experience, I know it's really important for us to let our wonderful straight friends come in and stay in our lives. We need them. They need us."

Friends, straight and gay, are particularly significant to us because of the exile we face all too often after coming out to our families, particularly our parents.

Coming Out to Parents

We are all bound to our parents, and to a lesser extent to other family members, by a thousand conscious and unconscious strands of potent emotional connection. How can we really be ourselves if those all-important bonds are based on a lie about our deepest self? No matter how active we are in the gay community or how out we are in our workplace, we are not yet truly free if our parents don't know the truth about our personal lives.

But coming out to our parents is not without significant risk. There's a price to pay for telling them the truth and defying the heterosexist notions forced on every child in every culture. Most parents will react to the news with shock, disbelief, rage, and denial. At first, many will reject or ostracize the gay child (although most do come around over time). The depth of anguish gay people experience as a result of parental rejection cannot be overemphasized. No single fact of gay existence is more painful than ostracism by our blood family. Even though we experience it alone, individually, the pool of anguish is so vast and so common it forms a shared cultural experience for an entire community. The accumulated sorrow induced by familial rejection lies very deep indeed in our queer collective soul.

Nevertheless, despite the pain of separation, coming out to our parents is absolutely essential to our personal empowerment and psychological freedom. We can't truly grow up if our folks don't know who we really are; we can't truly be ourselves if we can't "bring it home" to Mom and Dad. Each of us who has walked this tough part of the coming-out journey knows what a major burden is lifted when our parents know, no matter what the immediate results. "Almost eight years later, I still reread that coming-out letter I wrote my parents if I'm feeling down on myself or scared about something," says Ernest, a thirty-four-year-old political consultant in Washington, D.C. "It still inspires me, because, boy, it was the toughest thing I'd ever done. My hand shook writing it; I rewrote it a hundred times; I delayed weeks sending it. And, it took them a year even to talk to me once they got it. But, you know what? When I dropped that envelope in the mailbox and sent it on its way to Dallas, I felt a release I'd never known. Walking through that fear empowered me forever."

Banishment from the tribe. Our rejection by families takes myriad shapes, ranging from minor slights to horrendous acts, and varies across economic and cultural lines. Often it is sharpest in middle-class and upper-middle-class families, where there is the most concern with social status—with what Aunt Tillie or the neighbors will think—and where there are assets from which one may be cut off in the will. Working-class or poor families, who rely more heavily on family bonds to protect against hardship, often feel the family can't afford to lose even one member. Ostracism in those families may simply take the form of subtly reinforced silence. The gay son or daughter may still be welcomed home for Thanksgiving, even with a lover in tow, or may live at home with that lover for years, but there will be no overt talk about her or his life, and no acknowledgment of the relationship. A friend of mine lived with his gay partner in his parents' blue-collar house for over five years, sharing a tiny bedroom, but not one word was ever spoken about the real nature of their relationship.

Other forms of rejection include an interruption in family rituals or habits—the end of Sunday evening phone calls, a drop in status in the family, or a cousin's wedding invitation somehow lost in the mail. Greater sanctions include disinheritance; wills do get rewritten once kids come out as gay or lesbian. Sometimes lesbian or gay children are not allowed home unless they shut up about their lives, or are not allowed home with a lover, even a longtime partner. After I came out to my parents, I was forbidden to bring my lover home.

In the very worst cases, gay children are beaten or brutalized, or forced into mental institutions for so-called reparative therapy. Or they become "throwaway" kids, declared dead forever by families and kicked out onto the streets. Although a small minority, those stories of permanent rejection are agonizingly sad.

———

Lauren, a college teacher and longtime activist, tells this terrible tale:
"I first met Eric in Phoenix about ten years ago when he was

fifteen, going steady with my teenage daughter. He was a lovely young man, with bright eyes, never a hair out of place, eternally open and curious, possessing the most generous and loving heart I have ever known. As a lesbian activist, I couldn't help but notice the telltale signs: the fact that he loved to clean my house for me, his ironing his jeans before leaving for the grocery store, the wide-eyed wonder shopping on certain hip streets. Later he and my daughter broke up, and quite soon I heard the not surprising news he had come out as gay.

"That news sent his already abusive and nonsupportive family into a violent frenzy. The gentle, loving misfit son was literally kicked out of his home. As of this year, Eric had not spoken with his family in five years. My daughter and he remained best friends and as close as busy lives and the distance between Phoenix and Philadelphia would permit. When she last saw him, during the summer, he seemed happy: he had a good job, he was making payments on his first car, and he and his lover had bought a house together. But, we learned last week, Eric, still devastated over the separation from his parents, couldn't overcome his demons. He took his own life at the age of twenty-four this past Thanksgiving weekend."

———

On the other hand there are equally rare happy surprise stories of instant and full acceptance of our homosexuality by parents. When my former partner, Sheila, told her parents she was a lesbian, her mother smiled lovingly, patted her daughter's hand, and said, "It's okay, honey. We always knew you liked girls better." (Sheila always chuckles as she relates those words, etched indelibly on her brain, and sighs: "Why I waited until I was thirty-nine years old to come out to my parents I'll *never* understand!") As time goes on, these happy stories become not only more prevalent, but more amazing.

———

The other day I was sitting in my favorite Washington, D.C., coffeehouse when an acquaintance, Jerry, a quiet Capitol Hill staffer in his late twenties, bounced up to my table and, with uncharacteristic excitement, shared the following anecdote:

"I'd been putting off coming out to my stodgy parents for years now, but after they invited me home to Virginia last weekend, I decided it was time to face the music. I figured Mom would be easier to talk to, so on Friday night while she and I were cooking spaghetti in the kitchen, I just blurted it out: 'Mom, I want you to know—I'm gay.' Instantly, she wheeled around to face me, a big broad grin on her Irish face, and said the last words I ever expected: 'Honey, do you really think I didn't know this? I've been wondering for years when you were going to tell us. Your father and I love you, no matter what you do with your life. In fact, I have something to tell *you*, Jerry, honey. . . . You see, your dad and I have been going to P-FLAG [Parents, Families and Friends of Lesbians and Gays] meetings for several months now, and' —a mischievous look zipped across her face— 'well, we've met lots of new friends, and one couple is coming over for dinner tonight . . . and, um, we invited them to bring their son who's just moved to D.C. and is about your age.' . . . I was utterly speechless. I thought, This can't really be happening to me. My mother is not only fine with my being gay, but is fixing me up with another guy. I swear to God I thought I was dreaming . . . and, Torie, to make a long story about a wonderful weekend short, the topper is that Chris and I got along great and we're going out again tomorrow night."

Parental Acceptance Usually Takes Time: The Grief Reaction

Stories like Eric's and Jerry's are both rare; most of the time, as it turns out, the result of our coming out to parents is neither permanent parental abandonment nor instant full acceptance. Mostly, the result of coming out is growing acceptance—*over time.* Anecdotal evidence suggests that 75 percent of the time parents do achieve full or substantial acceptance of their gay children in from three to five years, regardless of economic, educational, or cultural background. My own parents underwent such a total change of heart over the years that when I broke up with my former life partner after nine years together, they sent her a warm letter of reassurance that she was still a member of the family.

Acceptance seems to be happening at a more rapid rate as gay and lesbian lives become more visible, spurring more and more discussion of an issue previously considered strictly taboo. I meet more and more parents who tell me they waited years for their children to tell them what they already knew. A Lincoln, Nebraska, mom recently told me: "It drove me crazy that Mary wouldn't tell me. I knew she was gay for probably ten years before she finally came out to me at age twenty-eight. I wanted to support her, but every time I broached the issue, she clammed up."

Coming out to our parents almost invariably induces what's called a "grief reaction" on their part. Heterosexuality, with the "inevitable" path toward marriage, kids, and "happiness," is unthinkingly assumed and desired by parents for their children. This notion is so deeply rooted in this society that parents experience a feeling of enormous loss when we come out to them. Right or wrong, it's a trauma, like being hit by a truck, from which they need time to recover and heal.

One experience illustrated clearly to me the depth of grief that parents may experience. I was on vacation a few years ago at a health resort, lounging in the hot tub one evening with a friend. My friend and I were chatting, and I must have made some casual reference to being gay that was loud enough to be heard by the only other person in the hot tub, a woman in her mid-fifties. After my friend left to take a class, this other woman paddled over my way and said "Excuse me. Did I hear you talk about being a . . . um, a lesbian?" "Yes," I said, "I'm a lesbian." And she said, "Well, my daughter just told me a few months ago she's a lesbian, and I'm having so much trouble with it." Her voice broke and she started to cry.

Her story spilled out. Divorced from her husband, she had worked hard to raise her only child. She had an enormous amount of hope invested in her daughter; she was counting on her to complete the college education she was denied, to become a successful professional, and, of course, to marry and "give her" grandchildren. When her daughter came out to her, she felt utterly betrayed. Her whole set of expectations toppled. She poured out her anguish to me: how she now thought her daughter wouldn't marry and produce the grandchildren she desired. For some irrational reason, she was even convinced her daughter would forgo graduate school—as if being gay destroyed professional ambition. She was overwhelmed by anger and shame, by grief and her own isolation. Over and over again she said to me she had nobody she could talk to about this; she was afraid of rejection even from her best friend.

Sitting in the moonlight, in that hot tub, I gained insight into parents and their own pain. They feel tremendous guilt that they must be responsible for this "problem." They experience shame and fear of rejection, and a compelling desire to run into their own closet. As one friend put it, "I walked out of the closet, and my mom raced right in." I could empathize with this woman's pain and grief, and see that she was really struggling with it all. In the ensuing hour, during which we both got as wrinkled as raisins, I did some consciousness-raising about the fact that lots of lesbians and gay men do become parents, and certainly have rich family lives. We talked about the wonderful, productive life her daughter was most likely destined to have. Most of all, though, as I listened, I tried to point out the gains that were involved here, as opposed to the losses—that what she experienced as a loss of social approval and the heterosexual "normal" life was really the gain of an honest and fulfilling life for her daughter.

In recent years, I have heard more and more parents talk about their own closets—using that term—and their own processes of coming out about having gay children. I've heard more and more stories of parents reaching acceptance not only of their gay kids, but of themselves as fathers and mothers who fully succeeded in that role, and who can talk proudly about their lesbian daughter or gay son to neighbors, friends, and family members.

But the parental "grief reaction" is often intense. Getting through it is multi-staged, sometimes taking several years. Acceptance comes only after a very difficult process of grieving and letting go of old expectations and of self-doubt. Shock and denial, anger, bargaining, depression, and sadness slowly give way, we can hope, to acceptance. It is not an easy journey. A myriad of jumbled feelings coexist; years can pass between steps.

The one absolute truth is that all of our parents will go through some version of most of these feelings, whether articulated or not. Most will get through it. How many people have said, as Richard did, "I can't tell my Mom. It will kill her!" The process is complicated for parents because of society's taboos on sex and homosexuality, and the extent to which gayness has been stigmatized. There is also the very real fear of AIDS. Because of these factors, it's been very hard for parents, stumbling through their own psychological process of mourning, to seek help from clergy, friends, and other family members. But parents are rarely as fragile or as unforgiving as we fear.

Taking responsibility for helping our parents. When I came out to my parents in 1973, it was a "come out and run" situation, like a lone lesbian guerrilla action. I went home on a vacation weekend, told them, and we spent all of one day arguing, crying, and slamming doors. Then I beat a hasty retreat back to my safe and nurturing lesbian community in Burlington, Vermont, with no follow-up communication for almost eighteen months. I was so wrapped up in my own drama that there was no possibility of empathy for my parents, let alone comprehension of their grief. It was only much later—in that hot tub—that I realized there even *was* another side to the story, and that perhaps I could have helped guide my parents through their grieving.

Today, a greater sophistication and maturity in our social-change movement have led to a positive change of tactics. Empathy is a revolutionary emotion, as Gloria Steinem says, and leads to a greater capacity for taking responsibility for our actions. As the openness, visibility, and collective self-confidence of gay people grow, we are more capable of experiencing empathy for others even as we walk through our own fears. More and more of us, particularly young lesbians and gay men, are able to empathize with our parents and even take some responsibility for helping them through their grieving process. Today, gay people help identify resources for parents, like the numerous books available at all gay and feminist bookstores, or point them in the direction of local chapters of P-FLAG, the wonderful national group devoted to supporting our parents and boosting their support of us.

Most significantly, gay people coming out to parents today are more willing to hang in there and answer the inevitable questions, particularly after the shock has worn off. As one young man, Joe, told me: "I'm taking a trip back to Indiana this summer; it's been a year since I came out to my parents and I sense they have questions and feelings they want to share with me. I feel for them and want to do my bit to help them. I already introduced them to P-FLAG; I sent them *Beyond Acceptance*.* Now it's time for me to sit down with them and see what else I can personally do to help bring closure to their process." This confident young man, twenty-three years old, is a real leader in the "Gay Nineties" way of doing the coming-out business. Extraordinary maturity and a sense of responsibility like Joe's are more and more widespread, thanks to growing self-respect and higher self-esteem among young gay people. This is a magnificent development.

There is still always the danger, however, that the power of parental influence will compromise us. That insidious closet may suddenly close in like a dark tent over our relationship with them, and we'll find ourselves agreeing not to bring our lover to our sister's wedding, or not to use the "L" word, or not to say "we" too much. After all, no matter how old we are, we regress if we spend enough time with our parents. . . . But, in general, I think it's healthy to find a bit of generosity in our hearts for their struggle, just as long as we are not catering to the ever-looming closet. We must never give up our own sense of boundaries and truth and self. We don't need to wear a "Fag" or "Dyke" button to the family reunion, but we don't have to hide either, no matter how much pressure our folks bring to bear. It's important to recognize that they need time, and that another, also difficult, kind of coming-out process faces each member of the family. We must remember all the years it took each of us to accept ourselves; we, too, went through many of the stages of the grief reaction, as we came to acceptance of our gayness, mourning the loss of privilege and social affirmation. We don't need to worry more about them than we do about ourselves, but just be aware of what they are likely feeling.

Over the years, I have developed a militant belief that we should come out to parents as early as possible, no matter what the consequences, so that we can enjoy as many years as possible of reconciliation on the other side of any separation that might occur. Too many people have come out to their parents in later years, only to see them die before reconciliation could occur and any loving

*Carolyn Welch Griffin, Marian J. Wirth, and Arthur G. Wirth, *Beyond Acceptance: Parents of Lesbians and Gays Talk About Their Experiences* (New York: St. Martin's Press, revised edition, 1996).

relationship reconstructed. I came out to my parents when I was twenty-two, and we went through six long years of icy separation before my first awkward homecoming as an out lesbian, with my lover, in 1979. But the glacier finally melted and our relationship was reestablished. We've now enjoyed more than seventeen years of a mature, healthy relationship of full acceptance. It's taken time, but my parents have even found far more than tolerance; they've found a deep pride in my work as a lesbian organizer and spokeswoman. It has been a fulfilling part of my life to have rebuilt that relationship, on my own terms, without compromise or denial. I shudder to think of how crippled my life would have been if I'd not come out to them at twenty-two, but waited until I was thirty-two, or forty-two. . . .

While coming out to our parents is the most loaded and scary— and the most empowering and significant—act of telling, all the other members of our family need to process the information, too. We need to spend some time with sisters and brothers, grandparents, and aunts and uncles. The more people in our family we deal with directly, the more control we have over, or input into, the collective storytelling (and myth-making) that occurs in each and every family.

Bigger Circles: Coming Out in the Workplace

Next to our parents' home, the workplace is the most important venue for being honest and open about our identity. It is also the place where furthering greater understanding of our lives helps move us forward to the broader goal of eroding homophobia at large.

Twenty-two years ago I was an English teacher at a community college and I remember how hard it was to come out on the job. It was simply not okay; every inch of the way was terrifying. Even though I was living with my lover and her son, out to my parents, an outspoken activist against the Vietnam war, and a member of a thriving countercultural lesbian-feminist community, I came out to very few of my colleagues. I, the radical, the activist, was frozen with fear every time I thought about bringing up the subject to a new straight person. I lived the same fragmented, compartmentalized, half-closeted, double-life existence common to the vast majority of lesbians and gay men. Every day I worried: Would I flub and call my girlfriend "honey" on the office phone? Was my stride too "dykey"? Anxiety, fear of discovery, and a constant sense that I was lying dominated my work life.

But the workplace closet is slowly, inexorably, melting. One of my favorite stories features a woman I met several years ago. Her experience illustrates a number of points about the fast-paced changes occurring in the workplace for lesbians and gay men:.

———

DJ didn't want to go to the 1993 March on Washington, but her lover, Alicia, insisted. Amazingly, she ended up having the time of her life. Her reluctance to attend stemmed partly from the fact that her new job as a marketing manager for a large midwestern corporation was so demanding she usually had to work weekends. DJ, thirty-two and African-American, was the eldest daughter of a poor family, and the first to go to college. Her drive to succeed was very strong. She wanted badly to move up the corporate ladder; she'd just moved from her hometown of Atlanta to take this new position.

A lifelong lesbian, DJ began a closeted life of lesbian dating in college and had been with Alicia for seven years in a committed relationship that looked as if it might last forever. Alicia was finishing up her practice hours to be a family therapist and was much farther out of the closet than DJ. Her large New Mexico Chicano family all knew she was a lesbian, as did her fellow students and teachers. DJ was not yet out to her mother and father, although her brothers knew, and she was certainly not out at work. She resented Alicia's openness with her family and work situation. She always felt a slight shiver of fear when Alicia called her at work: somehow Alicia might slip and give them away. To DJ's workmates, Alicia was her "roommate." There was nobody openly gay at her new job, although there was one guy, Vittorio, whom she suspected, in part because he took such great pains to avoid her. DJ dressed impeccably for success—actually, in a much more feminine style than came naturally to her tall, strong, athletic frame. She wore makeup and jewelry, which she thought would help "straighten her out."

Broadcasting at work that she was leaving work early on Friday to go on a camping trip with "the girls," DJ headed off with Alicia to the March on Washington. Once she was there, the sense of joy and optimism, the party spirit that permeated the weekend, overwhelmed DJ—and throughout the weekend she and Alicia held hands in public for the first time ever. Although she saw the media everywhere, she felt she had been transported to an alternative universe of freedom and openness sufficiently disconnected from her everyday life that she could abandon her normal fears of exposure. As it turned out, a TV camera, panning the crowds, had filmed her and Alicia on the fringes of the wild Lesbian Avengers' "Dyke March" of twenty thousand women the night before the big march. Pictures of the happy couple were beamed out to the nation. For a few seconds, they were front and center on America's TV sets, hugging and dancing in the streets of D.C. to the disco strains of "We Are Family."

When DJ arrived at work on Monday morning, she instantly knew something was up. People treated her differently. Some people offered knowing smiles of amusement and quiet warmth, but others averted their eyes or gave her questioning looks. She had no idea what had happened until her best work buddy, Tom, pulled her aside and said, "So, your camping trip was to Washington, D.C., huh?" Before DJ could respond, he quickly went on to say that everyone had been watching coverage of the march and they were generally sympathetic to the cause. There had been talk in the office about it even on Friday afternoon because of all the national publicity, but this morning everyone was talking about it because they'd seen DJ and Alicia on TV—and people were mostly supportive. "It's really okay," he told her. "Most of us had already figured it out, anyway. I mean, you and Alicia have been 'roommates' for seven years, right? Even the boss seems okay with it."

DJ's first instinct was to deny everything, saying that she must have had a lookalike in Washington, but events had clearly gone too far for a cover-up. She'd been "outed."

Over the months that followed, things changed slowly. DJ's initial wariness dissolved and she began to grow into a new sense of freedom. She dressed differently, adopting a more tailored, more "butch" look, which was more natural for her. She was surprised to discover an instinctive physical response: she held her head up higher and was more relaxed and comfortable in her body. The lessening of fear—fear of discovery of her hidden life—and the release of suppressed energies freed her considerable productivity and leadership abilities. She was more successful on the job than before; her skills and confidence grew more quickly than she had ever imagined.

Not only was she personally empowered, but DJ found that her work colleagues were actually bursting with questions and thoughts about the gay and lesbian issue. Her own previous awkwardness had projected outward and actually inhibited conversations that would have been natural, given the high profile of the gay and lesbian issue that spring because of the gays-in-the-military debate of 1993. Most people had already guessed DJ was a lesbian, but no one felt comfortable initiating conversations about the matter. Her personal closet enveloped the entire issue within an even larger closet. Once DJ was out, she found she was treated as quite the specialist on all things queer. She would often laugh and remind people that she was not an expert on every gay topic known to humanity, but no one believed her. When the k. d. lang *Vanity Fair* cover story came out that August, everyone wanted to know if she somehow personally knew k.d.!

———

DJ's story contains several key lessons:

- *Passing, or attempting to pass, at work has been an age-old lesbian and gay coping mechanism.* DJ's attempts to look straight, to corset her true nature, are a sorry but widespread part of gay life in a homophobic society.

- Because of the current level of visibility of gay and lesbian issues, people are no longer blind to gayness. *The "glass closet" is far more prevalent.* If we're in our thirties and aren't married with kids, or if we have a longtime same-sex "roommate" or look gay in any way, people are simply going to guess. There's no hiding place anymore.

- *Our own attitude about ourselves signals others.* If we are awkward and uncomfortable with ourselves, in or out of the closet, others will be too. If we are happy with ourselves, and comfortable with our personal style, no matter how much we transgress traditional gender roles, for the most part others will be comfortable too.

- *Often closeted gay people are the most homophobic.* DJ's experience with her gay co-worker, Vittorio, is all too common. It's as though we might give ourselves away by association. Vittorio's snubbing of DJ was a way to protect his own closet; it was directly linked to his own fear of being discovered. Once she was out and there was no subsequent discrimination, he was able to inch out of his closet, too.

- *The workplace closet affects productivity.* Hiding takes enormous energy; lying diminishes potential. Openly gay people are less alienated, more productive, more successful workers. We are more able to reach our own potential to achieve. A recent book, *Straight Jobs, Gay Lives,* actually documents this.* The authors studied the careers of a hundred lesbian and gay graduates of Harvard Business School; those who were out of the closet were more successful in their professional lives. So much, again, for the Big Lie.

- *The fear of overt discrimination is almost always worse than the actuality.* There are countless examples of people who stayed closeted for years and years because they feared losing their jobs, only to discover greater tolerance than they imagined when they finally come out.

- *Double or triple identity issues add to the complexities of lesbian and gay life.* DJ's burdens of race and class made her situation more complex, and the risks and fears greater. A black lesbian from a poor background, who feels enormous pressures from her family to succeed and has responsibilities not just to herself and lover but also to her family of origin and her ethnic community, does not just leap out of the closet without a lot of forethought. It's important to recognize what academics call intersectionality—multiple pulls on us from different parts of our backgrounds and cultures.

---

*Annette Friskopp and Sharon Silverstein, *Straight Jobs, Gay Lives* (New York: Scribner's, 1995).

- *When lovers are at different stages of coming out, a relationship can suffer serious stresses.* DJ and Alicia lived in very different personal psychological states before DJ came out at work: Alicia was free in all facets of her life, and DJ was uptight in most of hers. Once DJ came out, those differences dissolved. They were both relieved, and their shared values and experience brought them much closer together.

Our workplace revolution. DJ's story is emblematic of a dramatic shift that has taken place over the past few years. My own experience two decades ago continued to be the norm until very recently. It's been perfectly acceptable within the gay and lesbian community to be closeted at work, despite the significant peer pressure to come out to family members. Today, there is a coming-out revolution spreading like wildfire through America's workplaces. "I'm more than my job," says Karen, twenty-nine, a secretary in New York City. "It's no longer negotiable. If I can't be out at a workplace, I'll go find somewhere I can. Life's too short to be closeted at the place I spend all day, five days a week."

Employee support groups for lesbians and gay men coming out on the job have proliferated everywhere, in both the public and private sectors of our economy. They provide all-important support for coming out at work, and also lobby for formal antidiscrimination measures, diversity training to combat homophobia, and health coverage and other benefits for domestic partners. More and more employers—not surprisingly led by the high-tech firms that rely on rapid-fire, peak-performance creativity from highly engaged workers—officially endorse these groups and respond by actively fighting job bias. Even the conservative entertainment industry has been mobilized in recent years; as of 1996, every major studio in Hollywood but one has domestic partner benefits for its lesbian and gay employees.

The Clinton administration made historic progress in 1993 by eliminating official job bias in all federal agencies. In 1994, I attended the inaugural meeting of a gay and lesbian staff affinity group for a huge government agency in Washington, D.C. Over 250 gay *and* nongay staff members sported festive rainbow ribbons of solidarity. In his remarks, the agency's director said: "The success of our collective enterprise depends on each of you being able to participate optimally in our workplace. That means each and every one of you being able to bring your full selves openly to work. We are pleased to support our gay and lesbian employees."

There are, of course, still risks in coming out at work. Studies show that one third of gay men and lesbians have experienced some form of direct employment discrimination, and antidiscrimination laws exist in only nine states and a hundred municipalities. Given the current conservative climate, federal protection is on tomorrow's political horizon, despite a heroic lobbying job by the Human Rights Campaign that has garnered 160 cosigners in Congress for the Employment Non-Discrimination Act (ENDA) introduced in 1994. Along with the losses of promotions, jobs, and college tenure that still occur, we must also count the more silent but insidious forms of discrimination such as social alienation and isolation, and the loss of normal pleasures like sharing freely in the office discussion about family life. Too few desks sport the framed smiling face of the staffer's gay or lesbian spouse.

But the risks of direct discrimination and the closet's oppression are fading fast as more and more of us come out on the job. Business and government are beginning to recognize widely that discrimination at work leads to lost dollars and opportunities. Increasingly, the case is being made to employers that, along with the human cost, there is a huge economic cost attached to the workplace closet and to the discrimination that has kept it in place for so long. A 1993 study by M. Lee Badgett of the University of Maryland estimates that between $1.4 billion and $2.7 billion in productivity is lost annually because gay workers spend a rough average of five minutes each day worrying about whether their boss or co-workers know they're gay, or actively lying about or hiding their gay lives, making up stories about their weekends or figuring out how to get out of the office to privately phone home to a sick lover.

Whether driven by humanitarian or economic incentives, corporations and government agencies are coming around at last, thanks to the leadership of individual gay people no longer willing to abide the Big Lie of the closet at work.

6. COMING OUT IS A LIFELONG COMMITMENT—GET USED TO IT!

Once we've decided to do it, coming out is a constant, complex, and never-ending process. Coming out is a lifelong event. Every time we meet someone new, every time we start a new job or move to a new neighborhood or town, we make a choice as to when, how, or if to come out to every single person or set of people. We may not choose to be gay, but we constantly choose whether or not to come out as gay. This is often exhilarating and always interesting, but even in the best of times, it can be occasionally overwhelming. It may well be the hardest work we've ever done, and it is stressful, so it's very important to be kind to ourselves.

Be Sure to Get Support

The American cultural tradition of rugged individualism is ingrained in all of us. It's a notion that I believe denies people's natural need for social support systems. Self-help and personal courage are positive—and something we gay people know a lot about—but toughing it out alone, macho-style, is often dysfunctional, not to mention needlessly lonely. Reaching out for help and support through all the phases of our coming-out process makes a lot of sense; it really lightens the load. Reading that parental coming-out letter to a good friend before we mail it can ease our anxiety. The community support groups that can be found in most cities now are great places to find out we are not alone in our feelings. Gay- and lesbian-affirmative therapists are widely available, and there is a rich and varied network of community-based organizations that have arisen from our need for emotional support. We should grab hold of every bit of it we can find.

Coming Out Constantly Can Be Exhausting

It's not necessary to come out in every situation. It's okay to rest occasionally. I don't often have to contrive opportunities to come out since I've been a professional lesbian activist of one stripe or another for twenty years, and whenever I'm asked what I do, I get to tell. A few years ago, however, I had a brief period of retro-rebellion: I can think of several airplane rides during which I actually got a kick out of inventing an identity as a straight person just because of the cumulative weariness I felt from being so out for so many years. The odd looks, the intrusive questions, the feigned tolerance, the overt disgust—all the varied responses straight people have to us—can be highly irritating. I was fed up with it all. I told one guy chatting me up on a cross-country trip that I was a nun fighting for women's rights within the Catholic Church.

I don't want to encourage straight-wannabe fabrications or passing here. I do, however, want to acknowledge the human truth that coming out constantly can be downright tiring. This is true whether we are "professional queers" whose careers or volunteer passions have involved being out of the closet for many years, or whether we are the moms who just came out to the first-grade teacher and now have to do it all over again to the seventh-grade teacher in the next building. Occasionally, we all should get to take a break from coming out to someone new all the time. It doesn't make us sellouts, as long as we are out to all the people who are important in our lives, and as long as that circle continues to widen, even if slowly, over the course of our lives.

We Must Respect People's Complex Lives and Responsibilities

The coming-out process demands of us personal courage and a lifelong commitment. It also should demand respect for the multiple demands of people's real lives. Particularly when we are basking in the new glow of leaving behind our own closet, it's natural to want company—and on our timetable. But our responsibility to shut down our own closets does not extend to imposing our timing on others.

Family and friends to whom we come out go through their own coming-out processes. If we ourselves are parents, we face very special sets of challenges about coming out, because our openness can automatically bring our kids out of their own special closets as children of lesbians or gays. In this homophobic world there are still very real consequences for our kids; they may face all kinds of embarrassment and harassment. Sure, they sometimes have their own homophobia and they sometimes want to keep our identity quiet for the wrong reasons, but they also have the right to negotiate with their lesbian moms and gay dads about their differing concerns and needs.

———

Polly, a Chicago computer programmer, longtime lesbian activist, and mother of two daughters now in their twenties, says:

"My coming out was wonderful, essential for my own development as a person, but I always had to balance it with my kids' needs. Especially during their teenage years, with all that peer pressure to fit in, they begged me to be "discreet" when their friends were over. So sometimes I made the tough choice to leave my openness at my own front door. This was not without its embarrassment and confusion, but my parenting instincts were clear—I needed to give my kids some safety and build some trust. Eventually, on their own timetable, they came out to their friends about being daughters of a lesbian. And they became outspoken on the issue of gay rights. But it felt important that they grow at their own pace. There would have been nothing positive about my insisting on them coming out about my life a year or two earlier than they were ready."

———

Of course, there's no one right answer here, no prescription for perfect gay parenting. Plenty of gay and lesbian parents come out fully and remain out throughout their children's lives with no discomfort or disruption of their family life. The watchword here is respect. We must always try to respect each other's complex lives and responsibilities.

Outing Is Not the Same as Coming Out

Another example of the need to apply some ethical—as well as commonsense—guidelines to the coming-out issue involves outing. I happen to think outing is delicious political revenge on our proven enemies. If, for example, the longtime, repressive FBI director J. Edgar Hoover—a deeply closeted gay man who promoted vicious homophobia as well as other bigotry—had been alive and powerful during the time of the active gay movement, we wouldn't have had a pang of conscience about outing him. Recently, openly gay Massachusetts congressman Barney Frank has cleverly parlayed the threat of outing actively homophobic, closeted gay Republican colleagues into good votes on AIDS and gay rights issues in Congress.

Outing our proven enemies is one thing, but since outing always alienates the person involved it's ultimately a lousy organizing strategy for our friends. In addition, outing as a concept alienates other potential allies—straight gay-friendly conservatives, liberals, libertarians, and feminists—whose support for our equality flows from their natural support for privacy rights or belief in the core concept of self-determination. And we need every warrior we can recruit into our army for this long-term cultural war.

The phenomenon of outing is actually more a social indicator of gay and lesbian explosion into visibility than it is a helpful strategy for promoting social change. The widespread dialogue on the outing issue over the past several years has represented a drastic paradigm shift in the value system of a critical mass of the organized gay and lesbian community. After fifteen years of the agony of AIDS and many more years of marginalized existence, we have shifted from general tolerance of the closet to general intolerance of it.

That's a good thing. But our ethical responsibility to speak out about the awful costs of the closet does not extend to subverting people's freedom of choice. It is easy to understand the frustration of many who feel that individuals' fears are holding us all back, but outing or threatening to expose any but our worst enemies diminishes the moral force of our message: *Choosing to come out of the closet is the only answer to the call of our truest individual selves.*

"Come out, come out, wherever you are" are children's teasing words. Our goal should be to build a movement that is ever widening, and as broadly based and inclusive as possible. Smart and savvy organizing most certainly involves challenging the closet, because the closet is a destructive force. In that message we should be militant and uncompromising. We must untiringly rattle others' closet doors by cajoling, inspiring, enticing, and, above all, leading, through the authentic example of our own lives. All of us who have come out know well the soaring sense of freedom gained from being honest about who we are to ourselves and others, the permanent strength of character generated by coming out to our parents, friends, and colleagues. We know well the depth of love and friendship we can find only outside the closet's perimeters.

Coming out empowers and invigorates our daily lives in multiple ways. It also has a powerful impact on the lives of the nongay people in our spheres of influence, who learn ever greater tolerance and experience glimmers of new understanding for those whose lives they once denied or ignored. When we come out, we each become key players, witting or not, in the unfolding epic of social change happening all around us at the turn of the twenty-first century: the beginning of the end of that ancient bigotry, homophobia.

2

DO ASK, DO TELL:
BRINGING THE
REVOLUTION HOME

I. "SPHERE OF INFLUENCE" THEORY:
COMING OUT WINS HEARTS
AND MINDS

Coming out to ourselves, and to our friends, family, and co-workers, is always empowering to our sense of identity, self-worth, and potential. In addition, our individual act of coming out reverberates into the world around us, setting in motion a dramatic chain reaction in the lives of people we know and the organizations we affect. In the wake of our personal honesty and courage, powerful, positive, and often permanent changes ripple their way through people's lives and the various arenas in which we travel.

1. WE EACH MAKE A DIFFERENCE

Helen was a feisty, outspoken woman in her late sixties. Her causes (civil rights, anti–Vietnam War, abortion rights) were the much admired centerpieces of conversation for many years at her suburban Columbus, Ohio, weekly bridge game. Lesbian and gay rights, however, was one issue that went just too far, and silence reigned on the subject. But one day, in the middle of the explosive 1993 national debate on gays in the military, one too many antigay cracks were made at the bridge table, and Helen's own closet blew open: "My granddaughter is a captain in the Army, and she's a lesbian. Doesn't she deserve freedom from discrimination, too?"

When Helen told me the story, she added proudly, "That sure shut them up!" But she herself was shocked at how powerful antigay bigotry was. She, a longtime fighter on so many other issues, had found it much, much harder to face this one. "How well I know that homophobia is still acceptable—I know because I had my own to deal with," she sadly told me. But Helen's own "coming out" about having a lesbian family member changed things. She became more and more comfortable with the issue, at her bridge table and elsewhere, and went on to speak in favor of lifting the military ban on lesbians and gay men to several civic and church groups.

When Helen's granddaughter came out to her, she was simply sharing her life with her favorite grandmother. She had no idea how many people's lives would eventually be touched by that piece of information. But the fact is that once you come out to others as a lesbian or gay man, you become a revolutionary in America's newest social change movement, whether you choose to or not. When you come out to your married sister in Oklahoma, to your co-worker at the auto plant or office typing pool, or to your old high school buddies at your tenth class reunion back in Missoula, you are changing the world. You may be the quietest, most private person in the world, someone who never would identify as political or aspire to be an activist, but the fact is that once you come out, your own personal act of empowerment has a transformative impact on the individuals in your life. The personal *is* the political, as we used to say in the early days of the contemporary women's movement.

An old community-organizing maxim says that every person has a sphere of influence of at least two hundred people—friends, family, neighbors, co-workers, local store owners, classmates, and on and on. If we are active in our local community—volunteering in our church, Girl Scout troop, or PTA—that number multiplies. Given the mobility of contemporary life, as well as the capabilities of communications technology, our sphere of influence could easily include thousands of people over a lifetime.

Each and every time we communicate our identity, whether softly or loudly, we help break down stereotypes and educate people. We help them overcome their prejudice by putting a real-life picture over the distorted or sketchy image of gay people that this society fosters. We help paint in living color a brighter vision of true diversity. We play our part in battling the ignorance that still predominates, and therefore we also fight back against the vicious disinformation campaigns of right-wing political religious extremists. Those campaigns portray us as sick and sinful, and, worse, as desperate, sexually obsessed child molesters. These lies survive because people don't know who we truly are. The lies scare people and then are parlayed effectively into fund-raising mailings and political organizing tactics that elect bigoted officials and build the ultra-right's organization. When we come out to those who don't yet know that we are gay, we take a vital first step in stopping this growing menace to ourselves and to America.

Lesbian and gay community-building for support and conscious and strategic political organizing to defeat homophobia must, of course, occur as well. But for too long we have ignored the real and substantial social impact of each brave individual act of coming out. As we each walk along our individual path as an open lesbian, bisexual, or gay man, let us remember the words of singer/songwriter Holly Near: "Can we be like drops of water, falling on the stone, splashing, breaking, dispersing in air? Weaker than the stone by far. But be aware that as time goes by, the rock will wear away." That rock of prejudice *will* wear away. As we live our usual lives, hour by hour, day by day, as open lesbians and gay men, we are not only bringing new talents and previously repressed creative energies into this world, we are performing the deeply important job of wearing down that seemingly impenetrable rock of bigotry.

The 75 Percent Solution

Polling data show that most Americans—at least 60 percent—don't want us to suffer job bias. We have essentially won the public-opinion battle on the basic issue of discrimination, at least in the workplace. There is also a clear correlation between those who know us and those more likely to favor nondiscrimination: 73 percent of those who know someone gay favor gay rights in the workplace, versus 55 percent of those who don't.

However, poll after poll has shown two additional things: that only about half of Americans today think they know someone gay (although, significantly, this figure has doubled in a decade, up from 25 percent in 1985). More important, the simple fact is that about 60 percent of Americans still consider homosexuality to be immoral. That is, only about 40 percent of Americans define gay people as morally equal to nongay people. This is the truth of where we stand today. People do not want us to suffer discrimination on the job, but they just don't yet fully accept us as equal.

That last statistic is the rock we must wear away in the coming years, and I believe there is a direct correlation between our utter invisibility to 50 percent of the population and the fact that we're not yet considered equal. History has shown that law and policy follow public opinion on matters about personal life such as abortion, women's roles, and birth control. We have our work cut out for us: to come out, come out, come out, in sufficient numbers to achieve a sea change in the fundamental acceptance of us as equal. True and lasting social change in the legal and political arenas, and real tolerance and even affirmation, will follow only when the great majority of Americans experience the real truth about us—about our differences, which give us uniqueness, and our similarities, which form enduring commonalities with them. To break down stereotypes and ignorance and to educate people, we must bring them ever closer into our lives and show them the wonderful truth of who we are. Only then will we crack that final crucial statistic and convince people of our humanity, our basic moral equality.

The noted psychologist Greg Herek recently conducted research which shows that heterosexuals with the most favorable attitudes toward gay people are those who know at least two gay people, and are good friends with them. In addition, his research shows that coming out directly, in person, to nongay people diminishes intolerance more than letting them learn at second hand. One 1994 poll showed that only 23 percent of Americans said they had a close friend or family member who is gay. Now, we know that *every* American has a family member or friend who is gay, lesbian, or bisexual. It seems we have achieved far greater general visibility than ever before, but we are still too hidden; our lives do not yet intersect fully enough with the lives of straight people to break down core prejudice. It's time to up the ante. I propose the "75 percent solution": if enough gay people come out to enough people in our circles of acquaintanceship so that instead of 50 percent of straight Americans knowing that they know one of us, 75 percent do, then that figure for true tolerance could very well go up, from 40 percent to 51 percent or higher.

When a simple majority of the public accepts us as morally equal, we will mark the beginning of the end of homophobia for good. Just as we have won people over on the basic discrimination issue during the past decade by coming out in record numbers, our goal should be to increase by another 25 percent the number of us who come out over the next decade. It would, of course, also measurably help if we built friendships out of those acquaintanceships as well, and made sure we told people directly ourselves—so have your straight friends over for dinner more often and see hearts be won over and minds be changed in the years to come.

The giant collective project of changing America on a tough issue is exciting and complex. It's very important to understand better, to examine more closely, how the unique challenges and joys of our individual coming out to others, starting with our families, contributes to this vital social change project.

2. NEW CLOSETS AND NEW COURAGE: OUR FAMILY'S SPHERE OF INFLUENCE

W hen we come out to our parents and family, for example, new closets spring up. Our family now has to face a stigma: one of their own family is gay in this homophobic, heterosexist society. Family members have their own coming-out process. It's certainly not as direct or intense or threatening for our mom or brother or cousin to face telling someone that we are gay as it is for us, but it is a similar experience. (I'm not talking about the process of accepting us, but rather about public acknowledgment—their coming out to others about us.) The very process of this acknowledgment requires its own brand of personal courage, too. Walking through the stigma and internalized bigotry to a place where family and friends can be comfortable about having a lesbian sister or daughter, or a gay cousin or uncle or son, is not easy. But once it happens, the effect enlarges the sphere of influence further and further.

———

Betsy talks movingly about "being in the closet for five years about my son being gay." She talks about the shame she and her husband felt, the inability to share their "little secret" with friends, other family, members of their church. "We had to find our own courage," she says, "and, while I wish it were different, I'm embarrassed to admit that it took us a very long time." For Betsy, the process was gradual; there was no precipitating incident, just a slow coming to terms with the truth. "I finally felt I was going to burst. Like any secret or lie, it began to chafe on my conscience, to gnaw at my soul. So I told my sister, and she was very loving. Then my husband and I told our close friends. I laugh now, we made such a big deal of it. We gathered our circle of best friends together, as if we were making a very big, serious announcement. Well, I guess in fact we were. 'Wade's gay. We want you all to know.' Of course, it turned out most of them had figured it out, and the rest were fine with it. I think our own fears and shame enlarge our closets."

Sasha's younger sister, still in high school, was a lesbian. Sasha recalls that she practically whispered this fact to her college roommate. "I don't know why, but I was frightened I would be rejected. I thought it would affect me negatively somehow. Guilt by association, I guess. I'd held it in the whole school year, but I just had to tell someone." It turned out that the roommate's best friend in high school had come out to her. In fact, as the word spread through their college dorm, it turned out that virtually everyone had a gay or lesbian relative or friend. "Bursting the bubble of silence was amazing. Everyone realized they had kept a secret about someone gay in their life. We all realized we were closeted about our gay relatives and friends, even when they weren't. It felt great to come out about it. We had something special in common."

Kathy's mom had come out as a lesbian when Kathy was ten years old, but Kathy always hid it from her friends. Her mom, who lived alone and not with her longtime lover, made her peace with being closeted to Kathy's friends throughout Kathy's high school years, even though she was very active in a local lesbian social organization. But when Kathy was applying to colleges, she was looking for a "unique selling point," a new angle to write about in her application essays. As a white, blond cheerleader, varsity athlete, and president of her high school class, with good grades, Kathy was not too distinguishable from many of her similarly high-achieving classmates in her upper-middle-class Florida suburb. At her mother's suggestion, Kathy took a chance and wrote half her college essays about growing up with a lesbian mom. Kathy disclosed her own closet, and described her own complicated ambivalence—her simultaneous resentment and respect for her mom. Surprise! Kathy was accepted at exactly those schools to which she had come out about being a lesbian's daughter. Though she had at first been suspicious of the idea, the process of being accepted by those colleges emboldened Kathy. She came out to several of her friends one by one that last spring of her high school senior year.

———————

Families and Allies Fight Back Against Bigotry

Sometimes a relative's or friend's decision to break down his or her own closet door happens as a result of getting fed up with the still-pervasive ignorance or prejudice against gays and lesbians. This is one of the most wonderful results of coming out to family members and others: we unwittingly recruit warriors in the fight against anti-gay bigotry. Their contribution can take the form of responding to a homophobic remark, or of more direct activism.

———

My sister, Ann, once stopped at a coffeeshop off the freeway in Oregon. Sitting at the counter, she heard the man next to her mutter "Goddamn queer" under his breath about a young man behind them who was leaving the restaurant. The waitress behind the counter also heard the remark; she looked a bit startled but said nothing. My shy, sweet sister saw that the waitress was upset but unwilling to say anything, so Ann said loudly, though in a slightly quavering voice: "I'm offended by your prejudice. My sister's gay, and she's wonderful." The waitress, buoyed by my sister's intervention, stepped forward and said, "Yeah, we don't like prejudice in here. My brother's gay, too. You'd better get out!" The man was completely taken aback, and left, we hope, with consciousness raised.

Much earlier we saw a young man named Paul work up the courage to go into the Los Angeles Gay and Lesbian Community Services Center. He came out to his parents several months later. His father, an emergency room doctor, seemed to be especially numbed by the information. But less than a week later, Paul Senior walked into the doctors' lounge at his hospital and heard a colleague telling a "fag" joke. After a moment's hesitation, he spoke up, told them that his son was gay, and said, quietly, that the insults had to stop. From then on, Paul Senior's silence was broken; he talked openly and increasingly proudly about his son's life and actively educated his colleagues and friends about gay and lesbian issues as he learned about them.

Mark, a young actor in Los Angeles, was inspired by the openness of the TV actor Dick Sargent, best known for his role on *Bewitched.*

Sargent came out publicly on *Entertainment Tonight* on National Coming Out Day in 1991, a few years before he died of cancer. Shortly thereafter, Mark came out to his parents, who live in Kansas. Not only were they immediately supportive, but, after the 1992 Republican convention's open and nasty homophobia, his father started a one-man weekly letter-writing campaign to Kansas senator Bob Dole complaining about the antigay Christian Coalition's growing influence on the Republican party.

Donna's work as a nonprofit organization consultant brought more and more gays and lesbians into her life over the years. "I guess I just fell in love with a few gay people I met, and now I see myself as an ally to the gay community. I take that role very seriously. I'm always aware that I can go off and march in the lesbian rights march—and chant and shout and join in with my sisters—but then I go back to my safe, straight world. I consciously do ally work often. Just today my brother confided in me that he was worried his five-year-old son might be gay because the boy wanted to play with a doll the other day. I gently but firmly pointed out his homophobia, and how destructive it is to that little boy, as well as himself."

3. ACCIDENTAL ACTIVISM: A GROWING PHENOMENON

Our individual acts of coming out often have the unintended consequence of transforming us or those around us into activists. As the right revs up its fund-raising and political engines with explicitly antigay campaigns, as more and more gay men and, increasingly, lesbians die of AIDS, and as more people recognize the natural connection between individual empowerment and political action, stories like the following are increasingly common.

Robin, thirty-three, and Tracie, thirty, both grew up in conservative Modesto, in central California. Their parents were friends, and they themselves became good friends at ages seventeen and fourteen, although neither ever shared with the other her personal suspicions about being gay. Robin went off to college in Vermont and Tracie finished high school, becoming a "heavy-duty Christian" during the years before she left to go to cooking school in San Francisco. The two young women stayed in touch through letters and holiday vacation visits at home. After cooking school, Tracie moved back to Modesto to live with her family.

The year she was twenty-one, Tracie visited Robin, who by then was living in Santa Clarita, outside Los Angeles. A few days into the visit, a magical moment happened: Tracie found herself cooking a particularly special meal for Robin, while Robin, a pianist and composer, was playing some new music for Tracie. They looked at each other and realized they were falling in love. When Tracie went back to Modesto, she started telling everyone she was in love with a woman. "I was so ecstatic, I just had to share it. My sister must have told my mother, because she called me into her room one night and berated me for an hour and a half about nothing in particular, just generalized rage, and then asked me, 'Are you and Robin in a relationship?' 'Yes, and I'm very happy,' I said. She said all the usual awful stuff—that I'd burn in hell, that she'd rather be dead than have a lesbian daughter; how could I do it to her, et cetera. She finally gave me twenty-four hours to break up with Robin or to get out of the house. That was a simple choice for me—I chose Robin, and packed up and left the next day."

During years of wrenching estrangement, interspersed with a few tearful, terrible holiday visits and a particularly tense encounter at her grandmother's funeral, Tracie's mom, Linda, repeatedly sent the couple Bibles with highlighted passages, and letters that were little more than antigay diatribes. Robin and Tracie's philosophy was simply to continue to send love her way. "We'd tell her, 'We love you' whenever we got the chance," says Robin. "We called often. We wrote. I'd call when Tracie visited her folks, the few awkward times she did. We deeply believed her mom would come around, if we just believed in her, and sent unconditional love her way."

It took four long years for Linda to reach out. She came to Los Angeles for a visit and the three of them went to a P-FLAG meeting. It broke the ice, and Linda bought and read *Beyond Acceptance,* a book by three P-FLAG members, which "raised her consciousness a mile and a half," says Tracie.

The next thing they knew, Linda wanted to go to the 1993 March on Washington. There, two incidents changed her permanently: Linda was leaving a P-FLAG reception, wearing a bright purple P-FLAG sash covered with buttons, and on the streets gay women and men started coming up to her, hugging her, crying, thanking her for being there, and pouring out their own stories of being rejected by their mothers. Linda was amazed by how much they appreciated her. Then, later that night, a pickup truck filled with drunk young thugs careened toward the three women. The boys, assuming Linda was a lesbian too, screamed at her: "Filthy dyke—fucking *DYKE!*" The violent rage and harassment shocked, infuriated, and then politicized Linda. She spent every day of the next week walking Capitol Hill, lobbying Congress. When she returned to quiet, conservative Modesto, she immediately founded its first-ever chapter of P-FLAG where today over forty people attend monthly meetings. Robin's parents are now also members; Tracie's mother is the president, and her aunt the treasurer. Modesto hasn't been the same since.

Linda went from rabid antigay bigot to progay activist in a mere few years. Her transformation surprised no one more than her daughter and her daughter's lover. And nobody is prouder of Linda's commitment to changing straight minds in her hometown than Robin and Tracie. "Accidental activists" like Linda are sprouting up around the country like so many blossoming wildflowers—people transformed every day into vital organizers for lesbian and gay freedom at this crucial crossroads time in history.

4. AIDS, HOMOPHOBIA, AND FAMILY TRANSFORMATION

Nothing has spawned activism and fostered change in families as much as the AIDS epidemic. In bittersweet irony, this horrific plague decimating our community has been a potent force leading us—and many of our families—out of closets and into city halls, streets, and service centers, with a greater commitment to change our lives and the world we live in.

I vividly remember seeing an older, distinguished, fatherly-looking man standing on the edge of the giant Names Project AIDS Memorial Quilt spread out on the Mall in Washington, D.C., in October 1987. He was alone, still and rigid, hands clasped tightly against his face, with his head thrown back up toward the sky in a gesture of frozen supplication. I was drawn to approach him; I'm not sure exactly why. "Forgive me, forgive me, forgive me," he was quietly chanting. "Can I help?" I asked, and his story—so common—poured out. His gay son, Tad, who lived in San Francisco, came out to him and his wife as gay at the same time he came out about having AIDS, only a year before he died at age thirty-one. Neither parent could deal with it. They didn't even visit Tad while he was sick, and they spoke to him on the telephone only a few times. "We're Catholic, and we just went numb," this man explained. "Then Tad died. His friends cared for him; he didn't die alone, but we never saw him again, and now I miss him so much. . . . And I have so many regrets." He broke down, sobbing and sobbing. "I came here to see the Quilt patch his friends made. I just hope God can forgive me for abandoning him." I must have hugged that guy for an hour, though I never saw him again. I hope the Quilt gave him some closure and some peace. And I hope his remorse translated into some activity against AIDS and homophobia.

AIDS has hit hardest in the gay men's community, with more than 230,000 American gay and bisexual men dead and another estimated 800,000 HIV-positive. There could be four full Vietnam War Memorial walls engraved with names of gay men who have died of AIDS to date, and there is no end in sight. Because of the relationship of AIDS to the gay community, the stigma of homosexuality in a homophobic culture has been, unfortunately, carried over to the disease. "AIDS-phobia," a catastrophic epidemic of its own, has taken countless lives by delaying government and medical response in the early days, promoting hysteria about contagion, and continuing to foster irrationality in public policy.

AIDS-phobia has generated a fierce political backlash. There is ongoing job and insurance discrimination (despite the passage of the Americans with Disabilities Act in 1990, which includes prohibitions against HIV-related discrimination), as well as continued barriers to aggressive leadership and public health campaigns for safer-sex education. The distribution of lifesaving condoms, the progress of research, updated and relevant prevention methods, needle-exchange programs for IV-drug users, and reasonable widespread public discussion about the disease have been stunted because of homophobia-induced AIDS-phobia. This has certainly been compounded by cultural taboos on death and sex in general, as well as by racism and sexism and by distaste for drug users. But there's no doubt that the core problem has been and remains simple homophobia. Homosexuality itself is still seen by too many people as a mysterious and terrible disease that is somehow both dangerous and contagious; the stigma has simply been "transmitted" to AIDS.

Irrational fear and hatred of gay people, of gay men in particular, has resulted in genocidal neglect in the past, and denial and timidity in the present. The blood of massive numbers of gay and bisexual men (and so many others) is on the hands of homophobes, both witting and unwitting, who have blocked a rational, public-health response to this holocaust.

But, while the horror continues, dealing with AIDS has also quietly wrought many positive effects on the families of origin of people with HIV. There are, of course, many ugly stories reflecting the rejection and ostracism that gay people already face. Families dealing with the double whammy of sons coming out both as gay and as living with AIDS have all too often responded by freezing them out—although, like the weeping father I met at the Names Project Quilt, they may have regretted it when it was too late. Silently and steadily, though, during the fifteen years that gay men have been dying of AIDS by the thousands, their nongay families and friends have also had scores of life-changing experiences. They have become sudden, serendipitous witnesses to the horror and pain of discrimination, self-hatred, social disdain, and irrationality, as well as to the immense courage and love exhibited by sick and dying gay men and their friends and lovers, doctors and nurses. For tens of thousands of parents and siblings of gay men with AIDS, facing the death of child or brother has forced them to stare down their own homophobia and to change attitudes and behaviors toward gay people.

Stories of the impact of AIDS on families are myriad, moving, and, unfortunately, multiplying on a daily basis. One day a few years ago, Sam, a short, pudgy, red-faced Irish bricklayer from Boston, wandered into my office at the Los Angeles Gay and Lesbian Community Services Center. Sam's only son, twenty-nine-year-old Johnny, had died of AIDS a few months before. As a former staff member and then client of the Center, Johnny had talked to his parents glowingly about the organization; it had given him a lot of personal and professional pride, as well as medical and emotional help facing HIV in his life. Sam sat in my office for hours, awkward, guilty, dazed, grieving deeply—another parent who didn't know his gay kid at all, who was now desperately sucking up information about his life, hoping to find some answers to old questions and some salve for the pain.

Sam peppered me with questions: What was Johnny like? Did I know him and work with him directly? What kind of support did he find? Why are people so scared of AIDS? And on and on. Sam reminded me of the saying that when a heart breaks, it sometimes breaks open. His heart was opened up by his grief. This conservative old guy wanted to learn everything he possibly could—about the Center, about the gay world, about AIDS. I got a Christmas card from him a few months later, with a check for the Center enclosed, and this note: "The death of my Johnny has changed me for the good. I speak out for you gay people like I never did before. You do wonderful work, and the world doesn't know about it. Thank you for giving my sweet boy some happiness in his short life."

Every time I hear someone say "you gay people," I have to smile even as I bristle reflexively at the casual objectification inherent in that phrase. I can't help but think of Sam and the changes he has made.

Some families affected by AIDS become active volunteers in AIDS work. One director of an AIDS service organization told me that he was sure that almost all of his nongay volunteers (amounting to over seventy-five total) were family members of people who had died of AIDS. Still other family members have become even more activist. "Mothers' Voices" began as a New York City support group for mothers whose sons and daughters have AIDS. Group members lobby for health care reform and march regularly in New York's Gay Pride celebrations. They hope to be America's conscience on an issue that people, particularly political leaders, want desperately to ignore. Their annual Mother's Day card lobbying project is touching a chord: in 1994, over 250,000 cards, bearing the message "We can't truly celebrate Mother's Day until you help our children," were delivered to the White House.

———

After Gabe came out as both gay and HIV-positive to his retired working-class British parents, they both began to volunteer at a London AIDS services organization as "buddies" to persons with AIDS. Their whole circle of longtime family friends, all in their sixties and seventies, took up AIDS volunteer work as well. It was a means of connecting more closely to Gabe's life and helping out with a cause that had suddenly become their own. In addition, Gabe's sister, her husband, and seven-year-old daughter (named Gabby after Gabe) became quiet AIDS activists, writing eloquent letters for increased funding at the state and national levels.

Marnie had been a closeted lesbian in a Mormon Utah family. When her gay brother developed AIDS, he was emotionally rejected by their family, and Marnie became his primary caretaker, spending every minute with him in the hospital. Bobby never worked through his own self-hatred about being gay, and as he got sicker, he became obsessed with self-shame, listening night and day from his hospital bed to a Christian Right radio station that blasted out antigay sermons. Marnie could do nothing to help him come to terms with himself, and he died sooner, she felt, than he otherwise might have, in great part due to his self-loathing.

As she hadn't been able to change her brother's life, Marnie's response was to change her own. She came out to everyone she knew, and she also changed her profession from high school teacher to radio producer and deejay, putting together programming that would blast gay-positive messages across the airwaves. "It's what I had to do for my baby brother because he couldn't do it for himself," she explained to me, tears running down her face.

Debbie is a twenty-five-year-old lesbian living with AIDS, infected through sexual abuse by her HIV-positive stepfather twelve years ago. She is a nurse who lectures widely on AIDS education, and is a charismatic, happy, dynamic woman. She has been out as a lesbian to her Idaho family all her life. Her best support system in her fight against HIV is her eighty-four-year-old grandfather, who accompanies her on her lecture trips whenever he can. "He's become a one-man AIDS education operation in Idaho," Debbie says. "He's proud of who I am. He's learned that disclosure about this disease and fighting back are keeping me alive, and he does it on my behalf. It's also revved up his life to become an AIDS activist! We're a team, in this one together."

Hugh and Mary Sweeney are devout Roman Catholics in Billings, Montana. When their son Mark got AIDS, they took the brave step of forming AIDS Spirit, a support group for people with AIDS and those affected by the disease, through their local Catholic church. Despite ignorance and heavy initial resistance from the church, they patiently persisted. Mary involved her local Catholic women's Circle of St. Rose of Lima in putting on a rummage sale that raised $300 for AIDS Spirit. Then the couple organized an unprecedented AIDS Mass, with appropriate music and liturgy, as well as talks that embraced diversity and openly challenged AIDS-phobia. An astounding 250 people attended. During the Mass's "Offering," Hugh and Mary stepped forward and spoke; Hugh's opening line was "The silence must end."

When Mark died, the obituary in the Billings paper ran a photo, mentioned he had died of AIDS, and described him as a "proud gay man." Over $2,000 was raised locally in his name for AIDS Spirit and the Yellowstone AIDS Coalition. Hugh and Mary's courageous commitment to being completely out and unashamed about their son's gayness and his illness—and unwaveringly proud to celebrate his life within the context of their devout Catholicism—drew much media coverage and admiring local support. About the couple's brave work fighting the stigma and silence shrouding AIDS, Hugh simply shrugs and says: "We just tried to express our love for Mark in the context of our faith."

New York gay AIDS activist Tim Sweeney, another son of Hugh and Mary Sweeney, says: "My parents' story is not unique. There are hundreds of thousands of people like them across the country whose lives have been fundamentally transformed and opened up by AIDS. Together they are quietly altering our social fabric in key ways—challenging traditional faiths to enlarge their vision, expanding and enriching the idea of family."

The loss of each individual life as well as the overwhelming impact on the social ecology of individual families, gay and nongay, is infinite and incalculable. So, too, are the spiritual and emotional growth and the political commitment that have evolved from the agony of loss, the rage, the revelations, the love. AIDS grief resting within the hearts and souls of an estimated ten million affected families and friends is an enormous and cataclysmic social force waiting to surge into collective and organized action. The shared sorrow and love of those moms and dads and siblings and cousins and grandparents who have so much in common but are cut off from each other by the separateness of their lives could be a vast reservoir of political power. It only needs the right catalyst. I like to believe that those private lessons of love and commitment will ultimately be shaped into public protest and new social values. I can't wait for that huge force to burst into vivid and living social action, and link up with lesbian and gay people whose loss has been equally intense or even greater.

5. MAKING CHANGE WITHIN MAINSTREAM INSTITUTIONS

Our coming out, and our sphere of influence in combating homophobia, can and should extend far beyond our families. We don't live in isolated lavender bubbles as lesbians and gay men. The arenas and worlds in which we work, volunteer, attend religious services or college—and more—reflect the dominant heterosexist culture. Coming out in those worlds has an enormous impact. I'm not talking about becoming conscious organizers with an agenda of political change. I'm talking about each of us simply telling our story about being a lesbian or gay man in America. We can make a huge difference within those worlds, those institutions, those areas, in which we spend big chunks of our lives.

Coming out within organizational settings is critical because these are naturally circumscribed worlds that can change, that can absorb and process new information. The ripples flowing outward from our coming out can reach the very edges of the institution, which can be a kind of microcosm of society at large, a self-contained sphere within which interactions between members can make a real impact. An institution often has a culture—shared values or language—that reverberates widely when one of its members is affected. As with any web, touch one strand and the whole construct moves. And as that culture shifts, as the institutional changes go into effect, either informally or with formal rules or guidelines or procedures, we can each leave a permanent legacy of increased openness and lessened discrimination for others who come after us.

Coming Out on Campus

A proliferation of gay men and lesbians coming out on college campuses in recent years has led to wide-scale consciousness-raising among nongay students, faculty, and staff. The University of Nebraska dean of students' office recently sent out pink triangle decals to every faculty member. (Pink triangles were used by the Nazis to distinguish gay men.) Faculty were asked to put the decals on their office door if it would be safe for a gay or lesbian student to come out to them.

Coming out on campus has also led, of course, to direct organizing of lesbian and gay student, faculty, and staff affinity groups for support, for fighting against antigay violence and harassment in school, and for obtaining antidiscrimination provisions, including even domestic partnership coverage. The National Gay and Lesbian Task Force includes nearly a thousand such groups in its national network. National Coming Out Day, October 11, coordinated by the Human Rights Campaign, the Washington, D.C.–based national gay political group, has become National Coming Out Week on thousands of college campuses, with wider and wider participation by nongay allies in various programs to fight homophobia.

On October 11, pink triangles are worn on campuses all over America by many students, faculty, and administrators, gay and nongay, to express solidarity. It is a grassroots tradition that I love, now spreading rapidly across campuses, which mimics the solidarity shown during the Nazi occupation of Denmark by many Danish people who followed their king's example and wore the Jewish yellow star, so that Danish Jews were indistinguishable from Gentiles.

A few years ago, I went back to my own alma mater—Middlebury College in Middlebury, Vermont—on National Coming Out Day. It warmed my lesbian heart to see hundreds of students and faculty members walking around that campus all day sporting big bright pink paper triangles on their jackets and sweaters. I did notice that an awful lot of those triangles bore bold print announcing that the wearers were "Straight but Not Narrow." Obviously, lots of people still feel the compulsion to protect themselves from the supposition that they might be gay, but as time goes on, fewer and fewer of our straight allies will find the need to write those words.

Coming Out at Church, at Work, at School and Beyond . . .

The effects of coming out in mainstream religious, educational, civic, and workplace settings are deeply revolutionary. They crack entrenched homophobic policies and create permanent change. One person can make a huge difference in his or her synagogue or church, or, of course, at work.

———

While she was in rabbinical school, many friends knew Denise Eger was a lesbian, but she was afraid she would lose her career if she were publicly gay. After her ordination, however, Rabbi Eger did come out publicly, and in 1990, the Central Conference of American Rabbis voted to uphold the rights of gay men and lesbians to become rabbis, in great part because of Rabbi Eger's openness and lobbying. The report read in part: "We endorse the view that all Jews are religiously equal and we are aware of loving and committed relationships between people of the same sex; so we call upon rabbis and congregations to treat with respect and to integrate fully all Jews into the life of the community." Rabbi Eger, who now serves Kol Ami in Los Angeles, a lesbian and gay Reform Jewish congregation one of whose copies of the Torah was rescued from a town utterly destroyed by Hitler, says: "I believe the power of personal transformation is a part of the Torah. We see that power when we are public and normal about who we are. The more we challenge who the mainstream thinks we are, then the more our personal power transforms how they think of us."

In 1994, Rabbi Eger and her partner, Karen Siteman, brought their newborn son, Benjamin, to a major West Coast conference of rabbis. After showing the assembled rabbis *Chicks in White Satin,* the Oscar-nominated documentary about a Jewish lesbian wedding, Rabbi Eger asked how many would perform such a ceremony themselves. Seventy-five percent said they would. "Three years earlier, that number would have been twenty-five percent. My being out and active, my bringing Karen with me year after year to the conferences, and now, sharing our son, our growing family, with them, changed their hearts," says Rabbi Eger. "Once again, it's the power of each of us to inspire personal transformation in others."

Elizabeth Birch, now head of the Human Rights Campaign, was in charge of litigation for Apple Computers when she came out of the closet at work in 1992. She made a point of spending extra time with her boss and mentor, Apple's then-CEO John Sculley, explaining why coming out was so important and sharing information about her life. Within weeks of Elizabeth's coming out to Sculley, he instituted domestic-partner benefits at Apple. And a few months later, on the morning of April 25, 1993, with no fanfare and no warning, he flew his private plane to Washington, D.C., to quietly show his personal support for gay and lesbian rights at our huge national march, standing with Elizabeth backstage at the rally for hours.

Alisha was formerly a shop steward and is now a professional trainer and organizer for the International Brotherhood of Teamsters. It had been tough enough being a Latina woman moving up in the ranks of the Teamsters. Deciding to come out as gay in her work was not easy, but Alisha felt her organizing job would benefit if she shed the lie of the closet. One by one, she told her co-workers, and found that her honesty was actually strengthening her leadership. Her popularity made acceptance relatively painless. It turned out that there were lots of questions from her fellow organizers, particularly since many UPS drivers were lesbians. People knew it, but hadn't felt they had the language or the license to discuss it. In 1994, thanks to Alisha's quiet visibility as an out lesbian, nongay workers spearheaded the inclusion of a nondiscrimination clause concerning sexual orientation in the regional union bylaws. "Alisha's openness pushed me to get off my duff and initiate this new clause," says Joanie, the straight union leader who led the drive.

Rachel was a recovering alcoholic who was an active member of the Twelve-Step community in Chicago. When she was a guest speaker at Twelve-Step meetings, she would focus solely on her story of breaking the stranglehold alcohol had over her life for over twenty years. She would not come out as a lesbian. But, increasingly, as she watched her friends die of AIDS and found herself impelled to come out more and more in her own life, she also told the fuller truth of her life within the recovering community. She saw it as a sort of life-affirming antidote to the sorrow and death around her. The first time she told her full life story, at a meeting with over a hundred people attending, she found herself making connections she had never publicly made, connections between her drinking and her internalized shame as a lesbian, connections between a more honest and open recovery process and her own shedding of the closet. She spoke with a new kind of wholeness, reflected in her words and her confident tone of voice. Afterward, she was overwhelmed by the number of people who lined up to thank her, and who tearfully shared their own stories from their multiple closets. Several people came out to her about having gay or lesbian siblings, or children, and one recent transplant to town told of having carefully hidden her mother's lesbianism from her new friends.

Over the following years, Rachel noticed a veritable coming-out revolution in her recovering community. More and more gay-specific meetings became officially sanctioned and lesbians and gays were increasingly open and found a welcome embrace within the recovery world. "Despite its adherence to tradition—and because its overarching mission is helping people stay clean—the Twelve-Step movement is a flexible, changeable culture able to be affected by those who speak from the heart," Rachel explained. "People respond to honesty; it's part of the program. I have seen ignorance and bigotry melt before my eyes in those meetings, and I'm proud to have been a small part of it."

Virginia Uribe is a science teacher at L.A.'s Fairfax High School who during the 1970s and early 1980s informally counseled a number of struggling gay and lesbian students who sought her out. "I guess they figured out who I was despite my determined closet," she says in retrospect, chuckling. In 1984, a gay youth was harassed so severely that he dropped out of school. That was the catalyst, says Virginia. "I was furious, and knew I had to act. I had to help those kids so that this would never, ever happen again. So I organized a little lunchtime rap group where kids could feel safe to come and talk about their fears and concerns. About the same time, I leapt out of my closet, appearing on a local TV show about gay teachers. Then I scrunched up my courage to come out directly to the principal so I could talk to him about formalizing this program somehow. He was great, and immediately gave me a green light to develop a real program, a model that could be copied at other schools in Los Angeles. We created Project 10, a school counseling program for kids who are gay, lesbian, and bisexual. Over the years, the word has spread. We work with the department of guidance to train counselors, and work with teachers and administrators to raise their consciousness about this invisible population. Today, twelve years later, we have the Los Angeles Gay and Lesbian Education Commission, with a paid director and an office at the board of education, spreading the word to fifty high schools, seventy-five middle schools, and hundreds of elementary schools in the L.A. Unified School District. We run formal Project 10 support groups with trained teachers and counselors at thirty high schools, creating a safe environment once a week for these kids to talk about everything on their minds. We do speaking and training; we refer parents to P-FLAG. There's a Project 10 now in

Cambridge, Massachusetts, with similar programs in Santa Cruz, San Francisco, and about a dozen other cities across the country."

———

Look at the systemic impact of these lesbians on major institutions in our country. Their courage, their calm pride in their gayness, and their decision to act have changed the course of life for hundreds, if not thousands, of other people, straight and gay, coming behind them.

Virginia Uribe is one of our great heroines, an early and accomplished pioneer in a particular struggle that must escalate dramatically in the years to come if we are going to win our freedom: coming out and challenging systemic homophobia in our nation's schools. Our schools remain a bastion of stigma, silence, and secrecy for our gay, lesbian, and bisexual kids—and for countless gay teachers as well. With schools targeted for vicious attacks by the radical right, it's all the more important to fight for visibility and equality in the educational arena. A major step will be to work to free our teachers.

Gay and lesbian teachers are everywhere. It wasn't a coincidence that Tom Hanks thanked two teachers for being significant gay role models in his life when he accepted his Oscar (for *Philadelphia*) at the 1994 Academy Awards. There are probably more gay and lesbian people working as teachers in this country than are concentrated in any other profession (except maybe health care). We are positive and nurturing teachers of young people in large numbers; we always have been and we always will be.

I don't know anyone who hasn't had several gay or lesbian teachers in their lives. Lesbians and gay men pour enormous dedication, creativity, and love into our teaching work. I find it maddening and ironic that this group of us—such positive role models for young people, so influential in young people's lives, so hardworking and committed—is so widely oppressed. One former school principal, a straight man, recently told me: "The many gay teachers I've known in twenty years in education are probably the brightest, most dedicated, most gifted teachers there are." If all the gay and lesbian teachers in America were to come out tomorrow, and if the right were to have its way and they lost their jobs, an inescapable crisis would hit the U.S. educational system. There simply would be too many vacancies and too much talent to replace.

Gay and lesbian teachers have a particularly vital role to play, because they belie the most dangerous stereotype about gay people: that we are bad for children. These lies—that we recruit, molest, and otherwise harm children—cling like sticky old glue to our community's reputation. Because of them, teachers face extraordinary obstacles to coming out. Even though studies show that 97 percent of child molesters are heterosexual, usually married, men, the manufactured terror about gay teachers persists. (Harvey Milk once said, "If it were true that teachers recruit, there'd be an awful lot of nuns running around.")

Despite increasing evidence that genetic factors influence sexual orientation, despite studies by the National Institutes for Mental Health and the Kinsey Institute showing that sexual orientation is largely formed by the early preschool years, the lying about us persists. Despite the overwhelming evidence that gay parents—far more influential than teachers during those critical early years—have zero impact on their kids' sexual orientation, our teachers are tarred with the brush of homophobic paranoia. Public opinion is still mired in bigotry; many Americans still don't want a gay teacher teaching their kids. In the nine states that do protect our jobs, peer pressure at school and the fear of backlash from parents and administration still create a powerful and pervasive fear of coming out.

Bringing the coming-out revolution into the schools has taken time, but it's finally in full swing. Spurred on by recent vicious right-wing homophobic assaults on school curricula, progay books, AIDS education, multicultural programming, and the like, gay teachers, school staff, and administrators—and their straight allies—are finally coming out all over the place. Along with Project 10, which harnesses new energies of teachers, administrators, and staff in service of our kids' safety and self-esteem, a vital new leader in the national battle against homophobia in the schools is the Gay, Lesbian, and Straight Teachers Network. GLSTN is a federation of local grassroots groups in twenty states in public, private, and parochial schools, from kindergarten through twelfth grade, working to create a safe environment for gay and lesbian teachers and students through training, media advocacy, and community organizing. There couldn't be a more important arena for the coming-out revolution.

II. COMING OUT CREATES UNINTENDED CHANGE IN THE WORLD

Like the proverbial stone thrown into the pond, the ripples of our coming out can transform the life of everyone who learns we are gay. Our individual coming-out process changes hearts and minds throughout our sphere of influence, affects the lives of those we know, love, and volunteer and work with, and often translates into permanent and concrete political or systemic change.

In addition, many other people, even further removed, are influenced by our coming out because our acquaintances, friends, coworkers, and family members then come out to others about knowing us. Because of our coming out, consciousness is raised, bigotry diminishes, and behavior changes in positive ways in places that we have no idea we've reached. There are often marvelous, far-reaching consequences to our coming-out stories, beyond our wildest expectations. We inadvertently bring a transformational touch well beyond the world we move in daily.

By just being ourselves, by living our lives openly, proudly, lovingly, we model strength and a fight-back spirit for other gays and lesbians we don't even know. We inspire all kinds of people to speak out against injustice. We motivate people to more closely examine their lives or to bring more truth-telling into them. We inject new vibrancy into the definition of family and into the hallowed institution of marriage. We, the pariahs from society, the scapegoats of the ultra-right, become extraordinary agents of change just by living our ordinary lives. Our creativity, our caring, our daring send ripples of empowerment out into the universe, into broader circles of influence than we ever imagined.

1. ROLE MODELING FOR OTHER GAYS AND LESBIANS

Role modeling is an amazingly potent consequence of each individual's coming out. Since isolation and invisibility traditionally have defined gay and lesbian lives, just living life out of the closet has a positive, empowering influence on other gay men and lesbians who are fighting the fear of exiting the closet.

Practically every lesbian or gay man who has emerged from the darkness of the closet has gained vital strength in his or her personal odyssey from seeing the example set by someone else who is gay. It may be a visible spokesperson, an elected official, a community activist, or a celebrity. More likely, it's someone they know or run into by chance through community connections, whose story is inspirational. Often that story is tucked away for a future time when one is ready for its moral to get to work in our consciousness. For us as a newly emerging minority, the importance of this cannot be overstated. We are born into enemy territory and often grow up in hostile or at best indifferent surroundings. For these reasons, role models play an essential part in inspiring and encouraging us. Role models lead by example, even when they are surprised to look back and see a parade behind them.

Anthony knew he was gay when childhood crushes on other boys became even more intense as he entered puberty. By the time he went off to college, he was a sullen withdrawn youth. Despite high grades, his self-esteem was low. He was a loner who hid in books. His freshman English teacher, Professor Timmer, however, was openly gay, a fact he made known to his class on October 11, National Coming Out Day, by wearing a pink triangle and taking a few minutes from his lecture on D. H. Lawrence to talk about the special day and reveal his homosexuality. Anthony sat there in shock, surprised and thrilled. Immediately after class he made an appointment with the professor. When they met, Anthony awkwardly came out, and Timmer quite matter-of-factly informed him about a number of resources available to him: the name of a gay-sensitive counselor in the student counseling center; the men's rap group sponsored by the Gay and Lesbian Student Association. But even more significant was the role modeling that Professor Timmer provided. He was confident, smart, accomplished, and articulate. He was not militant, but he was totally out and comfortable with it. He referred to his spouse, Stephen, just as a straight faculty member might, casually and with affection. In class, he occasionally referred to the huge lesbian and gay literary heritage. He explored gay sensibilities and the impact of sexual identity on writing, just as he did with the issues of race, class, and gender. The material was fully integrated into his larger intellectual work and his professional presentation. Being gay was fully "normalized" for Professor Timmer, and that was the most impressive and inspiring fact for young Anthony.

Previously trapped in a silent world of self-loathing, suffering thoughts of suicide and feelings of shame and self-doubt, Anthony found his teacher to be a lifeline to self-esteem.

Gloria was a young nurse, a second-generation Filipina, just out of school and working in the emergency room of a Houston hospital. She had left an abusive husband and had a two-year-old son to support. She occasionally dated men as cover but had a quiet lesbian life, with a diverse circle of mostly lesbian and some gay male friends. She was active in an informal network of some eighty lesbian mothers and gay dads around the city. She wasn't out at work or to her family, and she more or less assumed her life would remain half-closeted forever. Her divorce had so badly upset her family that she couldn't imagine coming out as a lesbian to her rigidly conservative Catholic immigrant parents.

One day a young Latino man named Lorenzo, who had been the victim of a vicious hate crime, was brought to the emergency room. He'd been stabbed by a gang of white skinheads who yelled racist and antigay slurs as they attacked him. He was close to death and remained in the intensive care unit for several days. Something in the fighting spirit that was keeping Lorenzo alive attracted Gloria. She visited him when she could find time, and they struck up a friendship. In the course of one early conversation, he came out to her, and then she to him. He also came out to everyone else at the hospital—he wore his gayness as a proud badge. He was a member of the AIDS activist group ACT UP, had been to both recent gay marches on Washington, in 1987 and 1993, and was more proud of his gay and AIDS activism than of anything else in his life. His pride gave him the life force he needed to fend off death, get back on his feet and out of the hospital in record time.

Gloria and Lorenzo remained friends, and his pride slowly began rubbing off on her. She asked to be assigned to the AIDS ward. She told more and more people she was a lesbian, beginning with the gay men with AIDS she met, and then, over time, her co-workers. She found that her new openness positively affected her professional esteem. She started taking more responsibilities at work, asserting herself more and more. She and another nurse—also a lesbian, as it turned out—helped reorganize the AIDS ward so that it was more patient-friendly and more comfortable for the extended families of the people with AIDS. If it hadn't been for Lorenzo, Gloria told me, she would never have come out, or grown so much professionally and personally.

Bradley couldn't believe his eyes when he watched the TV news on April 16, 1993. At the top of the news in Chicago was coverage of the first group of gays and lesbians ever to meet with a president of the United States. More incredibly, in the chair right up front next to President Clinton in the Oval Office was a black gay man, Phill Wilson, who also acted as spokesperson for the group after the meeting. Bradley couldn't remember ever seeing a black man as a gay spokesperson. While he went to the black gay bars in Chicago, and had a circle of black gay friends, he had imposed a lavender ceiling on his own life. When he was a kid, he had harbored dreams of being a lawyer, even a politician. But once he realized he was gay, he had dumped those dreams. Although he believed he could possibly overcome racism with the support of his family and home community, he felt it was absolutely impossible for him to be black *and gay* and successful. He believed that the threat of discovery would naturally limit his options, and that he would never be accepted if he was open.

But that night in April 1993, he saw the glimmer of a new possibility in the smiling, handsome, open, proud face of Phill Wilson.

His dreams were reawakened, and he began making plans to go to college, a dream previously deferred due to fear.

———

Particularly for gay men of color and for all lesbians—whose utter invisibility over the years testifies to the double and triple damages wrought by sexism and racism interweaving with hetero-sexism—role models are extraordinarily important. In a world where most media images of black men are as criminals being handcuffed by white police, the power of a positive image of a black man like gay and AIDS activist Phill Wilson is transformative. Bradley was not the only black gay man whose life was touched by Phill's visibility in that photo, beamed around the world to millions of people. That photo represented a small step toward setting the record straight on just how diverse we are as a people. (In addition, President Clinton's own acceptance and respect for us in that room was another kind of role modeling: leadership on a still-unpopular issue that signaled commitment to a vision of America that includes us.)

Because they see and are aware of role models—gay people who are living freely and happily and proudly, whether they are personal acquaintances or more distant figures—thousands of gay people are coming out at an ever faster pace to ever wider circles of people. They are getting involved personally, professionally, politically—and openly—in their communities. In their own time, they will take their place as role models for others coming out behind them, teaching by example, helping to build esteem, planting new hopes, smashing stereotypes, and jamming the homophobic radar of people who have preconceived notions of who we are.

A special part in the drama of growing gay visibility is played by public figures who are open and by celebrity role models from all fields. Sheila James Kuehl, my former partner of nine years, is a TV actress turned feminist attorney who became California's first openly gay state assemblyperson in 1994. She inspired hundreds of people to come out for the first time and volunteer on her campaign, including gay people who had never even voted before. Virtually all openly gay candidates comment on the role-model aspect of their campaign and (if they are elected) their job. Zeke Zeidler, a thirty-year-old gay man who was elected to the Manhattan Beach,

California, school board in 1995, says, "The best part of running for office openly gay—especially as a first for this area—was how many closet doors I know I helped open all over town, even if I never met the people."

The openness of famous role models—celebrities like k. d. lang and Melissa Etheridge—adds breadth and credibility to our fight, and helps save countless years of shame and pain in the closet for lots of people, particularly young people. "Coming out became possible for me because my longtime hero had come out," a twenty-nine-year-old Latino man told me as he waited patiently in line with hundreds of other people to meet Greg Louganis when the Olympic diver's autobiography, *Breaking the Surface*, appeared in 1995.

2. EMPOWERMENT IS CONTAGIOUS: MAKING CONNECTIONS

As more and more people begin to see lesbians and gay men in a positive (or at least neutral) light, our influence begins to extend beyond our own struggle.

Recently, I overheard a conversation between two people standing near me on the subway. One young woman said to an office colleague: "That's it; I've had it. I'm going to human resources tomorrow and complain about Ed's sexual harassment. I'm not putting up with it anymore." Her friend: "What pushed you over the edge? You've been putting up with it for months." The first young woman: "Last weekend, my sixteen-year-old brother came out as gay to the whole family at Sunday lunch. He had such guts; it was awesome. And I decided if he could do that, I can stand up for myself at work."

I have no idea how many comings-out have inspired others to take up the cause of their own liberation, but I do know that empowerment is a contagious thing. When you feel stronger and better about yourself, it is inspirational. My younger sister, Ann, credits my giving her Rita Mae Brown's *Rubyfruit Jungle* as a formative and empowering event in her life. She was fourteen years old and read and reread the book, treasuring it but keeping it hidden for many months, afraid my parents would take it away from her. (In those days, *Rubyfruit Jungle* was published by a tiny women's press, Daughters, Inc., and not available widely.) My parents were apparently afraid the book might recruit my sister to lesbianism. That it did not do, but it did recruit my definitely heterosexual sister to a stronger sense of her own self at a critical age, and to a lifelong commitment to women's equality. The family controversy about the book only served to highlight its impact. Ann, a top-notch athlete, recalls, "I remember feeling so good reading about another tomboy girl—I loved the character's strength, and I loved that my lesbian older sister, whom I admired for being open, had given it to me. That book empowered me like nothing else did in those years."

Making connections between issues, between forms of oppression and discrimination, happens often. A moving section in an educational video, *Straight from the Heart*, produced by the prominent San Francisco lesbian psychiatrist Dr. Dee Mosbacher, features Tracy Thorne and his parents. Tracy is the Navy lieutenant who came out publicly on television in 1992 and was kicked out of the military. In the video, Tracy's father poignantly relates a story from his own youth: working behind a pharmacy counter with a "whites only" policy, he followed orders and kicked a young black woman nurse out of the store. As his own tears flow, he connects the pain of discrimination that he himself perpetrated, and now deeply regrets, to the pain of the homophobia his son is suffering. His empathy for his son's own plight awakened empathy for the victim of his own racism so many years earlier.

And the ripples go on: Dee Mosbacher's 1996 film *All God's Children*, made with Dr. Sylvia Rhue, an African-American lesbian psychologist and filmmaker, exposes the radical right's wedge-driving between the black and gay communities in service of a pernicious agenda of bigotry. The film has inspired bridge-building and consciousness-raising across the country.

———

Michelle, a straight African-American social worker, saw *All God's Children* at a lunchtime showing at her workplace. "A lightbulb went off in my head. As black people, our trust for white people is fragile, and since the gay movement has always seemed so white, many of us couldn't relate. I remember the uproar in my neighborhood when the film *The Color Purple* came out. Ladies at my church were protesting the lesbianism and the portrayal of black men as wife-beaters, and they set up picket lines outside the theater. Never mind that there's plenty of black wife-beaters—we're just not supposed to talk about *that*. Showing the lesbian relationship as well seemed like a slap in the face of the black family. I supported that protest. I equated gay rights with the breakdown of our black family, and I resented it when wealthy gay white men said the civil rights movement and gay rights movement were alike.

"When I saw *All God's Children,* though, I saw that my church sisters on that picket line were wrong. I saw how fighting gays has been the conscious strategy of the same people who supported segregation in the South. They know how to divide and conquer. I saw how racism and homophobia are similar. We may not all like each other's lifestyles, but we're all God's children here to share this world, and we can find plenty in common if we try."

———

Connections between issues pop up at surprising moments. Recently, I was the invited guest speaker at a meeting of the diversity task force of a large western corporation with an excellent track record on all diversity issues. I noticed right away that the audience (about half gay and half straight) at this voluntary brown-bag meeting seemed preoccupied, too quiet, and a little edgy. I couldn't figure it out. It wasn't the issue I was addressing; all present were informed leaders in fighting discrimination, including homophobia. I tried every speaker's trick to capture their attention—telling jokes, asking questions, moving around the room—to no avail. Over an hour into the two-hour session, I was talking about what lesbian psychologist Linda Garnets has termed "AIDS trauma syndrome," the untreated psychological epidemic found increasingly in lesbian and gay urban AIDS-affected communities. I was describing symptoms many of us experience, which resemble post-traumatic stress syndrome: psychic numbness, panic attacks, migraines and other physical symptoms, serious depression, survivor guilt, and more. Suddenly, the group got eerily still. Then an older woman in the front row said: "I don't mean to belittle what you're talking about with AIDS, but everything you're describing applies to us here. You see, the company is undergoing 'reengineering,' a fancy name for laying off over twenty percent of us and retraining the rest of us to totally new jobs. People are completely traumatized—everyone. All of us thought we had jobs here for the rest of our lives."

The group then exploded into a passionate, active conversation about the situation, and, needless to say, the next hour was spent processing their own intense pain and anger and grief. I found I became a very different kind of organizer than I had expected to be that day, urging my audience on not in the struggle against workplace homophobia but instead to fight against disempowerment in a time of turbulent economic transition. The common ground we found was unexpected, but it was there.

Yes, empowerment is contagious; fighting one injustice opens up our empathy for others. Making connections between and among issues is a powerful and unexpected result of our individual coming-out process. There are many others.

3. CHANGING THE WAY THE WORLD WORKS: INCREASED SELF-EXAMINATION AND COMMUNICATION

The impact of our visibility and our way of being in the world as out and proud gays and lesbians often extends beyond directly combating injustice, including homophobia. I was first alerted to the varied and profound kinds of effects that coming out has on our blood families a few years ago, when I made one of my periodic visits to a regular youth support group at the Center in L.A. We were having a rambling, fun conversation about coming out to our parents—focusing, of course, on the process's relationship to us: how long their acceptance took, their immediate reactions, and so forth. Then one young man said thoughtfully: "You know, I think my coming out to my parents last year really changed my family's whole communication pattern. It's kind of subtle, and it took a while, but now people listen to each other more. I think there's now a better, healthier connection between people, all the way around."

Lots of the kids in the room nodded in agreement at this, and a whole new conversation was sparked. Too often, we don't see the impact of our own coming out on the people in our lives, particularly when there's that initial shock, anger, and rejection. Naturally, we are caught up in our own pain, focusing on our own issues. We are blind to the subtle but powerful ways that our honesty reverberates out and prompts others to be honest about a host of issues. We don't see that our act of coming out has a life of its own, *separate from the reaction to us*. When we look closely, we can see that, quietly but powerfully, the quality of relationships in many families of gay people changes for the better after one of their own comes out.

Caroline is a surgeon who is married to a highly respected professor at a medical school. He is bisexual, and they have worked out their marriage over the years. "I am most struck by the level of thought and self-examination that Geraldo and his gay friends bring to their own lives," Caroline says. "Sometimes I don't think they are aware of exactly how unusual it is. Theirs are lives well examined. There is a quality of absolute authenticity and honest reflection about life that sometimes takes my breath away. It has forced me to look at myself in all kinds of ways—to reflect on my relationships, to examine my own sexuality, to think about my secrets, my own various closets. I'm very grateful to Geraldo for this. I know his bisexuality has caused him pain, but it's also been a great gift he has shared with me, and others who are straight."

"When my older sister came out in my black, middle-class, midwestern suburban family it ricocheted around like a wild Ping-Pong ball," Charlene, age fifteen, told me. "Everyone went nuts—anger, tears, slamming doors. But, you know, somehow the anger and the tears chased away some of the mistrust of each other. Over the couple of years that followed, people opened up to each other. We listen to each other more caringly. Melanie didn't get the benefits because she had left home already, but our family is definitely more loving now. We hold hands and say grace before dinner now, and, believe me, that wouldn't have happened before."

Ron's dad was almost fifty when Ron was born, and as an Old World German, was conditioned to a stoic inexpressive demeanor. He never expressed love openly, and had been very shut down and disapproving of Ron's gayness when his son came out to him at twenty-five. Although his father had always expressly forbidden Ron to bring his lover, Willy, home, Ron persisted in calling his dad regularly and made a point of talking about his relationship, and how much he loved Willy. When Ron Senior was diagnosed with terminal cancer in his early eighties, he called Ron on the phone and asked him to come home to Tucson to visit. At the very end of the phone call, he said words that shocked Ron: "I would very much like it if Willy could come as well." When Ron and Willy spent what turned out to be a deathbed visit at Ron's parents' home, Ron Senior healed years of hurt by apologizing with tears in his eyes for his lack of acceptance of their relationship. He looked his son in the eyes and said words Ron Junior had never thought he would hear: "I love you." Then, he turned to Willy and said, "You are a good man. I wish you the best of luck in your legal career, and I ask you to take good care of my son for me when I'm gone. He is a special man." Deathbed reconciliations are an old story, but Ron is convinced that the depth of change in his father's character was a result of his own emotional openness about his love for Willy. "My not being closed and uptight about emotions, like a man was supposed to be in my family—my openly expressing love for my lover—allowed my father to open up when he was ready," says Ron.

Debbie, the young Idaho lesbian with AIDS we met earlier, says that her lifelong openness as a lesbian has definitely changed the level of openness among some members of her family as well. Her wonderful eighty-four-year-old grandfather, widowed a few years ago, recently started dating a seventy-eight-year-old woman. He called Debbie for advice on dating and sex. "Should I kiss her on the first date?" he asked. "You know about women and it's been so long since

I did this," Debbie believes his honesty and forthrightness about personal issues are due to her own openness about her sexual orientation.

———————

These are great gifts indeed that we give to our families and the world—honesty and courage that inspire others to greater openness and daring as well.

4. BRINGING DEMOCRACY HOME: EXPANDING THE DEFINITION OF FAMILY

For years, lesbians and gay men have formed brave, varied, wonderful families—largely closeted and out of society's view. The radical right tries to demonize our families because they do not fit a traditional mold, but our creative families of choice do in truth embody the best, most basic, "family value" of all: *love*. In fact, our various queer family configurations often have succeeded in achieving unconditional love and support in far greater measure than many of the so-called traditional families in which we grew up.

Our Families Are Different

Family love comes in lots of flavors in the gay world. Some gay people—more than is generally understood—form lifelong, committed relationships, many of them monogamous. (A 1994 *Advocate* magazine survey showed that a surprising 71 percent of its male readers sought lifelong, monogamous love partnerships.)

Many gay people, though, live perfectly happy lives *not* in lifelong, monogamous relationships. We may have several long-term committed relationships in the course of our lifetime: serial monogamy. We may, in addition or instead, form extended families that often include our former lovers and partners. Or friendship circles become our families. I even know a long-term, loving, live-in relationship among three gay men, still happy and thriving after thirteen years—a "ménage à trois gay marriage," my friends call themselves.

Gay men and lesbians are entering creative co-parenting family arrangements together in countless permutations. Or take the example of two lesbian friends of mine, together for over a decade in a committed life partnership, who have each had a child by the same sperm donor, a straight man who is an active co-parent to his son and daughter. The three adults and two kids live on the same block, in two small houses that seem like extensions of each other, and form a wonderful and loving family unit. After many years of foster-parenting several children, my dear friend, AIDS activist and actor Michael Kearns, has officially adopted eighteen-month-old Tia, who is well cared for not only by Michael, but by a well-organized, highly committed extended family of ten of Michael's friends, gay and straight, single and married. "Sometimes I feel less like a dad than the busy artistic director of a huge, multicultural tribe," Michael says with a loving laugh.

Our experience as exiles from our families of origin has taught us how to be free from the strictures of convention that can too often narrow human potential. Yes, our families explode traditional patterns and prescribed roles. Yes, they are wonderfully diverse—and we should be nothing short of exuberantly proud of that diversity. We are contributing in positive ways to the evolution of the human family, which is broadening to encompass ever greater diversity and democracy as time marches on.

One man in Wisconsin actually set out to create his own family structure. Feeling isolated, he consciously formed what he called a tribe. He chose specific gay and lesbian individuals to join, people he wanted to get to know and who he felt shared common values. They share meals, provide emotional support for each other, share in child care, and even help each other out financially in tough times. His new, consciously invented, happy, and healthy extended family has continued to work for its members for many years.

Lesbian society is filled with women whose best friends and closest family members are our exes, our former lovers and partners. I remember a poignant evening just before Christmas over a decade ago: Sheila, my life partner at the time, was suddenly called to the hospital because Kristi, her former lover (of seventeen years) and now best friend, had a deadly heart attack. Kristi's folks were both dead, and she was estranged from her two brothers. Sheila and I rushed to the hospital, and there the two of us sat for hours with another of her closest friends; together we were Kristi's only true family. But when the doctor came out in the middle of the night to tell us that things were really bad, and to ask how to contact Kristi's family to make "pull-the-plug" decisions, she had a bit of trouble comprehending the situation. Thus began the litany that so many gay people have had to endure: "Is she married?" No. "Children?" No. "Parents?" No. "Siblings?" Yes; two brothers she doesn't talk to. Sheila kept saying: "We *are* her family." The doctor kept trying to find other, "real" family. Finally, Sheila said, "Look, Kristi and I lived together for seventeen years. I'm her ex-partner and best friend. I *am* her family, damn it." The doctor grasped the situation at last, although as it turned out no life-and-death decisions needed to be made: Kristi died later that night, aged forty-five. And we had to go through this ordeal again later when a different doctor, on duty when Kristi died, insisted on going off to call her brothers to "officially" inform them of her death, leaving Sheila standing there in tears waiting for her moment alone with Kristi to say good-bye.

Family Diversity Is Everywhere

There is no single correct family form. Period. The human family flourishes in as many forms as the human imagination can create; it is simply a lie to say otherwise. Of course everyone needs family, and everyone values family. Everyone builds family, one way or another; family is what we create. The lesbian and gay family message is loud and clear: family diversity is here; get used to it. We are merely adding our proud chorus of voices to those of many others— women, single fathers, seniors, disabled people, and young adults— who have all in various ways pointed out the limits of the so-called traditional nuclear family, even as we reaffirm the profound importance of the notion of family itself.

All of us should demand respect for our families—and all families—in their full creative bloom, as long as they are positive and nurturing. We should recognize that the contemporary "traditional family values" crusade is nothing more than a flailing—and temporary—backlash against women's equality, gay liberation, children's rights, and the idea of diversity in general. This reactionary backlash is based on the fear of change, change that is inevitable with economic and social evolution, change that can promise more, not less, freedom for the vast majority of us.

It's no secret that the family is rapidly changing these days. Only 7 percent of Americans still live in the old-fashioned family structure with a heterosexual man as breadwinner, a woman as stay-at-home wife and mother, and two kids. In fact, it's odd that this structure has come to be seen as traditional, since the nuclear family unit defended by the right as a sacred, immutable form has only existed for roughly a hundred years—and has been steadily shifting and adapting to economic and social changes. The nuclear family, with woman as unpaid emotional worker whose primary jobs are reproduction and maintaining daily life for the paid male worker and "his" children, hardly needed lesbians and gay men to challenge it in order to begin to die. The 1960s feminist revolution did that job first. Its genesis lay in women's isolation, in their rejection of their second-class status and the dependency and passivity inherent in it, and in the economic changes pushing women into the labor force. But major evolutionary changes in women's roles and family structure, created by economic forces and rising social expectations, have been met with ferocious resistance.

Change is never easy, and the disintegration of the patriarchal nuclear family ideal has brought with it understandable insecurity and confusion. This confusion, and the sense of loss that accompanies all change, even causes some people to perceive feminism and gay rights as more threatening and destructive than liberating.

The backlash against family diversity expresses itself in a sentimental and nostalgic attempt to retreat to vague notions of 1950s happy heterosexual family life. But the fact is that an awful lot of burdensome mythology has been piled on that little nuclear family unit, and as the world gets more mobile, more complex, more economically difficult, that unit has proved fragile and impermanent indeed. Even if one doesn't count the colorful families of gays and lesbians, the American family is radically different these days from what it was only a few decades ago.

Family diversity is here, and it's growing, in a natural process of adaption to human change and evolution. Divorce rates of 50 percent result in reconfigured "blended" heterosexual families; there are step-parents and step-children, and foster parents and foster children. (And, as feminist psychologist Harriet Lerner points out, a failure rate of 50 percent should mandate profound reassessment of the fundamental vitality of the heterosexual marriage institution regardless of other issues.) There is a proliferation of single heterosexual parenting, as well as of alternative, chosen families of heterosexual disabled and older people. All that makes for a country desperately in need of an accurate and expanded definition of "family," one that matches reality and embraces the diversity of forms in this most ancient human social structure.

Because gays and lesbians in general are not yet widely accepted as equal, we are a convenient scapegoat and target for conservatives who are trying to promote a return to the "traditional family." Gay and lesbian families face daunting and aggressive opposition from our enemies, fueled by fear of change combined with widespread ignorance. That is why recognition of our families is such a cutting-edge issue for both sides. Those of us who come out publicly about our relationships, who insist on acknowledgment and affirmation of those relationships, and those involved in parenting are vitally important revolutionaries in this new era.

Promoting Real Family Values

We face fierce resistance. Seventy-two percent of Americans still disapprove of gay marriage; 62 percent oppose domestic partnership benefits. Sixty-five percent don't support us raising children, and 62 percent don't want their kids playing with ours. A blanket of negativity still shrouds the truth. Ignorance, sex phobia (fear of sex and sexuality), and those dusty old stereotypes still promulgated by the right—gays as child recruiters, pedophiles, and sex fanatics—combine with the closet to hide the real truth of our lives: lesbian and gay people create and thrive within happy, wonderfully vibrant, loving families.

Fortunately, the clock of human progress ultimately ticks in only one direction: forward. There may be one step backward for every two forward strides, but it's not possible to return to the largely mythical heterosexual nuclear family now that we are out of the closet and women are demanding their rights alongside men. When people taste freedom, they do not go back permanently by choice. Despite aggressive campaigns by the right, the evolution of new kinds of families will continue, not only because of economic pressures but also because the so-called traditional family is not a perfect and happy place for many of its members. Modern feminism has allowed long-silent voices to be heard—those of women, and, increasingly, of children. And the "traditional" family has been found to be often a place of terrifying levels of violence, incest, and neglect as well as loneliness and alienation. No wonder it is disintegrating. The only question is how long it will take for honesty to set in, for acceptance of the changes to come about, and for social policies to arise that really do help nurture liberating, loving family ties.

The old social order in this country has been dying since people challenged the conformity of the melting-pot ideal in the 1960s, and began to welcome the mixing bowl of diversity—including diversity within the family. A new, evolved, modernized social order based on democracy and pluralism is struggling to be born, but we are still in an awkward transitional phase. Out of the current chaos and backlash against change will come substantial and positive change, in the long term. To follow through on the American promise of fuller equality and democracy, these qualities must expand within the private sphere. With time, there will need to be new social policies to help support this natural evolution of human freedom.

In my view, a truly creative public debate about supporting and nurturing families in this country would require a paradigm shift from the current family debate, shaped primarily by right-wing think tanks. The first step would be to end the ridiculous enshrining of the sexist (and mythical) old-fashioned, patriarchal nuclear family. The honest, relevant discussion would be driven by real moral values, beginning by acknowledging that the true enemy of family is not the queer, the single teenage mom, or the welfare recipient. The enemy of family love is violence. Promoting real family values would involve aggressively fighting domestic violence, child abuse, and other forms of violence, including antigay harassment and discrimination in all its forms. Poverty, too, is a form of violence that destabilizes family.

In addition, family-centered values would put children first, across all social lines. We would place higher priority on a whole set of child-centered programs. We would provide teenagers full access to health care, and AIDS and sex education. We would attack the homophobia that murders the spirits of our gay and bisexual kids and distorts the minds of their straight classmates. We'd also develop after-school recreational programs to build teenagers' self-esteem so that having babies at an early age, or belonging to violent gangs, no longer provides major means of self-expression for our youth.

To strengthen and support families, there must also be dramatic changes in the workplace that would place value upon family life as much as work output. Technological advances make this ever more feasible; it's a matter of political and social will. The United States already lags far behind European nations in government and public support for a humane work life that prioritizes family; we are still a nation of workaholics and moonlighters, too defined by the workplace at the expense of attention to home and family life. Public policy that would enhance a family-centered workplace would include shorter workweeks and longer vacations; safe, affordable, and accessible child care; parental and family caregiver leave time and domestic partnership benefits; diversity training programs; flextime and other progressive quality-of-worklife policies. These and other forward-looking policies would enhance and expand *real* family values.

5. CLAIMING OUR RIGHT TO LOVE: GAY AND LESBIAN MARRIAGE

In 1996, the conservative British newsmagazine *The Economist* came out in favor of legalizing lesbian and gay marriage—an absolutely unheard-of position within traditional mainstream circles only a few short years ago. There has been a flurry of media attention as the state of Hawaii moves toward legalizing gay and lesbian marriage. The legislative response has been the Defense of Marriage Act, which defines marriage as being between a man and a woman and would deny federal recognition to same-sex marriages for Social Security, federal tax, and immigration benefits. It has attracted wide bipartisan support, including that of President Clinton and a lengthy list of Congressmen who have normally been gay-rights supporters. DOMA is effectively an attempt to undermine the Constitution's full faith and credit clause by affirming that states would not be required to recognize same-sex marriages if legalized by another state. The issue is red hot. Virulent opposition from ultraconservatives resulted in attempts to ban gay marriage in thirty-four states in 1995–1996 alone, but gay marriage has gained strong support from surprising quarters, both liberal and conservative, ranging from the neoliberal *New Republic* magazine and the libertarian Cato Institute. A much-heralded lesbian wedding occurred on TV's top-rated *Friends*; the popular episode was pulled from the air only by one small-town Texas NBC affiliate. The marriage issue cuts to the very core of whether our humanity will be recognized, and this topic promises to be with us for a long time.

A few years ago, I was on a plane trip cross-country, squished in the middle seat of three between two older businessmen. I opened my *New Yorker* and started to read, and was suddenly stopped in my tracks by a headline: "Tom and Walter Got Married Last Week." The article was about the wedding of New York City lawyer and national leader Tom Stoddard to his life partner, Walter Rieman, also an attorney, who had recently made partner in a major law firm. Tom is a good friend of mine, and I'd been invited to their ceremony, a big New York event, but was unable to attend.

My heart started beating hard, and I was so excited about reading this long, positive, upbeat article in *The New Yorker* that I couldn't contain myself: I turned to my seatmates, both older gray-suited men, quite conservative looking. I showed them the article, beaming: "These are my friends Tom and Walter. Look! Their wedding was in *The New Yorker*." Both men read the article, I think mostly to humor me.

In that article, Tom and Walter came across as men that those guys could in some way identify with, and their marriage certainly challenged the notion that two successful professional men could not possibly fall in love with and want to marry each other. One guy finished the article, said nothing, avoided eye contact with me, and turned back to his book, his body language indicating clearly that the conversation was over for him.

The other man smiled somewhat and managed to mutter something like "Those guys are gutsy," but I noticed he was suddenly nervous, shifting about uncomfortably in his seat. The words to a Holly Near song suddenly danced across my brain: "Why does my love make you shift restless in your chair? . . . It's simply love, my love for another woman." Not wanting to miss the opportunity for an organizing challenge, I asked him: "Why does this make you so uncomfortable?" "I don't know," he answered. "It's just wrong." That sparked a several-hour-long, sometimes awkward conversation about the topic of gay marriage, a conversation that was very instructive to me.

The bottom line was that reasoned arguments about equality seemed useless in moving this fellow forward. To him, gay marriage was purely, simply, morally wrong. But he did change during our conversation, and what moved him was not intellectual argument. What brought a flash of responsiveness across his face was my sharing with him the story of Tom first telling me about Walter. I described the scene: Tom and I were sitting in a car in a parking lot in Los Angeles waiting for friends, and Tom just started passionately pouring out to me his feelings about Walter. Tears flowed from Tom's eyes as he—usually a rather reserved man—described his deep feelings for Walter and his amazement at discovering with him a depth of love he had never imagined. His passion and tenderness filled the air between us. As I was telling this story to this total stranger on the plane that day, my own eyes teared up and my voice choked—and then this guy's heart opened up. In that moment, some small piece of reflexive bigotry just melted. He said to me, softly: "That sounds really touching. I guess maybe it's just new to me. Could I take your *New Yorker* home? My wife helps me understand things sometimes—I'd like to show it to her." From this interaction, I was reminded that prejudice is illogical. Often, the only way to open others' minds is through their hearts.

Most Americans oppose gay marriage, and resistance is fierce. The moral certainty with which heterosexuals claim their right not to share the institution of marriage with us is astoundingly strong. But this is not new; we are only the latest minority group to experience an intense struggle over this issue. The right to marry has always been controlled by those in power. Once, only nobility—not peasants—were permitted state-sanctioned marriage. People of Chinese and Japanese ancestry could not marry whites in America until the 1950s. It took until 1967 for the Supreme Court to declare state bans on interracial marriage to be unconstitutional. The contemporary right-wing race to outlaw gay marriage is exactly analogous to the racist rush to outlaw miscegenation after the Civil War. To exclude a group from the institution of marriage—from legal and social recognition of human love—is probably the most powerful way society can deny basic humanity to its members. And, of course, once our humanity is denied, the possibilities for discrimination and degradation are limitless.

Ultimately, as my story shows, resistance to our right to marry remains irrational. Coming out about our relationships, our love for each other, and about the wonderful, quirky ways we reinvent the notion of marriage and that most hallowed of social customs—the marriage ceremony—are essential to the process of changing public opinion. On this very tough issue, the best weapon in the battle against fierce fear is fierce love.

———

The crowd at the wedding was very mixed. Many of the guests at Michael Kearns and Philip Juwig's "ceremony of union" in 1992 were straight friends and family from their Midwest hometowns. In addition there were radical AIDS activists who identified much more with civil disobedience and "die-ins" in public protest than with the private rites of love. ("Who ever thought we'd love a wedding so much?" gay writer Paul Monette asked me there.) AIDS fighter and playwright Jim Pickett's usually acerbic and irreverent wit melted into purely sentimental paeans to gay love as he emceed the event. The stillness in the air was palpable as Philip, an art curator and international traveler now emaciated by AIDS, and Michael, an openly HIV-positive and gay actor, serenely stood there and looked into each other's eyes in front of their friends and families and said their sweet, funny, simple vows of commitment, which ended with "I'll be Ethel to your Lucy" and "I'll be Lucy to your Ethel."

No heterosexual wedding I have ever been to, whether traditional-with-trappings or hippie-style on a mountaintop, could match the sweet and forceful love that emanated from Michael and Philip that day, three months before Philip died. Radiating from those two men was a love so powerful that it fundamentally contradicted the notion that gay people are somehow less capable of loving relationships than straight people are. Everyone there was affected, from the jaded queer radicals to straight colleagues and family members who experienced profound new respect for gay love. As Michael's mom said to me: "I wish their love could be broadcast around the world. Straights would stop beating up on gays if they could experience this feeling." A straight guy, a friend of Philip's, said to me, with a shy smile of embarrassment crossing his face: "I came thinking this would be a kind of gay theatrical spectacle or something, not anything relevant to my own suburban heterosexual life. But my mind is blown—in fact, today makes me think about my own marriage, my level of commitment to it. I get to take marriage for granted; these guys have fought against bitter odds for it. Here's my old pal Philip near the end of his life. His love for Michael has clearly kept him alive longer than anyone expected, and this ceremony today is the high point of his life. I have a lot of thinking to do after this."

Largely because of AIDS and its constant lessons about the fragility of life itself, increasing numbers of lesbian and gay men want to publicly acknowledge their committed relationships through such ceremonies of union. Lesbians started having commitment ceremonies in large numbers in the 1970s. The phenomenon has now become widespread among both gay women and men—and, as was not the case in the early years, more and more such ceremonies involve straight friends and family. Our "marriage" ceremonies, therefore, inevitably become organizing tools, ways both to teach about the true texture of our relationships and lives together and to craft new boundaries for the meaning of marriage in this society.

The marriage issue is controversial even within the gay and lesbian community. Some people fear that adopting the right to marry like heterosexuals will divide us into "good" gays, who live more assimilated, traditional lives, and "bad" lesbians and gays. The "bad" lesbians and gays are those who have no interest in marriage or who live in nontraditional families—nonpartnered, unusual families that would never receive social sanction in a world still only officially honoring lifetime, supposedly monogamous marriage. (Think, for example, of my friends in that long-term threesome.)

But this debate is mostly academic. The fact is that lesbians and gay men in huge numbers are living in committed relationships and want to get "married," in part for the sake of the very real economic benefits that accrue to married couples. The gay and lesbian impulse to get married in ever greater numbers, and to flaunt our committed relationships by adopting the language of marriage, is not necessarily a conservative trend at all. Because of who we are, is it not possible that we in fact transform the institution as we adopt it and adapt it to our own lives? Do we not have the power to "queerify" marriage (as I fondly call it) when we apply it to our own lives? What straight couple would model their relationship after Lucy and Ethel, and write poetic vows declaring it? That is not only campy and funny; it's a touching, not-so-subtle shift to a softer, more egalitarian, sisterly notion of relationship.

In taking on marriage as our own, as a social institution, as a legal and religious convention, we will not merely be assimilated into a static structure. Like everything else we touch, marriage will be transformed. It will take on a broader meaning; it will be expanded, enlivened, dusted with fairy sparkle. The right is right to fear gay marriage—not because heterosexual marriage will be undermined, as they claim, but because the notion of marriage will be extended, broadened, invigorated, and democratized. And democracy is not what the right wants.

Our relationships, even our partnered, committed relationships, *are* often different. Equality between gay and lesbian partners is, arguably, more widespread and natural than it is between heterosexuals, who are still battling the institutionalized sexism that permeates private life.

———

In fact, lesbian psychologist Linda Garnets reports:
"Research findings consistently show that partners in gay and

lesbian relationships have greater equality, reciprocity, and role flexibility than partners in heterosexual relationships. Most gay male and lesbian couples value power equality and shared decision-making as a goal for their relationships. And in general, lesbian and gay male couples often adopt a peer-friendship model of intimate relationships, thus creating, on a widespread basis, new models of intimate relationships. Such relationships reduce the traditional gender role power imbalances and role inflexibility found in heterosexual relationships, which are so oppressive to women and limiting to men."*

———

Our relationships are also freer from some of the oppression and abuse that plague too many heterosexual marriages and relationships. Remember, one out of three heterosexual women faces a pattern of violence in the home from her boyfriend or husband sometime in her life.†

As exiles from heterosexist society, we lack romantic mythologies to support our relationships. The good news about this is that gay people probably suffer fewer delusions than our heterosexual counterparts about romantic love lasting forever. The bad news, of course, is the lack of societal support for our relationships. And isolation, invisibility, and ignorance about them feed our lowered expectations. As this changes, as we ourselves grow to validate our committed, long-term relationships, we naturally want to celebrate them in ever more publicly sanctioned ways.

The desire to celebrate our committed relationships is a natural process, especially, as my rabbi and minister friends tell me, during a time of such widespread death. Wherever I go, I see the hunger among lesbians and gay men for acknowledgment of our relationships and the right to the legal and social benefits attached to marriage.

Resistance to gay marriage is often based on the idea that gay marriage undermines heterosexual marriage. How is this possible?

*Linda Garnets and Doug Kimmel, *Psychological Perspectives on Lesbian and Gay Male Experiences* (New York: Columbia University Press, 1993), pp. 31–32.
†Mary Koss, et. al., *No Safe Haven: Male Violence Against Women at Home, at Work, and in the Community* (Washington, D.C.: American Psychological Association Press, 1994), p. 44.

In an eloquent speech in early 1996 about an anti-gay-marriage bill, nongay Iowa state representative Ed Fallon said: "What are you trying to protect heterosexual marriages from? There isn't a limited amount of love in Iowa. It isn't a nonrenewable resource. If Amy and Barbara or Mike and Steve love each other, it doesn't mean that John and Mary can't. Marriage licenses aren't distributed on a first-come, first-served basis here in Iowa. Heterosexual couples don't have to rush out and claim marriage licenses now, before they are all snatched up by gay and lesbian couples. Heterosexual unions are and will continue to be predominant, regardless of what gay and lesbian couples do. To suggest that homosexual couples in any way, shape, or form threaten to undermine the stability of heterosexual unions in patently absurd."

Indeed, that idea—repeatedly asserted by the right as if it were definitive truth—is downright illogical. But, again, this is not about logic. Not so very long ago, the antimarriage diatribes, citing biblical chapter and verse, were hurled against interracial marriage; now the target is us. History is on our side. In the long run, we will prevail on this issue, but not until a critical mass of us come out about our proud and loving relationships so the world can view the truth of our lives together. I think we have a moral imperative to talk them up all over the place, and when the spirit moves us to publicly acknowledge our commitments, we must invite every straight friend and acquaintance we have to laugh with us, to cry with us, to celebrate with us at our "marriage" ceremony.

6. WIDENING THE SPHERE EVEN FURTHER: LESBIAN AND GAY PARENTS

The current "gayby boom" is burgeoning, despite a persistent myth that lesbians and gay men can't have or don't want to have children. There are currently between 6 million and 14 million kids who have a gay or lesbian parent. An estimated 10,000 more are being born to lesbians every year by alternative insemination.

Thousands more are being adopted or foster parented by gay men and lesbians. Too many kids are still being taken away from gay parents during bitter custody disputes, but as a generation of gay people, particularly lesbians, reaches its late thirties and decides to parent, more and more children are born or adopted into gay families. And once again, the true gay and lesbian experience shows that, contrary to our enemies' disinformation about us, we are excellent parents who model highly conscious, evolved, and loving parenting—in part because of the obstacles we must overcome to keep, have, and adopt our children.

Thirty-five studies over fifteen years have shown that kids raised by gay people are as well adjusted as or even better adjusted than kids raised in straight families. That is partly because so many kids of gay people are, by necessity, the result of real "family planning"— extensive preparation and very thorough self-examination that take place *before* the pregnancy or adoption. Never has any group of people put so much concerted, thoughtful work into the project of having kids. These children are truly wanted. Moreover, studies show that children raised in lesbian and gay homes are better at tolerating diversity; they are more comfortable in general with all kinds of people. It is possible, then, that the lesbian and gay parents of today are quietly raising the leaders of tomorrow's multicultural world.

These kids are also, incidentally, no more likely to be gay than their counterparts in straight families. Study after study of the possible influence of gay and lesbian parents on sexual orientation shows that there is none. This provides strong ammunition against those who argue that other adults, such as teachers, actually influence children's sexuality.

We bring our queer creativity, of course, to the parenting task; some wonderful new institutions are growing up around our kids' needs for support. An example is Camp-It-Up, an annual two-week family summer camp in Yosemite for alternative families. It draws 250 kids and their parents, three-quarters gay and lesbian and one-quarter straight, for the standard summer camp offerings of hiking, sports, drama, arts and crafts, and fun, food, and fellowship. There are workshops and support groups of all kinds: for gay dads, for lesbian moms, and for their children, on a host of issues, such as "Coming Out at School About Your Gay Parents."

Nancy, an economist, college teacher, and lesbian mom, has attended Camp-It-Up every summer with her two young sons. Last summer, she talked to numerous straight parents about why they choose to go there as well. Nancy reported: "They feel that lesbian and gay parents are really good role models for them, more than the average straight family. Because gay parenting is such a conscious choice, we don't just fall into parenting. It takes conscious decision-making. We don't take anything for granted. The straight parents I spoke with feel that, as a consequence, there's often more thoughtfulness and care in our parenting. They also feel the kids raised by gay and lesbian parents are great role models for their own kids."

Nancy also says that the camp can really help to "normalize" gay life for the kids. "My new girlfriend's twelve-year-old son was really uncomfortable with his mom and me showing affection for each other openly when we first got involved. Then he came to camp. He saw so much natural and open affection between lesbian partners, as well as nongay people totally comfortable with it, that he relaxed. Now, he comes into the bedroom when we're cuddling, and is perfectly fine with it."

Nancy's own son, eleven-year-old Jesse, has been to Camp-It-Up for five years. He says: "Every year, I miss it when it's over. I love camp because I don't have to worry what people will think about my mom being gay. I love talking openly about it. I can't do that at school. Once, I told a friend my mom was a lesbian and he dropped me. But every summer, I get to go somewhere and hang out with people who understand. It makes me happy. It makes the school year easier for me."

Gay and lesbian parents are a dynamic force for change. Every time a gay or lesbian parent or his or her kid comes out to another person in the course of just being themselves, another critical piece falls into place in this huge jigsaw puzzle of truth-telling about our lives. Our daily interaction with neighbors, school officials, other parents, and the broader community is vital social-change work, particularly because of the continuing right-wing disinformation perpetrated about us in relation to children. Our families promote the best of values that build family stability and contribute to the community and society at large—love, honesty, child-centered support, and respect for each other.

Marcia, a children's book illustrator and muralist in Denver, had always wanted to be a mother. Although she dated men, she hadn't met anyone she wanted to settle down with, and when she found herself pregnant at age thirty-three, she decided to have the child alone. Just after she got pregnant, she met a sister artist, cartoonist, and illustrator named Meg, whom she began to date. Meg herself had always wanted to parent, and became Marcia's birth partner, faithfully attending Lamaze classes with Marcia, and helping with Celia's birth.

Meg and Marcia have raised Celia as open lesbian co-parents now for fourteen years. "We don't wear 'Dyke Mom' buttons or go to demonstrations for gay rights," Meg explains. "We frankly don't have the time as moms and artists struggling in this economy to make it. But our little family does its bit for the cause. We vowed to be open from the time I went to those Lamaze classes. We both believe honesty opens hearts, and, naïve as that may sound, it has worked for us for fourteen years."

Meg and Marcia, and now Celia, are tall, blond, striking women—funny, warmhearted, generous people who make and keep friends easily. Meg and Marcia both work at home, and their family life with Celia (and their cat, Bette, and rabbit, Phoebe) is the center of their existence. "We've had to evolve our own ideas about lesbian parenting. We are proud to have deeply egalitarian ideas; we believe kids have rights, too," Meg says. "We insist on being open and loving about being a family, but we also respect Celia's right to tell her friends when and how she wants to. She has an equal vote in this household." That and knowing she is loved so much has built up her confidence. Celia is a mature, centered, calm, accomplished girl—the valedictorian of her class and Most Valuable Player on her volleyball team—who unfailingly refers in any situation to Meg and Marcia as "my parents." They say they have never faced any discrimination that they are aware of. They celebrate "Meg's Day" on Father's Day every year.

Each year, Meg and Marcia have told Celia's teachers: "You know, we are partners. We are a family." They attend her parent-teacher conferences together. For the first few years, they anxiously probed Celia's teachers for any evidence of problems at school. Every year they were told she was a totally happy and productive child.

One day Celia came home and excitedly reported that her teacher had heard one of the kids calling another kid "lezzie" in a derogatory way. Her teacher stopped everything going on in the class to say, "I know some lesbians, and they are among the nicest people I know. No more name-calling in my class." Celia knew that Mrs. Jones was talking about Meg and Marcia, and was really proud. Now Celia baby-sits for that teacher's kids because the teacher wants them "to grow up like Celia."

Meg and Marcia love to have visitors stay at their home in Monterey, California. On one occasion, Dotty, an eighteen-year-old woman who had been nanny to Meg's niece and nephew in Philadelphia, arrived for a weekend visit. She had come from a strict Baptist family; her church youth group burned rock-and-roll records as works of the devil. Her eyes were opened that weekend. She asked questions nonstop once she realized she was in a lesbian household. Dotty left a changed person; she is now getting her Ph.D. in women's studies, doing her dissertation on lesbian motherhood.

Meg and Marcia paint a large number of murals and giant artworks together, always openly as "partners in life and art." This past year, they have been designing and painting high school theater sets for a number of schools in the school district. They are always open about who they are as they work with ten to twenty kids at a time. "I love how the gay kids gravitate to us; we've made a number of them very happy," says Marcia. "They'll come back to work with us over and over again, just to be around us. Usually we don't need to talk to them specifically about being gay, unless they bring it up; they just want to be around us. We know that's the most effective pride builder there is: seeing two happy, open women loving each other and working together, and having one of the happiest families in the world."

———

Meg, Marcia, and Celia together form one of thousands of loving lesbian and gay families quietly remaking America today. They are heroines, all three, whose courage to come out, to be role models, and to create a loving alternative family has transformed their families of origin, their friends, their neighbors, their broader community, and the very notion of what family can be.

The power of personal example to create change is vital, particularly on a tough issue such as homosexuality, which was strictly taboo until recently. Let us not forget that only thirty years ago, gays and lesbians were almost universally considered sick, sinful degenerates. We have come a very long way in a relatively short time, but we still have the big task ahead of convincing an enduring majority of Americans of our basic humanity and equality. Gays and lesbians are still invisible to at least half the people in this country, and there is simply no better, stronger, more powerful way to open up and change their minds than by reaching their hearts. We do that best simply by being our most free, most honest, most alive, most wonderful and natural selves—fully out of the closet.

Our individual coming out is the exciting and revolutionary cornerstone act for this public education strategy, which will diminish homophobia significantly in our lifetimes. Our personal act of coming out has wide-ranging political consequences, whether intended or not. We catalyze dramatic improvements in the quality of people's lives all around us. We help eliminate bigotry in our workplace, our church or synagogue, our college campus or favorite civic group by sparking new support and insight among our colleagues, and we help democratize the notion of family by simply sharing our loving ways with those people we know.

We must never, ever forget the amazing effect that each of us has on the broader society. The gay and lesbian experience teaches this lesson well—that individual, ordinary lives can be forces for extraordinary social change just in the course of everyday living. Simply telling the truth about our lives, and living them freely and unafraid—though not unaware—of the consequences has a dynamic effect on the world at large. We send reverberations of courage, love, and leadership as we model new, freer ways of living and thinking that act not only to help push forward our own movement for equality but to transform the rest of society as well. Together, over time, one at a time, we are steadily wearing away that rock of homophobic prejudice. That's a sphere of influence!

3

BUILDING COMMUNITY:
A HOME OF OUR OWN

1. CREATING COMMUNITY,
OUR HOME BASE

Each individual gay, lesbian, or bisexual person adds to the total social wisdom about our people through all the energy he or she puts into touching those in our spheres of influence. Like individual pinballs, we careen off more and more bumpers, bells, and lights over the course of our lifetime. The result is that the collective score of understanding of lesbian and gay life grows steadily in the straight community. If each of us, however, stayed isolated from others in our own coming-out processes, we would fade away with loneliness. Fortunately, we are not alone; we are part of a growing and thriving —and quite extraordinary—lesbian and gay community. That's what we call it: the gay community, the lesbian and gay community, the GLBT (gay, lesbian, bi, and "trans") community, or simply "the" community. But what exactly is it, and why is it so fundamentally important?

The gay and lesbian community comprises the far-flung network of organizations we have built across the country, organizations that nurture individual self-esteem and identity, build a common culture, and fire the engines of our movement for social change. Beyond that, at its very best our community is also a spirit of collective purpose capable of unifying and mobilizing us in powerful ways.

When hundreds of thousands of us streamed back home from the March on Washington in the spring of 1993, or from Stonewall 25 and the Olympics-style Gay Games in New York in 1994, our busy, diverse galaxy of organizations was there to greet us. Maybe our town has a community center, or a gay bowling league, or a monthly lunchtime networking club for lesbian businesswomen, or all three. Maybe there's a gay Metropolitan Community Church, or a local chapter of the Gay and Lesbian Alliance Against Defamation, or a hotline for teenagers struggling with their sexuality. Or there may be a lesbian and gay chorus, a gay bookstore, or a coffeehouse where gays and lesbians and hip straights gather, with a bulletin board in the back papered with job and apartment referrals. There are probably a lesbian softball league and a country-and-western dance club. And there's likely to be at least one gay bar. These days, there's also a "virtual" community on-line, accessible from anywhere, with a plethora of gay chat rooms for asking advice or cyberdating.

Today, there are an estimated seven thousand to ten thousand gay and lesbian community groups that save, change, and enrich thousands of lives every single day. Our creation of a vast web of community organizations is our single greatest asset as a people, the crowning achievement of our work to date. This dense, varied set of groups and organizations collectively forms the vital home base of our movement for equal rights, and the launching pad for our steady migration into the mainstream. Our community is our autonomous base of resistance to oppression, our place to gain the tools to survive, and then to fight back against discrimination and hatred. It is the spiritual seedbed of our politics, our culture, our potential.

Community-building has been, and continues to be, the heart and soul of what we have done, and done best.

Building community organizations is a defining and integral part of our culture because community means survival for an exiled people whose core, shared experience from birth is isolation, invisibility, and ostracism. For us, finding each other and creating support for our individual journeys and for the development of our collective identity is a life-or-death undertaking.

America's queer exiles have been forced to build our own loving home—for ourselves, for each other—and we have undertaken this project with extraordinary verve, entrepreneurial zeal, and awesome creativity. Instinctively at first, as a survival mechanism, and then quite consciously, we have made our own "free spaces" of emotional, spiritual, social, intellectual, cultural, and political support in order to heal the multiple hurts of homophobia, to re-create our families, to nurture ourselves, to affirm our social identity, to create art and social vision, and to build political power. This is a dynamic and ongoing project. Every day new groups sprout up to cover the full spectrum of human-developmental needs: basic survival and safety; emotional support; friendship and recreation; affiliation and affirmation of gay identity; spirituality; culture and art; advocacy and politics.

Those organizations allow us to survive and thrive in havens safe from homophobia, and they provide the outlets and the basis for our independence and our creativity. As we move our values, our visions, and our very selves into mainstream America, the organized lesbian and gay community is where we gather strength to come home to America.

———

Emilie is a forty-seven-year-old attorney with a master's degree in business administration. She lives in Washington, D.C., and moves in powerful political and financial circles. She loves her job, but her face really lights up when she talks about her lesbian softball team. In ten years, she's never missed a game. Last year, she even talked her sister into postponing her wedding until softball season was over. Why? "Softball brings out the real me," says Emilie. "It's being a tomboy again, with a bunch of sisters. It's a kind of family."

Jack is twenty-three and leaves his rural Ohio hometown every week-end for the bright lights of Cincinnati. One night, he was badly beaten up outside a gay bar by a gang of skinheads. Alone, hurt, and scared, he dialed information from a pay-phone and was connected to the Gay Anti-Violence Hotline at Stonewall Cincinnati, a lesbian and gay advocacy group. Very quickly, a trained victim's advocate showed up, went with him to the hospital, helped him file a report with the police, and stood by as a new friend to help him through the trauma. "We have to take care of each other. Nobody else does," the volunteer told Jack.

Lydia is a young Native American woman who moved to San Francisco from South Dakota. She was certain she was a lesbian and hoped that a friendly and more anonymous city would allow her to explore her real self. Not knowing anyone at all in San Francisco, she rented a room. A few days later, in a routine self-exam, she was terrified to discover a lump in her breast. "I was so alone and scared," she says, "but I had seen a sign on Market Street, near the hotel, for the Lyon-Martin Women's Health Clinic, and I got an appointment for the next day."

The clinic was highly professional and friendly, and its staff was proudly and openly lesbian, as well as multiracial. Lydia, to her own surprise, felt totally at home. The lump proved to be benign, and Lydia found ongoing, top-notch primary medical care in a caring community-based setting. She also found much more: Lyon-Martin's bulletin board helped her find an apartment and a coming-out support group. It was her "gayteway" to a new community and to her first full sense of belonging.

At sixteen, Ben was thrown out of his ultra-conservative Christian parents' Philadelphia home for being gay. Months of forced "reparative therapy" ("religious and sexist brainwashing," he calls it) hadn't taken. He lived on the streets of New York, joining other homeless runaway youth who "squatted" in abandoned buildings. Some drive inside him kept him away from the survival sex, drugs, and alcohol abuse so prevalent among runaways, and he managed to find a job in a condom store. "If they'd only known where I was living!" he says.

His goal was to complete his high school education, but he couldn't figure out a way to do it until a pal told him about the high school diploma program jointly sponsored by the Hetrick-Martin Institute (New York City's gay and lesbian youth organization) and the New York Lesbian and Gay Community Services Center. "HMI and the New York Center gave me my future," says Ben. He was then able to move off the streets permanently, get a better job, and make plans for college.

Rhonda, age nineteen, was pushed out of her alcoholic, abusive, homophobic Seattle family. Aimless and lost, she ended up in L.A., jobless, homeless, and spending too much time at bars, both gay and nongay. Within months, she was trapped in the thrall of both speed and alcohol. Ironically, a caring gay bartender took her under his wing and connected her to a gay Alcoholics Anonymous meeting. The folks at AA got her in touch with the Alcoholism Center for Women. There, in a lesbian-friendly treatment program, Rhonda got sober, got off the streets, and began a new life.

---

2. OUR HISTORY OF COMMUNITY-BUILDING: THE EXILES CREATE OUR OWN HOME

Softball, safety, service, support, sobriety: these are great gifts our community organizations give us on our journey to personal and political freedom. Almost none of those organizations existed thirty years ago—except the bar and, perhaps, way underground, the lesbian softball league. Until 1969, gay or lesbian bars were virtually our only gathering places. Not surprisingly, this, coupled with hatred from within and without, led many of us to struggle with alcoholism and other addictions. In response, we began to provide services for our own; today, bars are only one of hundreds of institutions in our world.

The contemporary gay community is the proud and transformed heir of an earlier era of silence when (with a few exceptions) there was only a brave but secretive and scared sexual underground sub-culture of lesbians and gay men meeting in living rooms or seedy Mafia-owned barrooms. Terror marked gay existence as police ha-rassment raged out of control. People were regularly dragged out of bars, bathhouses, and even private homes and hauled off to jail; often, their lives were destroyed by the subsequent publication of their names, addresses, and places of employment in the local news-paper.

A pioneering band of visionaries in the 1950s and 1960s planted the seeds of gay liberation in the "homophile" movement, which, for the first time ever, asserted that gay people are a per-secuted minority, not sick, sinful, or criminal. A handful of groups, led by the Mattachine Society (founded in 1950 in Los Angeles by Harry Hay) and the Daughters of Bilitis (founded in San Francisco in 1955 by Del Martin and Phyllis Lyon) stressed education, and by word of mouth built a small, mutually supportive network of gay people. The groups, working under impossible odds from in-side the closet, were always tiny and fragile; in 1960, DOB had 110 members, the Mattachine 230. Nevertheless, they established sev-eral elements as important and permanent parts of our move-ment's culture: the use of direct-action protest tactics; the notion of autonomous organizing for women; and the essential signifi-cance of community organizations as the building blocks of our movement.

The radical gay liberation movement, unofficially launched by the Stonewall riots in 1969, made coming out of the closet its basic battle cry and firmly established the centrality of conscious com-munity organization-building for safety, support, affirmation, and advocacy as the very essence of the contemporary gay and lesbian movement and culture. In 1969 there were fewer than fifty gay and lesbian organizations; by 1973, there were a thousand. Our organi-zations meant survival, visibility, and, for the first time, the bare be-ginnings of political power to change attitudes, laws, and public pol-icy.*

---

*For more information, see the classic work by John D'Emilio, *Sexual Politics, Sexual Communities: The Making of a Homosexual Minority in the United States, 1940–1970* (Chicago: University of Chicago Press, 1983).

The "Gendered Seventies" and Beyond:
Two Communities Become One

The historian John D'Emilio has described the decade following the first few years of exuberant gay liberation organizing as "the gendered seventies" and has carefully documented the two very separate movements that together constituted our movement for social change during those years: gay male urban single-issue reform politics and lesbian-feminism. I well remember those years.

Twenty years ago, it seemed that gay men and lesbians lived on different planets, despite the fact that the outside world lumped us together. Attracted to our own gender, we gravitated to our own kind, creating same-sex social circles. We were often far more different from each other as gays and lesbians than we were from straight men and women. I shared a love of sports with straight men, but couldn't relate to gay camp. With straight women, I shared many experiences of growing up in this society. Gay men often had straight women as their closest friends, and socialized regularly with straight men in the male-dominated world of work.

Lesbians often resented gay men's economic privilege. I remember that in Chicago in the mid-1970s, there were over a hundred gay men's bars, and *four* for lesbians. Across race and class lines, lesbians were women first—subject to sexual harassment on the job and assault in the streets, carrying disproportionate responsibility for children, and facing severe economic barriers that white gay men did not share. We thought gay men were elitist and obsessed with sex; they thought we were humorless and antisex.

Occasionally, gay men and lesbians were drawn together, usually to fight common threats such as Anita Bryant's vicious antigay crusade in 1977 or the 1978 Briggs Initiative in California, which would have forced the firing of all gay teachers. When that era's political fights united us, I used to note wryly in speeches that lesbians and gay men were indeed the oddest political bedfellows, a forced marriage if ever there was one.

I remember trying to work with men when I was living in Chicago in the mid-1970s. I represented Blazing Star (the lesbian work group of the grassroots feminist Chicago Women's Liberation Union) to Chicago's main gay rights group, the Metropolitan Gay and Lesbian Coalition. At the meetings, there were fifty men and four women. The women's calls for child care at meetings or outreach to other, diverse communities were greeted with jeers. It was not a pleasant experience. I remember being horrified by a speech before a straight college audience given by a gay man who celebrated the "freedom from responsibility" of the gay life. He happily announced that gay men were "freer" because they did not have to support wives and children and therefore had more disposable income to spend on enjoyment of social life and sexuality. I, on the other hand, had a lover with a teenage son, was helping a straight single-mom neighbor with her new baby, and was active in the burgeoning "women's community." My lover and I struggled to make it economically. My lesbian-feminist political life was totally dedicated to the women's community and to increasing social responsibility among lesbians. I was spending evenings and weekends hammering Sheetrock at the new women's coffeehouse or handing out flyers at lesbian bars and softball games about one or another feminist or gay march or event. My gay comrade's notions of what constituted gay life and happiness simply bore no relation to my own. Because of such incompatibility in the worldviews of many lesbians and gay men, many of us said, "Good-bye to all that," and set off to work separately with our own, creating a busy, thriving lesbian separatist subculture that for a few years nurtured our spirits and built skills and self-confidence.

Ultimately, though (as John D'Emilio has brilliantly documented), both gendered movements reached dead ends, each in its own way being isolated and lacking in vitality. Lesbian-feminism became mired in its utopianism; gay male reform politics lacked a broad and compelling vision. Both had moved a far distance from the bright, bold gay liberation vision of radical transformation of gender roles and society at large. Says D'Emilio: "Take, for instance what may very well be the quintessential product of each; the elaborate, glitzy, high-tech gay male discos found in many cities, and the self-sufficient, rural communities of lesbian separatists. Here were men, in a public space, spending money, focused on themselves, and searching for sex. And here were women, in a private retreat, financially marginal, focused on group process, and nurturing loving re-

lationships. For all our talk about a brave new world of sexual freedom, or the building of an Amazon Nation, what I now see is how
thoroughly enmeshed such institutions remained in gender con-
ventions."* There we were, men and women living on different
planets, replicating our traditional gender roles, self-referential and
isolated from the world outside and from each other, and unable to
effect substantive social change.

Today, it's a different story: we stand together, at the other side
of that chasm of difference, partners in crafting a movement that
is vital and dynamic. In 1996, our friendship circles interconnect as
never before, and gay men and lesbians share leadership in our organizations and partnership in articulating our visions and strategies for the future. Of course, things aren't perfect; sexism continues to exist, and there is separatism remaining on both sides, but
we have achieved an unprecedented degree of unity. Today, lesbians
can chortle with pleasure at the campy drag antics in *Priscilla: Queen
of the Desert*, and gay men can appreciate raunchy lesbian comedi-
ans and powerful lesbian leaders.

How did gay men and lesbians change from suspicious antago-
nists representing different worlds to friends and collaborators
today? In large measure, the change resulted from the contemporary woman's journey to self-esteem, quietly but inevitably traveled
by so many lesbians alongside our straight sisters these past twenty-
five years, a journey that has given us the confidence and leadership
capabilities to take our rightful place next to gay brothers within
community-based organizations and political groups. But, ultimately, the defining and transformative issue has been AIDS.

We have fought a bloody war together; in the process of combating a negligent government, building health care services, and
facing AIDS-phobia and homophobia, a new unity was forged. This
was more than just lesbians taking places at a gay table emptied by
AIDS. The truth is far more complicated and interesting: Lesbians
have rightfully earned power and respect through working heroically side by side with, and often in front of, men. At the same time,

*John D'Emilio, "After Stonewall," in *Making Trouble* (New York: Routledge, 1992), p.
258.

fighting women for power and control of emerging gay community institutions became irrelevant as AIDS showed gay men where their real enemies were. Sexism decreased; lesbian power increased. AIDS transformed the relationship between the genders primarily because lesbians became key players in the fight against AIDS. There are a huge number of lesbians in the health professions, so we were precisely where the barricades of this battle were erected. In addition, AIDS changed the concerns and understanding of a huge cohort of gay men. For activist lesbians, the fight had always included a set of issues greater than simply fighting discrimination on the basis of sexual orientation. We were always aware of broader, systemic oppression and of the linkage between issues as we actively fought for abortion rights, child care, pay equity, health care reform, and recognition of alternative families, and against violence, sexual harassment, poverty, racism and other forms of discrimination. Because of AIDS, white gay men in huge numbers experienced ugly and systemic discrimination like that women had always faced; for many whose closets had preserved male privilege, this was their first such experience. In addition, AIDS expanded gay men's understanding of the pressing need for health care reform. And they passionately embraced family issues as their own after all too often facing pitiless homophobic parents who, with no respect for gay relationships, swept in to take charge of funerals, grab property, or contest perfectly clear wills.

Gay men also discovered linkages between forms of discrimination. I vividly recall walking into a fancy hotel bar in a gay neighborhood during the Anita Hill–Clarence Thomas hearings in the fall of 1991. The bar was packed with well-heeled white gay men intently gathered around the big-screen TV. I was completely taken aback by the crowd's raucous, militant, and totally unanimous support for Professor Hill; in angry, campy unison, those guys shouted, "Liar, liar, liar!" at Judge Thomas. That kind of clear identification with oppression outside their own simply was unthinkable before AIDS.

In the process of facing death, dying, repression, and a traumatic catastrophe together for over a decade, without adequate support from the nongay world, women and men learned to care for each other in very deep ways. We indeed became family. I remember the impassioned testimony I got one night from Danny, a chunky black bartender in a West Hollywood club. Danny has a huge heart and a winning way with everybody. One night he came up to me, tears filling his eyes: "I've seen just about everything in my day— outrageous drag queens with nothing to lose, the closeted businessman visiting here every month, so scared to death his wife would find out, the runaway kids who get ground down by the streets. And so many guys dying, one right after another. It's enough to make me permanently depressed. But, you know what? The other night I saw the most beautiful thing. There was this great big butch lesbian carrying this skinny, sick PWA off to the hospital in her arms. I just cried. . . . We never used to notice the women, or we'd laugh and joke about them—we thought they were prudish and humorless. We didn't really want them in here. But now they've become our heroines, our sisters for real. Boy, the times have changed."

Building Our Own Culture

A culture, says *Webster's New World Dictionary*, is the "ideas, skills, arts of a people communicated or passed along to succeeding generations." For exiles from society yearning for connection with each other and for a home of our own, culture is of fundamental significance and is inextricably bound up with our self-conscious creation both of openly gay and lesbian community and of our political movement.

Gay people have always offered our expansive creativity to society at large as leaders and innovators in forming and changing mainstream culture. We have always been artists, writers, poets, dancers, fashion designers, social critics. In addition, within our own world, camp and drag, and lesbian bar culture, for example, were significant forces in transmitting our values and ways of being to new folks coming into our subculture, even before Stonewall.

Since Stonewall, there has been a magnificent unleashing and channeling of our limitless creativity into building for ourselves a passionate, unique, multifaceted culture. Our culture takes myriad forms that collectively shape a vivid counterculture, a culture of resistance to the dominant heterosexual world's denial and distortion of our existence and its attempts to obliterate us from view. Our queer cultural spirit is fierce indeed, a dynamic, defiant life force that has been nothing short of miraculous in its power to keep us going through tough times and inspire us. "Culture 'R' us—with style!" a friend likes to say, and we bring amazing artistry even to daily life. A last-minute, casual gay dinner party can become a silver-candelabra'd thing of virtuoso beauty. Annual dyke Super Bowl parties in cities and towns everywhere are a prized, no-holds-barred tradition that happily enshrines butch-lesbian pride. We are nothing if not immensely creative.

Every social change movement has its music and art to stoke the fires of its vision. Because art is so powerful at uniting and inspiring people to want to help change the world, it is no wonder that the ultra-right attacks art, particularly homoerotic or gay art. There are no words to capture the healing and motivational power of the following examples, which make up only a minute sample of the autonomous gay and lesbian culture that has sprung up in the past twenty-five-plus years:

The annual Michigan Womyn's Music Festival, now twenty years old, continues to be an annual lesbian rite, an Amazon Woodstock drawing thousands of women to the woods to revel in the bacchanalian delight of each other and lesbian culture and politics.

Viva! is a Latino lesbian and gay performance-art group that nurtures writers and performers in the avant-garde and coffeehouse scenes in Los Angeles. "My father was a Uruguayan freedom fighter and musician who taught me that art's greatest function is serving social change, so I started Viva! to give my people their own place to express our voices so we can more firmly take our place in the performance-art world," says founder Roland Palencia.

None of the lucky folks who heard it will ever forget the sweet, soaring, angelic voice of AIDS activist and artist Michael Callen as he sang "Love Don't Need a Reason" at the April 1993 March on Washington, in one of his final, heart-wrenching performances before he died of AIDS. As Michael once told me: "Only remembering that this struggle is about love gives us the heart to fight it over the long term—that's why I sing my songs."

Our hope—personal, political, spiritual—is powerfully nurtured by the sheer force of the moral vision contained in Tony Kushner's play *Angels in America,* the AIDS-inspired dance of Bill T. Jones, the gorgeous poetry and writings of Audre Lorde and Adrienne Rich. Or, our flagging spirits are uplifted by the whimsy of Keith Haring's art, or the eroticism of the lesbian-vampire fiction of Jewelle Gomez. The list goes on and on. One of my personal favorites is writer Paul Monette's autobiographical work *Becoming a Man,* the first three pages of which form the most heart-stoppingly powerful argument against "the coffin world of the closet" I've read.

Our autonomous cultural and communications institutions have paramount significance. The independent gay and lesbian press interprets the world through our own eyes, frames issues, and analyzes our movement as it moves along. And there are small publishing houses, such as our beloved lesbian Naiad Press, which has been feeding the infinite lesbian craving for love stories, mysteries, and more since 1973.

These days, it's almost impossible to turn on the television and *not* see a lesbian or gay character. In addition, gay-themed literature, theater, dance, and other cultural forms are front and center in the contemporary American arts. The growing mainstream visibility of openly gay and lesbian culture and art is directly related to the proliferation and strength of our independent institutions and support networks—our presses, our film festivals, our gallery showings, our small theaters—within our home-base community. Our passions and pride, and our influence on the dominant culture, will continue to grow as long as the independent, community-rooted groups and institutions that support them do.

Community-Building for the Future: Beyond the Urban Ghetto

Social change movements evolve, growing more complex and passing through various phases over time. There are ample signs that the next major phase of our movement—one that has already begun—involves bringing our culture, community, and movement out of the big cities and into the smaller towns, suburbs, and rural areas of this country. An organic result of the contemporary mass migration out of our closets, this reversal of the trend for gay people to move to urban areas in order to feel safe in coming out is highly significant. Increasingly, we are building our community right at home, regardless of where home is. This trend probably began in earnest in 1987, when the second national March on Washington energized and mobilized people to create a wave of new organizations in the South and in smaller towns and cities. A period of vigorous activism and community organizing began then and saw exponential growth with the Clinton campaign and victory in 1992, and beyond. The "Gay Nineties" have been, essentially, about this remarkable new trend, bringing home our issues, our visibility, our daily lives to the heartland, to the suburbs—everywhere.

Community groups are sprouting up in all sorts of places where it was unimaginable to be "out" even a decade ago. Buck, a strikingly handsome Montana cowboy active in the gay rodeo circuit, told me he had recently come out of the closet to everyone he knew in his tiny town after he initiated a gay men's social group. He received tremendous support: "I've lived here my whole life, and they all know and trust me, and just accept who I am—the postmaster, the Main Street storeowners, everyone." To top it off, practically the whole town showed up at his commitment ceremony with his partner of twelve years—gays and straights, cowboys and cowgirls, all happily two-stepping together into the early morning. Craig, the Iowa college student who came out by purchasing a National Coming Out Day ad in his college newspaper, told me, grinning from ear to ear: "Sure, I'm moving to New York City. I want to learn everything I can from gay community activists there so I can take it all back to my small hometown in Iowa and start a gay and lesbian community center. I feel very lucky to have an option my elders did not have: to stay in my home state." Almost a quarter of all the nation's gay and lesbian community centers have been founded *since 1992*, in places like Caribou, Maine; Wichita, Kansas; and Fort Collins, Colorado.

The future success and vibrancy of the gay and lesbian movement will depend on continuing this upsurge in visibility and activism in cities and towns that have never been hotbeds of activism before. Salt Lake City, Utah, jumped into the headlines in 1996 when extraordinary leadership was shown by high school students fighting a bigoted decision by the board of education to eliminate *all* school clubs (such as, for example, Frisbee and Bible clubs) in order to stamp out one school's Gay/Straight Alliance. Seventeen-year-old Erin Wiser, a founding member of the Alliance, said, "We are accidental activists—our backpacks are our briefcases and our school lockers are our offices. Our first priority is to help each other. . . . Now, I want to see clubs like this at every high school in the state of Utah." Determination of steel has been fired in the heart of this young lesbian because right-wing forces moved to obliterate the only community that existed for her and others in her school. The conservative, largely Mormon state of Utah is in for an interesting few years ahead.

3. COMMUNITY-BUILDING FOR AFFIRMATION AND EMPOWERMENT

As we move to spread the word ever farther from urban gay ghettoes, we would do well to consider where our community-building instincts have led us in the past, as a partial blueprint for what can be brought to a wider sphere of geographical influence. By far the largest number of groups and organizations in the gay community exist to meet our deep needs for social belonging, for connection to one another, for affiliation and affirmation of our gay and lesbian identities. From sporting to spiritual, there are thousands of groups representing millions of members across the country. They exist because our greatest problem is isolation. Finding friends and lovers and meeting our craving for connection to others like us is our greatest need. Finding or creating affinity groups in our workplaces, neighborhoods, or ethnic communities is our first step.

———

Letitia lived alone, in the closet and struggling to pass as heterosexual at work. She was depressed and lonely, sometimes finding it hard even to get out of bed and make it to work at the insurance company where she was a secretary. Increasingly alienated from her East L.A. community, she wondered if she were the only Latina lesbian in the world. Then one day she saw a public service announcement on a Spanish cable station advertising Lesbianas Unidas, the women's section of L.A.'s Gay and Lesbian Latinos Unidos. She was amazed and thrilled—there it was, on television, in her living room. One phone call led her to an empowering community she hadn't known existed.

Billy was stunned. He was at his first National Black Gay and Lesbian Leadership Conference in Newark, New Jersey, and the hotel was bursting with the energy and excitement of hundreds of out and proud African-American lesbians and gay men. They were there from rural and urban settings, from every class, culture, and political persuasion. They could choose from poetry readings, keynote lectures by leaders such as politico Angela Davis, AIDS activist Mario Cooper, and gay-positive feminist writer bell hooks, and workshops on everything from leadership development to gay black history. For the first time in his life, Billy felt he belonged somewhere, his invisibility and isolation left behind for good. Back at work on Monday, Billy found himself automatically coming out to his closest colleague, with little fear and a new attitude about himself. He felt like a brand-new person—an out and proud African-American gay man.

Sandi is an assistant film director in Hollywood. When she and four other women nervously booked a room for LIFT (Lesbians in Film and Television), a new professional networking and support group, they were sure that fear of the homophobia rampant in the film industry would keep more than a few women from showing up. Imagine their surprise—and joy—when 350 lesbians attended that first meeting. Two years later, the membership of LIFT stands at 1700.

Al organized the Uptown Gay and Lesbian Alliance in the early 1980s after he noticed that a number of other gay men seemed to be moving into his L.A. neighborhood called "Uptown," a multiracial middle-class area of tidy, single-family homes. Over the years this neighborhood community organization has grown to a solid membership of 150 people—an even mix of women and men from virtually every ethnic group found in multicultural L.A. Like so many other gay and lesbian social affinity groups, this one has evolved over time, from hosting parties and brunches, to providing members neighborly services such as baby-sitting, pet care, and house painting, to holding regular programs of speakers on various topics from organizing to fight the right to volunteering to fight AIDS. They now even march in Los Angeles's annual Gay Pride Parade. Over time, active involvement and leadership have become more and more important and empowering in many members' lives, encouraging them to come out in other areas of their lives as well. As so often happens, UGLA has become a model for several other neighborhood groups in the L.A. area.

———

Ironically, because our community work has arisen from our very survival needs—and because we've been so busy doing it—we too often take it for granted, failing to recognize the creativity and magnitude of our achievement. I remember my straight aunt's astonishment when she came to visit me in San Francisco in the late 1970s. After a day that included a hiking trip organized by a lesbian outdoors club, a visit to a gay-owned laundromat, dinner in a totally gay restaurant, and a show at the neighborhood lesbian coffeehouse featuring an all-lesbian jazz combo, she exclaimed: "You-all have created your own entirely lesbian and gay world, haven't you?" Believe it or not, until she said that, I hadn't grasped the scope of the world I lived in daily. I took it for granted.

Some social and affiliation groups are permanent fixtures in the community, even if specific forms come and go. On the other hand, some groups rise and die with social trends or with leadership energies that move on. For example, the closing in 1989 of Maud's, a neighborhood lesbian bar in the Haight district of San Francisco, became a community event, memorializing and celebrating the long life and passing of a lesbian institution that gave way to changing tastes and times. As documented in the film *Last Call at Maud's*, there was a gala week-long party attended by thousands of patrons and supporters from Maud's twenty years, proving that this bar was a beloved San Francisco lesbian community fixture. Maud's was an important touchstone for the lesbian community, much more than a place to buy a beer and shoot pool; in the years before any such thing could exist, it was a kind of community center. As trends changed and a host of new organizations sprang into existence to meet various community service needs, its role was outgrown.

Pride Parades and More: Protest as Celebration

Gay people have made an art of getting together. We seem to like nothing better than gathering together, particularly in large numbers. Our yearly pride marches and festivals, beginning with the first commemoration of the Stonewall riots in 1970 and continuing to spread out into new towns every single year, are among our favorite annual rites of communal celebration.

Almost every political march or demonstration we organize becomes a party. Our coming together is necessary, powerful, and revolutionary, in and of itself—an elemental self-healing salve against isolation. The very act of defying the isolation thrust upon us by homophobia, the very act of gathering collectively, seems to generate a kind of group jubilation. Protest invariably becomes celebration. In the fall of 1991 thousands of gay men and lesbians hit L.A.'s streets, committing mass civil disobedience to protest California governor Pete Wilson's veto of a job-equity bill. After days of angry traffic-snarling marches, the energy on the streets changed from rage to collective exuberance.

Every year, more and more towns and cities host Gay Pride celebrations. A few years ago, I spoke at the inaugural Pride event of the Gay and Lesbian Association of Antelope Valley, California. This rural, conservative community is home to the church that produced the infamous homophobic disinformation videotape, *The*

Gay Agenda, which has been mass-marketed by the radical right. It's also the same area in which Dan Quayle made one of his most famous "family values" speeches.

It was a courageous and beautiful gathering at the local county fairgrounds—which was also hosting an evangelical church's fundraiser (a wrestling match) right next door. Despite virulent opposition by local right-wingers, who had even formed the Alliance to Prevent Immorality in Public to stop the festival, an amazing one thousand gay people attended. For many, it was their very first venture out of the closet, but their cheers and hearty whistles and applause soared to the top of that huge echoing concrete barn, in newly formed defiance and determination. I guarantee that Antelope Valley, California, will be a changed place in the future.

4. BUILDING ON THE BARRICADES: FIGHTING BACK

After college, Sarah worked as a publicist for her father's movie and television production company. Her family was very supportive of her long-term lesbian relationship, but in her dealings with other Hollywood business people, she became increasingly angered by the pervasive homophobia—and the mandatory closet. One day she heard a casting director, whom she knew to be gay, dismiss an actor with a glib "Oh, he's a poofter—too light on his feet to play in this movie." When she confronted the man, he warned her: "Honey, you won't make it if you rock *this* big boat." Fed up, she started working with the Gay and Lesbian Alliance Against Defamation in L.A., helping to build a network of behind-the-scenes entertainment industry writers and producers to protest homophobia in scripts and to insist on rewrites. Sarah also helps GLAAD mount public protests against movies and television shows that perpetuate negative stereotypes of lesbians and gay men. Today, she is also a proud supporter of Out There, a new and growing group of powerful Hollywood professionals fighting homophobia in their industry.

Sarah doesn't think of herself as political. But, as often happens, the simple act of standing up for fairness can lead someone right into the arena of politics.

Of course, most local gay groups are de facto political, even if they don't identify that way, simply because they affirm their members and empower them to continue coming out more and more fully. This is a political act precisely because it is likely to have a profound cumulative effect on gay people's spheres of influence. (The California Supreme Court recognized the inherently political nature of coming out when it ruled in 1979 that discrimination against openly gay individuals at work violates the ban in the labor laws against discrimination on the basis of political activity.)

Even purely recreational groups such as our bowling and tennis leagues build the kind of gay and lesbian solidarity that spills over into other aspects of life. One bowling league leader, who had previously been closeted for years, proudly told me how much fun he had coming out to straight bowling-lane owners, joking with them, and making them more sensitive to gay people. From bowling to beating bigotry—that's political.

People like Sarah join local lesbian and gay political groups because they're sick and tired of seeing discrimination around them. Some groups, such as GLAAD, are explicitly activist while others undergo a natural evolution so that, over time, they engage in more and more explicitly "out" or political activity, ranging from simply marching as a group at annual gay and lesbian pride celebrations, to more explicit organizing. Santa Monica, California's WAVES (We Advocate Visibility, Equality and Strength) was organized to mix social activities, such as weekly volleyball and bridge games, with organizing activities such as staffing a booth at the local shopping mall under a sign: "We're lesbian and gay: Ask us your questions." Asian Men United of Washington, D.C., began as a purely social support network, but, in time, they marched openly behind their banner at the Gay Pride Parade. The first year, six brave souls appeared, but by the third year, there were over thirty. Some of the members became increasingly active in their local straight-majority communities or in gay and lesbian political work. This kind of progression from Pride to politics is very common. Every day, more groups are forming in more small towns and cities. The founders of Ground Zero were well aware from the start that they existed right smack in the belly of the beast, when they started their group in Colorado Springs, a radical right stronghold. For their first large public event, they organized a Fourth of July picnic for gays and lesbians and their allies in the town square. They passed out pamphlets and publicized the fact that the patriotic hymn "America, the Beautiful" was written by a lesbian, Katherine Lee Bates.

Political groups take many different forms. There are effective single-issue advocacy organizations such as those comprising the proliferating network of lesbian health projects across the country agitating against the lesbian-phobic medical establishment and providing support for lesbians with substance abuse or mental health problems, chronic fatigue immune-deficiency syndrome, breast cancer, cervical cancer, and AIDS. (Since 1990 alone, hundreds of lesbian health advocacy, research, support, and coalition-building groups have been inaugurated.) The absurd and dangerous hypocrisy of the "don't ask, don't tell" U.S. military policy has been brilliantly exposed by the tiny, understaffed Washington, D.C.–based Servicemembers Legal Defense Fund, whose persistent work has paid off with front-page media coverage of the real and horrifying truth of this policy: that the codification of the closet within a supremely homophobic military has *increased* the number of antigay witchhunts by bringing the issue out in the open but not prohibiting discrimination. They have documented the bitter fact that *more*, not fewer, gay and lesbian servicemembers have been thrown out of the military since the policy was enacted.

Other groups, such as the Lambda Legal Defense and Education Fund and the National Center for Lesbian Rights, work through the courts, representing lesbian or gay people. For example, the case of Sharon Kowalski and Karen Thompson in Minnesota became a national rallying point for the rights of both lesbian and gay families and disabled persons. When Sharon became severely disabled because of a car accident, she was ripped away from the care of her lesbian lover, Karen Thompson, despite clear medical evidence that Karen's care was key to Sharon's recovery. Karen had to fight Sharon's homophobic parents in the courts for almost a decade before she won final custody of her longtime life partner.

Direct-action political organizing has been a tactical staple since the homophile movement. We have hit the streets in public protests—rallies, pickets, demonstrations, and civil disobedience. The year 1965 saw spontaneous demonstrations and organized pickets for gay rights in front of the Pentagon, the White House, the United Nations, and other sites. The Stonewall riots were, of course, a form of direct action; a few years later, New York's Gay Activist Alliance—a relatively moderate group in those revolutionary times—perfected the use of "zap actions" to disrupt homophobic academic events.

Civil disobedience, the most militant form of direct action, proves enormously effective during a time of great political ferment, like the early 1970s, when it ups the tactical ante, or else when it is clear to a critical mass of the community that every possible legal means of redress has been tried—that the system has so rigidly shut us out that we have no choice but to hit the streets. Then nonviolent, militant direct action can garner broad support within the community. The work of ACT UP in its heyday is a prime example.

The bitter truth of the federal government's indifference toward the national tragedy of AIDS resulted in broad-based community support for ACT UP's confrontational tactics, from die-ins to mass civil disobedience, from taking over Dan Rather's TV studio to guerrilla shock tactics such as inflating a thirty-foot condom on the roof of ultra-right-wing antigay U.S. senator Jesse Helms's house. ACT UP's bold style, savvy media and marketing skills, and passionate commitment to its message earned it fierce, widespread loyalty and high moral authority, both because of and despite its militancy. The community resonated to the simple truth of its message: "Silence equals death." Even to moderate, closeted folks around the country, it was clear that ACT UP's tactics were both necessary and justifiable in the face of the Republican administration's arguably genocidal neglect of the greatest plague of our time.

In my mind's eye, I can still see the smiling face of the three-piece-suited accountant bringing cups of water to protesters at one mass ACT UP action in which I was arrested in 1988. As we chatted for a few minutes, he said he was nervous; this was his first-ever demonstration. He'd been drawn there by his anger and grief at the loss of so many friends. As I and my affinity group of other local leaders went up to block the doors of the Federal Building in West Los Angeles, he jumped up and down at the front of the crowd, a big grin brightening his face: "Go, Torie! You're doing it for all of us!" His conservative clothes belied his newly radicalized heart.

ACT UP has faded to a shadow of its former vibrant self for several reasons. People were exhausted and burned out from the relentless death and endless loss of leadership. Ugly infighting and political purism—all too often the luxury of the powerless—pushed members away in droves. But ultimately, ACT UP faded because the system *did* respond; for better or worse, once the battle moves off the streets and into the government halls, broad support for radical direct action diminishes. While the Clinton administration has not met the high expectations of some AIDS activists, it certainly has taken giant strides forward.

We will be in the streets again in large numbers before our struggle is won. Nonviolent direct action, as well as the educational or mobilizing tools of rallies and pickets, will remain in our tactical toolbox forever. Our annual exuberant Gay and Lesbian Pride rallies are, in fact, a form of direct action.

Other kinds of political organizing have included mounting reactive short-term campaigns to combat the many attacks on our rights, such as the radical right's antigay ballot initiative campaigns. These assaults date back to the days of Anita Bryant's viciously homophobic "Save Our Children" crusade in the mid-1970s and proliferated with the current antigay backlash. The 1996 Supreme Court decision invalidating Colorado's antigay amendment will change the nature of future gay-bashing-by-ballot, but antigay legislative efforts will be back in some form. Count on it.

On a country-wide level, the National Gay and Lesbian Task Force helps fight the right, supports local activists' work on a wide range of issues, hosts our own movement-building convention—the hugely successful annual "Creating Change" conference—and sponsors a policy institute and think tank headed by gay historian John D'Emilio that researches key issues such as family policy.

A relatively new organization, the Washington, D.C.–based National Gay and Lesbian Journalists Association (NLGJA), has already carved out an all-important niche in the national scene. It is a fast-growing and increasingly powerful network of over 1,200 professionals working in print, radio, and television media. In this media-driven world, they have assumed a vitally important role as advocates for gays and lesbians working within their industry as well as fighting for accurate portrayals of us in the media at large.

Electoral Political Power

Because our movement is so young (compared to the women's and antiracism movements, each with over a century of history behind it), our electoral political work is relatively underdeveloped, even though local lesbian and gay Democratic and Republican party clubs have been around since the early 1970s. In fact, it is ironic indeed that the homophobic right raises the specter of an all-powerful "gay lobby," with a potent "gay agenda," in the attempt to paint a picture of a tiny minority wielding disproportionate financial and political clout (a caricature highly reminiscent of anti-Semitism). The truth is that our electoral political power lags far behind other parts of our movement such as our cultural influence and social organizing. This political area will see the greatest flowering of potential over the years ahead, as we come out in record numbers, bringing our messages home to America, and as the spotlight shifts away from urban ghettos to the rest of the country.

There are local and statewide political action committees that raise millions of dollars annually, and a dozen state-level lobbying groups, such as Action Wisconsin: A Congress for Human Rights, Empire State Pride Agenda in New York, and California's League for Individual Freedom and Equality (LIFE) Lobby, which fight repressive legislation in state capitals and lobby for state gay rights bills. Those organizations will undoubtedly grow in significance over the coming years, with the national trend to move funding and public policy decision-making away from Washington to the states. In the past couple of years, national groups like the Human Rights Campaign have begun to invest substantial energy in collaborating with and strengthening these state organizations, thus linking our national and state political work for the first time.

Our national electoral-political leader is the D.C.-based Human Rights Campaign, a lobbying group and political action committee that focuses on helping elect progay congressional representatives and lobbying on issues such as ENDA—the Employment Non-Discrimination Act—and AIDS funding. The Gay and Lesbian Victory Fund supports gay and lesbian candidates both by raising money and training campaign managers and strategists. The number of gay and lesbian candidates running for local office has risen enormously over the past few years. In 1991, there were 52 openly gay elected officials and the Victory Fund fielded inquiries from an additional 40; by 1996 there were 118 people elected, and inquiries came from 232 more. We now have viable state-level and congressional candidates, and Roberta Achtenberg's run for San Francisco mayor catapulted her into a new level of stature and leadership in the eyes not only of the gay community in California and the nation, but of the mainstream media and political-electoral worlds.

Building for electoral political power will become an ever more important part of our strategy as our movement evolves, but a strong case can be made that this task will be made much easier if we first focus our resources and attention on developing our local grassroots organizational infrastructure. Over the next couple of decades, our political power will grow decisively only in proportion to our ability to mobilize and galvanize our grassroots base to, first, come out of the closet, and, second, develop the vast array of local social and cultural groups that forms the backbone of our community today into an explicitly political force. That is our challenge for the new millennium. Then we will be able to translate our people into money and votes for real political power.

5. BUILDING IN THE HOLOCAUST

The devastation wrought by the AIDS pandemic not only ignited probably the most effective grassroots political action movement in America in the past twenty years but also spawned an entire new set of community organizations: AIDS service organizations (ASOs). Because of their organic link to grassroots activism, ASOs have given new vigor and a spirit of determination to the enterprise of lesbian and gay community-building.

_____

"AIDS work, AIDS activism, has prolonged my life by years," the intense and adamant man was saying. In his teens, Dave Johnson had been a brilliant and precocious gay liberation organizer, the founding leader of UCLA's gay student group. After graduation, however, he left his activism behind and went on to a successful corporate career as a computer whiz and information systems manager. In 1986, when his lover of ten years died of AIDS and Dave learned he was also HIV-positive, he discovered just how powerless and hated persons with AIDS (PWAs) were. Infuriated, he left the corporate world and turned to AIDS activism. Using his professional managerial abilities and dusting off his organizing skills, he became the dynamic first executive director of Being Alive, L.A.'s PWA advocacy group. After a brilliant tenure, he was named the city's first AIDS coordinator by Mayor Tom Bradley.

_____

In several respects AIDS work has been revolutionary, both in individual lives and for the society as a whole. Under agonizing circumstances, lesbians and gay men have built visionary new models of community-based health care delivery systems. Rooted in the activist and democratic principles of self-determination and patient empowerment—the proposition that those people directly affected should have a strong voice in their own care—ASOs integrate direct services (medical and psychosocial) with advocacy and with social and support systems in a holistic model (sometimes termed "the San Francisco model"). ASOs have collaboratively developed the "continuum of care" model of health care to address the full range of education, treatment, and ancillary services along the spectrum of the disease's progression, from prevention education to hospice care to the emotional work associated with death and dying.

Such a collaborative, full-service, patient-centered model is the blueprint for a progressive vision for community-based health care, to be implemented at some future time when our collapsing health care system is rebuilt along different, friendlier lines. A person coming for medical care to an L.A. HIV treatment clinic, for example, will not only see the neurologist or other specialist, as well as a trained nurse, but also will be offered access to a support group at the clinic (sponsored by Being Alive); will have access to the latest AIDS treatment and to acupuncture and massage; and will be assigned a social worker from the outset. If the patient is a Latina mother, for example, day care will be available, as will a Spanish-speaking weekly support group.

As Dave and so many other PWA heroes, like Michael Callen and Larry Kramer, have testified, thousands of people living with HIV have discovered the positive therapeutic effects of activism. Fighting back is a powerful antidote to the disease; it can actually extend life while improving its quality as well. AIDS activism has transcended the classic split between those inside and outside the "system," between the "suits" and the "radicals," between working "in the suites" and working "in the streets." In 1988, while I sat on the L.A. County AIDS Commission, and we were lobbying hard for an AIDS ward at L.A. County General Hospital, I and others on the commission were also on the phone with radical AIDS activists such as the late Mark Kostopoulos, L.A.'s legendary and brilliant ACT UP leader, helping to coordinate militant demonstrations against the county. This kind of "unite and conquer" strategy can be very effective and is a good legacy of AIDS activism.

The roots of this bi-tacticalism, as I call it, may be found in the two major influences on AIDS activism: radical grassroots organizing and the real-world power that privileged gay men, politicized by AIDS, brought with them to the movement. Never before active or out of the closet, an enormous cohort of successful gay professionals—stockbrokers, businessmen, film producers, doctors, lawyers, artists—brought to AIDS activism substantial financial resources, a familiarity with and fearlessness of power, and highly developed skills in media, lobbying, and management. They merged their resources and professional skills with the organizing abilities and radical tactics of activists with roots in the 1960s and early 1970s civil rights, new left, and women's health movements.

I think of Steve Kolzak, a highly successful Hollywood casting director (*Cheers*, among many television shows), who, after testing HIV-positive and losing his job because of it, became a fierce and passionate AIDS radical on the front lines of many an ACT UP demonstration. "I was the perfect Harvard golden boy who came to Hollywood and made it. I had everything; I benefited from the system," Steve told me a few months before he died in 1990. "Then I found out the impossible could happen—that I could lose it all because of AIDS-phobia, so linked to homo-hatred. First it made me nuts. Then it made me fight back."

One of the most profound ironies of the 1980s in America was this: while Ronald Reagan and George Bush were busy trumpeting volunteerism—remember the thousand points of light?—a community they hated was busy doing it. Our million points of proud, fierce, and brilliant light far outshone their pious rhetoric.

6. HARNESSING THE SPIRIT OF COMMUNITY

B uilding community is an exciting activity that is individually empowering as well as socially responsible. Every day, rap session facilitators, social or recreational group leaders, hotline volunteers, board members of community-based organizations, and "professional" lesbian and gay activists like myself get involved and then stay involved for years—and even decades. What is it about the project of community-building that is compelling and transformative in our lives?

Working for the Good of Others Builds Competence and Self-Esteem

First, creating community fosters tremendous personal growth. Again and again we hear: "I set out to help someone else and I grew so much myself." Almost inevitably, active involvement leads to a surprising and powerful outcome: individual development. On a practical level, service to community adds enormously to our individual toolkit of personal, psychological, professional, and leadership skills. As an extra added bonus, doing good *feels* good.

In my college days, I was shy and tongue-tied, utterly incapable of speaking up in class; I lacked self-confidence in every way. I honestly don't know who I would be today if I hadn't stumbled into Burlington's lesbian-feminist women's community in my early twenties, just coming out. My self-confidence was seeded by that experience.

As part of the culture and ethos we created then, with their deep connections to the burgeoning new women's liberation movement, we encouraged each other to develop as many concrete skills as possible. In one exciting year, I worked with a friendly feminist hypnotherapist to overcome my terror of public speaking, learned basic carpentry so that I could literally build a room of my own onto my lover's house, took apart my VW Bug's engine and put it back together, studied karate and judo for self-defense, played a conga drum (sort of), avidly studied *Robert's Rules of Order* to chair an endless number of meetings, and played in weekly dyke softball and basketball games.

The self-esteem I built through all those classes and activities is central to my sense of self today. It didn't matter that I discovered I was lousy at auto mechanics (beyond changing tires and oil), had a long way to go to be a good meeting chair, and lacked the patience to excel at carpentry. I learned that I could learn new things, and I learned about the richness of available knowledge when it's shared. I also learned things that in later years would become vital to me both personally and professionally—how to mentor and be mentored, how to take pride in accomplishment, how to take risks, deal with failure, think on my feet, admit my limitations, and acknowledge my strengths. In our lesbian subculture we pushed each other to take every opportunity to develop all kinds of esteem-building skills—skills that turned out to be highly transferable as the years wore on, even though I never, ever spent one more day tearing down my car engine.

In retrospect, although we weren't conscious of it then, we were incorporating into our very notion of community the mandate of individual empowerment through skill-building, the importance of taking responsibility for others, and the significance of developing leadership. Self-esteem grows directly out of accomplishment, learning competence, and actively affirming those things in each other—and those values continue to be a critical function of lesbian and gay community-building today. Leadership, too, is a vital and precious resource, of which we are finally more willing to be supportive and proud, and which we are more consciously developing.

I was not alone in my experience. Tens of thousands of lesbians, imprinted by that subcultural experience of lesbian-feminist community in the 1970s, have brought our ideas and our joyful experience of community with us as we have put the "lesbian" into "gay and lesbian" organizing, worked in the women's, disability rights, environmental, and other social movements, and developed our professional and personal lives. A whole generation of us are quietly, and not so quietly, bringing leadership to a host of areas in the 1990s, and we would not be the women we are were it not for that early shared community-building.

Hands across the community. This same process of personal development is occurring within gay and lesbian community groups every day. If you have been involved in a gay or lesbian organization over a period of years or even just a few months, stop and look at the personal growth among the members, and particularly those who have taken on leadership roles of any kind.

————

Carol was a middle-aged woman with two teenage kids who landed in a lesbian rap group at Connexxus, a lesbian center in L.A. in the mid-1980s. She had finally left the oppressive lie of a long marriage to an abusive husband, and she was working at a number of jobs. But she lacked confidence; she felt confused, unfocused, searching for a larger place to plug in and get inspired. Within a matter of weeks, she volunteered to take the rap group facilitators' training class, went on to conscientiously run the weekly rap group for a year, and then took a leadership position on the board of directors. In the course of this work, Carol not only developed facilitation and organizing skills, she also built substantial self-confidence, decided to become a lawyer, and went back to school. Today, she is a successful partner in a law firm, and a dynamic community leader.

Scotty was a shy, tongue-tied teenager, a regular member of the young men's rap group that meets Fridays at the L.A. Center. For two years, he struggled through shame and self-doubt; then, with the encouragement of one of the group's facilitators, he started volunteering in the youth shelter. The adult staff encouraged him to start college, and he continued to volunteer at the Center through his entire four years at UCLA. On graduation, he immediately took a staff position in the Center's youth services department, where he initiated a mentoring program to pass on the lessons and leadership skills he himself had learned.

This hands-across-the-community approach has brought hundreds of us into leadership and activism, and through that process we have discovered that we not only gain skills and self-esteem, we feel good. It feels great to work to change the world; it feels great to give back to the community; it feels great to be of service to others. Our sense of self, our estimation of our own value in the world, are heightened by the simple act of giving back. Pour out the cup and find it ever full.

Perhaps we get some quiet satisfaction by simply being out gay people involved in a gay group in this crazy, homophobic world. Maybe we like knowing we're active in America's newest social revolution, even if we didn't set out to do so. We still face such powerful antigay forces both within ourselves and from the world outside that we become freedom fighters just by walking out of our closet and into any gay or lesbian community activity. Simple participation can give a strong measure of pride and positive self-regard and has inestimable value in nurturing character and confidence.

The actual skill-building and the enhanced self-esteem that come from service to the community translate into increased professional success as well as personal development. Plus, there's an additional reward: whether consciously or not, when we help to build the local gay chorus, or facilitate the lesbians-over-forty group, or write a letter on behalf of our town's GLAAD chapter, we are acting as an ambassador of goodwill for our people. We are representatives of lesbians and gay men, providing an example of moral strength to the world. The message we send is that we are a people who value helping our own and building community. It's a message we send to ourselves as well.

Collaboration with others gives a sense of purpose. We develop useful skills and competence, we are altruistic, we feel fine. So far, so good. But there is a magnificent additional benefit to working with others to help craft community: doing so adds a heightened sense of meaning to life. In this patriarchal world, which overvalues rugged individualism, we are not taught to expect the powerful force created by working with others to build something socially useful. Life is often hard, and life for gay men and lesbians is even harder. It becomes easier, and infinitely more enjoyable, when we get active in building something greater than ourselves. Working collaboratively with others toward a social purpose feeds our deepest spirit.

People need to be part of something larger than themselves; this is just as much a part of our nature as the need for individual expression. Engaging in group activities, we are individually empowered, and often transformed. Sometimes this can operate at a pretty basic level. For example, sometimes just leaving that lonely apartment and going to the neighborhood gay potluck after we've spent the whole afternoon cooking our secret-recipe casserole can give us a warm sense of connectedness and even some perspective on our life.

Again and again, people say they stay involved over a long period of time in community or advocacy work because of their feelings of connectedness to others and to a higher sense of purpose. Above the individual benefits, the synergy created by a group project is enormously rewarding. Rather than detracting from the individual, the unifying energy thus created empowers the involved person, even when there is a diminishment of individual ego. This is one of those ancient paradoxes: willingness to surrender to a spirit of group cooperation energizes the individual.

Community-building endeavors can even be the highest form of sacred or spiritual experience. For a moment, an hour, a weekend, or a lifetime, community-building can put people in touch with a sense of transcendent purpose. This transcendent purpose emerges from the joyful experience of building community collaboratively. This feeling, this spirit, is transformational for the individual and for the group, capable of unifying people across great differences and moving us to true community. This transformational, transcendent quality is the brightest promise of community.

The "Glory of Community"

I first experienced this magical, transformational quality during my involvement with lesbian-feminist "women's music" in the early 1970s. Like thousands of lesbians coming out at that time, I will remember my first Cris Williamson concert forever. It was 1974; a raucous group of women friends piled into my baby-blue VW Bug and a few other cars and drove from Burlington, Vermont, to Boston to hear the West Coast folk-rock singer in concert.

As Cris sang, more than a thousand women linked arms and swayed in unison to that lyrical, soaring music. It was unlike any experience I'd ever had; it was sheer magic. Women walked out of that concert with a throat-catching, shining joy in being lesbians, a feeling far, far bigger than pride. New courage and confidence germinated in that music and in the revolutionary empowerment that came from gathering so many women-loving women together. Within days of that concert (and hundreds more like it over the years), women walked out of marriages or relationships with men that, they suddenly realized, had been nothing but a lie for a long time. They walked off jobs with no futures, or where they were being sexually harassed long before there was a name for it or a movement to fight it. They came out to themselves and to each other. They exulted in limitless new possibilities of a freedom never before tasted, and they made the decision to change their lives forever.

There was a spiritual quality to that music as well, a healing, hopeful, barrier-breaking quality that unified people with an energy greater than each of us. It broke down walls of separation among and between us and created a sense of collective higher purpose. That night, a staid concert hall at Harvard University became the seedbed in which sprouted a revolutionary new spirit that touched the hearts and souls of a brand-new community of women. That night, I knew my life would never be the same again; I'd discovered a compelling force with great power to mobilize people. For years already, marching and organizing against the Vietnam War, for civil rights, and for women's liberation felt important and empowering, but this new-found community touched my soul in such a different way that I couldn't wait to get active in the emerging "women's music" phenomenon. I spent the better part of the next ten years as a concert, festival, and record producer and promoter. So my own life was changed as well.

Over the years, I've seen that same transcendental, powerful force generated by the collective power of a group operating in myriad ways—at conferences, group retreats, rallies, religious services, AIDS memorials, staff meetings, and street demonstrations. With skilled leadership and facilitation, or even by chance when a lucky mix of people and circumstance collide, this spirit of purposefulness, this wonderful group intimacy, is achieved. One can feel the energy in a room, a magnetic force field of bonding that both energizes the individual and unifies the group regardless of differences. This energy can quietly vibrate or be electrifying, suddenly enveloping a room or rally site or restaurant table with a jolt of radiant power. Transcendent community spirit is an energy not sufficiently discussed because it has a magical, almost mystical nature. But, increasingly as people become more and more comfortable with the notion of integrating spiritual elements into our community or political work, we will develop a more sophisticated collective conversation about it. It is real; we've all felt it—we just haven't figured out yet how to sufficiently harness and use it.

From my own experience I know that this force is not a rarefied, occasional occurrence, but can be a kind of everyday magic. This transcendent energy occurs when a critical level of honesty and openness and a collaborative spirit are achieved. Because more and more of us are walking through the terror of coming out to new courage and open-heartedness, this spirit is operating more and more in everyday life—in our interactions with each other, in the way we do organizing or leadership work. It is happening more often because the simple truths of our lives—our great love, our caring, our creativity—shine out in stark contrast to the shrill din of lies about us and the growing violence against us. It is happening more and more because of the increased intensity and search for meaning we are engaged in as we daily face death and dying in this era of horrific plague. This quality we find in our community work has been called group intimacy or queer collective spirit. To me, that transformative synergy is the essence of what gay community can achieve—and it is exactly what we should strive to achieve as we shape our organizations and institutions, our culture and our movement in this challenging time.

Another powerful—but profoundly bittersweet—example of this magical, transformational quality associated with community-building has been conveyed by gay friends and acquaintances who are dying of AIDS. Dying is a time when we try to make some sense out of our lives, to take stock, to comprehend our place in the universe. I remember with great clarity a conversation I had with Rob Roberts, a friend and comrade activist.

Rob was tall, handsome, redheaded—a dynamic, strong-willed young man. He had successfully sued the employer who fired him for having HIV. He was a key founder and leader of Los Angeles Queer Nation and had even helped spark an uprising.

California gays and lesbians had lobbied hard for many years to pass a simple job-equity bill, AB 101, that enjoyed two-to-one popular support. It finally landed on Governor Wilson's desk in the fall of 1991. Wilson had repeatedly vowed to sign the bill during his close 1990 gubernatorial race against Dianne Feinstein. In fact, many credited his one percent margin of victory in that race to a strong gay vote for Wilson—a vote that was largely based on his support of AB 101. After fifteen years of educating and organizing on this centerpiece of its legislative strategy, the gay and lesbian community held its collective breath when that bill reached Governor Wilson for signature in mid-September 1991. But Rob Roberts did much more than that.

Rob, a lone PWA with enormous determination, set up a tent on a little green triangle of grass in the middle of West Hollywood and quietly started a hunger strike to keep an eye on the governor, who was showing signs of cozying up to the radical right. Sure enough, Governor Wilson betrayed his campaign promise and vetoed AB 101 a couple of weeks later. Rob's brave stance as hunger striker and lone watchdog over the governor set the moral tone for what was to become, to that point in California history, the most massive and sustained civil unrest since the nineteen-sixties. Rob single-handedly defined the appropriate response to a governor who capitulated to bigots against his own word and the clear will of Californians.

Rob was charismatic and quiet, a forceful moral example. People gathered spontaneously at his tent in West Hollywood on September 30, the evening of the veto; it was there that seventeen days and nights of protest began. He was our spokesperson, handsome and stunningly articulate. He was the hero whose example helped inspire 50,000 lesbian and gay Angelenos of every political, ethnic, and economic background to stay in the streets for almost three weeks.

Years later Rob was losing his battle with AIDS. On the day before he died, we spoke for an hour as he took stock of his own life. This tenacious man, this consummate individualist, artist, militant activist, and leader, said to me, "You know, Tor, the greatest lesson of my life was learning about the glory of community. I loved accomplishing work I was proud of, and I loved loving my lovers [Rob had a wonderful, supportive partner in his last few years], but my greatest joy was working with you and all the others building community together."

I was struck by his deathbed assessment that it had not been his individual acts of heroism that had lent the deepest meaning to his life. "What about your leadership in the AB 101 protest?" I asked.

"Oh, I just had to do that," he said. "It just naturally came out of me. . . . But what I remember best is the collective force of our spirit—of all of us out there together—that incredible magical strength we felt. That's what matters, Tor. That's the 'glory of community.' "

———

Our success in the future will be greatly enhanced by our capacity to generate and harness this empowering "glory of community," which strengthens us individually and unites us into a force far greater than we ever imagined possible. Critical to this effort will be recognizing and investing in those institutions that serve to foster a culture of community-building and this spirit of community. A prime example is the gay and lesbian community center model.

7. A CASE STUDY OF ONE GATEWAY TO FREEDOM: THE L.A. GAY AND LESBIAN COMMUNITY SERVICES CENTER

———

Tears of pride welled up in Morris Kight's eyes as the old man stood on a Hollywood street corner looking up at a four-story building with a rainbow of huge pennants hanging from its six front columns. How ironic, he thought. He remembered coming to this same building twenty-five years earlier to beg the Internal Revenue Service to grant tax-exempt nonprofit status to a gay group for the very first time. On that day, he entered the gray, forbidding building, terrified, to ask a hostile government agency to approve the very group that now owned the place—the Los Angeles Gay and Lesbian Community Services Center. "Today, this is our very own!" Morris exulted aloud to the world as he looked up at the building in amazement. "Doesn't that just show the bastards," he said with a twinkle.

———

The L.A. Center's $8 million purchase and renovation of that 44,000-square-foot building in 1992 was a symbol of the coming of age of the lesbian and gay community, a bold physical statement: we're out; we're proud; we're here to stay. "Out for all of us" was the Center's motto that year. By 1996 the organization housed in that huge building had already outgrown its new facility and had raised $4.5 million in trust to buy an additional 33,000-square-foot building nearby, to house its cultural and educational programs. The L.A. Center's annual budget now exceeds $15 million; 240 full-time employees work there, along with 2,000 volunteers. An amazing

420,000 calls for information and referrals are logged every year, and there are over 170,000 in-person visits annually by people using programs ranging from lesbian poetry classes to HIV treatment to housing for runaway youth.

This story, however, is not about a community building; it is about building a community. Early planning began in 1969, and the L.A. Center was officially founded in 1971 by a small determined band of gay liberation activists. Unlike much of the heady, anarchistic political activity of those days, this organization was founded on a simple, sober moral principle: *You can't have hope, let alone liberation, if you're hungry or homeless or hate yourself.* Then and now, many people in our community fit those descriptions. The core of the L.A. Center's mission was the notion that advocacy must be rooted in human services, that from the start the moral imperative of the emerging lesbian and gay movement would be to take care of our own. It was clear nobody else would. True to its mission, this organization became a home, in every meaning of the word, to the L.A. gay community.

The Center was first housed in Morris Kight's living room; it moved into a small house on Wilshire Boulevard, and then into a ramshackle building on heavily traveled Highland Avenue, its original core vision intact. Over the years its programs grew, and by the time I came to work there in 1987, they encompassed the full spectrum of community needs, from basic shelter, food, and clothing, to medical, legal, and crisis counseling services, to educational classes and artistic workshops, to coming-out support groups, to the city's largest information and referral hotline of any kind. I once estimated that over three million people were served by the Center during its first twenty years. Astoundingly, another three million had been helped by the time of its twenty-fifth birthday celebration, in late 1996.

The appellation "Center" is appropriate for an entity that draws in and holds together myriad strands of a diverse community. Trying to capture in words the vast range of programs and services on any given week at the Center is like trying to snap a picture of the Grand Canyon: it's impossible to do justice to the magnitude. Today, women go to the Center for a full range of cancer screening, gynecological, and mental health care at the Audre Lorde Lesbian

Health Clinic (proudly named for the visionary lesbian African-American poet who died of cancer in 1992), or for social activities such as a lesbian film series or hiking and horseback lessons. The Center houses painters, writers, and photographers in residence, has published books of poetry and fiction by community members dealing with HIV, and regularly exhibits sculpture and art. On any given night, a visitor could drop in on a gay fathers' support group, one of numerous lesbian and gay Twelve-Step meetings, a lesbian legal clinic on stepparent adoption, a class in self-defense, professionally facilitated group therapy for Latina lesbians, a class on "queer theory," or outside group meetings ranging from the Stonewall Democratic Club to the Police Advisory Committee to United Lesbians of African Heritage.

The Center's Jeffrey Goodman Clinic conducts significant AIDS research (including the nation's first acupuncture study), houses L.A.'s largest anonymous HIV test site—testing 80 percent of those who have ever tested HIV-positive in L.A.—and provides, in 5,000 client visits monthly, a full range of primary and specialty medical care and treatment services for people at all stages of HIV infection and AIDS. The Center's youth services program is the largest in the country, with a twenty-four-bed emergency shelter, a mentoring program that was the first in the country directed at gay youth, and an international youth pen pal program that has signed on 2,000 young people. (One high school student in Des Moines, Iowa, credits a Center pen pal with saving his life. He now corresponds with fourteen pen pals all over the world.) Gay teens find health care at the one-of-a-kind Pedro Zamora clinic, or can hear the warm voice of another gay teen over the nightly Youth Talkline, or get in-person support in weekly rap groups. A new satellite operation, the Jeffery D. Griffith Gay and Lesbian Youth Center, provides food, clothing, and showers; legal, educational, and job counseling; housing referral, and other services to L.A.'s estimated homeless population of 2,500–5,000 high-risk runaway and "throw-away" gay, lesbian, bisexual, and transgendered youth.

The Center is one of our national success stories. Its greatness derives from that original vision of melding basic human-service provision with all the other activities that provide support and meet the

community's needs for pride, community-wide organizing, affirmation, and advocacy.

In many ways, the Center models the very best of gay and lesbian visionary culture. Its vision and programs are so expansive as
to defy clear categorization; it transcends dualism, that "either/or"
notion so prevalent in our heterosexist society. The Center provides a living model of "both/and" thinking, of saying "Yes, this and
yes, that too." It is both public *and* private—depending on government funding and privately raised gay and lesbian dollars. It is both
grassroots *and* professional, a traditional nonprofit organizational
structure with roots and political identity in the community. It is
both alternative *and* mainstream, radical in its defiance of past categories and mainstream in its political influence. It encompasses
what is traditionally considered both conservative *and* liberal. Its organizational culture seamlessly blends the principles of self-reliance
and compassion.

Over the years of its existence as a fixture in L.A.'s post-
Stonewall gay and lesbian world, the Center has been a microcosm
of that world. Every issue, every political battle, every internal struggle has been mirrored within its walls. The Center has been the single place where all the collective pain as well as the hard-earned
progress of the community has played out. For example, during the
"gender wars" of the 1970s and early 1980s, lesbians fought the
sexism in the ranks of the gay liberation movement and left the
Center—not once but several times—to form our own autonomous
lesbian-feminist groups. But we kept returning to try again. For
years women fought to have the word "lesbian" added to the Center's name; I love the tales of the guerrilla midnight spray-painting
raid in 1979 by determined dykes who painted a caret and a big,
sloppy, lavender "AND LESBIAN" on the "Gay Community Services
Center" sign. On the cement outside the old Highland Avenue
building, you can still discern faded slogans such as "Lesbians ignite"
and "Free the Center!" The name was officially changed in 1985.
So was the sign.

Before there was even a name for the disease, L.A.'s first cases
of AIDS were discovered in the Center's STD clinic for gay men;
the very first "AIDS Prevention Clinic" was established in 1984. In
the fall of 1991, the Center was the mobilizing hub for street protests

against Wilson's veto of AB 101; at the Center, nightly civil disobedience by tens of thousands of L.A. gay men and lesbians was organized. For three solid weeks, Center faxes whirred, phones buzzed, and the switchboard spread the word on the nightly changing location of demonstrations, while the staff mediated between protesters and the city of West Hollywood. Town-hall strategy meetings and regular press briefings crowded the lobby. The Center organized "Freedom Buses" carrying hundreds to a Sacramento National Coming Out Day protest rally. The convoy left from the Center's front parking lot with great media and community fanfare. Of course, all the regular business of the Center continued as well.

The Center is flexible. It can act as a guerrilla base of operations when political conditions require, but it has also become a highly regarded, politically powerful, professional social-services organization. Among a long list of achievements, Center staff led in the development of the High Risk Youth Consortium housed in L.A.'s Children's Hospital. The consortium has become a national model of cutting-edge services to high-risk, homeless street kids. The Center's mental health services program is the country's most acclaimed and oldest professional gay psychotherapy program. It provides one-on-one therapy, couples counseling, and group counseling, trains therapists, serves as a top-notch psychological research center on incest, domestic violence, HIV, and addictions, and provides superb professional-development and sensitivity training to a host of mainstream service organizations.

The Center, because of its multiple purposes, has evolved into a truly diverse and representative community-based organization. The bold driving vision of social services and community programming has required it to involve a rich variety of people as volunteers, staff, participants, and clients. The Center bridges class, age, race, and gender, and is one of the most successful models in the country of true diversity and inclusiveness.

On a recent visit, I randomly approached people in the lobby and asked them how they found their way to the Center.

Peter, sixteen, had returned from high school baseball practice to his Indianapolis suburban home one spring afternoon to find his father pacing the living room in a terrifying rage. Peter's mom had found a copy of *The Advocate* under his bed and called his dad, who raced home. He came after Peter with his fists and chased him up the stairs, beating him and shouting, "No son of mine is going to be a faggot!" Without warning, he ran at Peter, lifted him up, and threw him out of the second-floor window, screaming, "Never, never come home again." Peter, miraculously only bruised by the fall made his way to a friend's house, borrowed some money, and boarded a bus for the only place he could think to go: Hollywood. At the bus station in L.A., Peter had no idea what to do, so he looked up "gay" in the phone book and found the Gay and Lesbian Community Services Center. The hotline told him they had a youth shelter for runaway and throwaway kids just like him, and he went there that night.

When I met him, Peter had graduated from the streets, found transitional housing, had a job, and was going to school and volunteering as a group facilitator at the Center's long-standing Friday night rap group for young people.

Erica, thirty-two, is a high school English teacher who has been with her partner, Lisa, for four years. Growing up in California's conservative Orange County, she always knew she wanted to have kids, but her hope had always seemed out of reach, because she knew she was a lesbian at age ten. Then, in her early twenties and in grad school, she heard about an informal network of over a hundred lesbian mothers who participated regularly in social events and networking in, of all places, Orange County. Erica decided to go to a conference sponsored by the group in 1987. It was an eye-opener. Over three hundred women attended programs on every aspect of parenting for lesbians. At that conference, Erica learned about the Center; after several years, when she was ready to get serious about parenting, she called the Center and heard about their regular "Maybe Baby" program for lesbians and gay men considering parenting.

When I met Erica, she was coming to the Center for her third meeting. She had already connected with a lesbian doctor who specialized in alternative insemination. She was talking with gay men she had met in the group about possible coparenting arrangements.

She was well on her way to creating one more lesbian family with children in this era of the "gayby boom."

Juan grew up in East L.A., and had early gay sexual experiences. His family was strict and Catholic. Juan, more and more terrified of his own homosexuality, followed a path taken by all too many latently homosexual men: he became aggressively homophobic. As was common in his Latino neighborhood, Juan joined a gang and actively urged his fellow members to participate in gay-bashings. More than once, he led attacks on gay men coming out of bars in the Silver Lake area (a mixed gay and Latino neighborhood).

Then a very unusual thing happened. Juan's mother intervened. Knowing of the gang's activities, she confronted him one day, gently demanding that he look at his own past behavior and the fact that he himself was probably gay. Realizing his mother was right, Juan came to the Center on National Coming Out Day in 1989 and told this story at the evening open-microphone speak-out. It was a cathartic experience that removed the weight of years from his shoulders, "just like confession. Once a Catholic, always a Catholic," Juan joked.

When I met him, Juan was a regular volunteer in STOP AIDS, the AIDS prevention peer-support program at the Center. He also worked on Silver Lake's annual "Sunset Junction Neighborhood Alliance Street Fair," organized by gays and lesbians to foster community spirit across cultural barriers and to have a good time as well. As an added and ironic bonus, Juan helped recruit Latino gang members from his neighborhood to work as security for the festival on an annual basis.

---

8. SUSTAINING THE GLORY OF COMMUNITY: A CALL TO ACTION

Creating and sustaining the glory of community will underlie much of our future success as individuals and as a movement for equality. This is a struggle that will not be won for decades to come, and as we wage it more and more on multiple battlefields never touched before—new geography, new issues—success will be measured in great part by our ability to foster a continually regenerating and vivid community spirit. We will need to cultivate increasing unity, determination, love, and vision to hang in there for the long run, and we will need to create the organizational foundation for that possibility.

We are in a new phase of the great and ongoing project of building our culture, community, and movement. We are moving "home to America," bringing ourselves and our issues out of the urban gay ghettoes and into the wide waters of the mainstream. We are coming out in huge numbers in small-town, suburban, and middle America. We are at last developing the possibility of a truly representative openly gay and lesbian grassroots presence everywhere over the next decade or two. This presence can be parlayed into permanent eradication of homophobia in the foreseeable future—but in order to accomplish that, a top priority must be to support and expand and deepen the power of our community-building, as follows:

We must support existing community groups. In order to keep our flame burning, we need to first make sure we each take some responsibility to maintain our existing network of sports, spiritual, service, social, and advocacy organizations. As we come out of our closets, our most powerful next step is to actively engage in service to community. Doing so empowers us with higher self-esteem and new skills, and it fosters a connection to an inspiring sense of purpose. Just as we have created a collective call to come out of the closet, our community culture should recognize this organic journey and encourage it for everyone. Out of the closet and into community work!

If you can't find the group you need, start it. As a people, we are blessed with enormous entrepreneurial skills and energies. If there isn't a lesbian softball league in the town you come out in, start one. If there's no church you can relate to, get together with friends and start a Metropolitan Community Church. If you want a lesbian two-stepping night in your local dance bar, organize for it. The lesson of three decades of gay and lesbian community organizing is that we have limitless capacity to create what we need, even against enormous odds and with slim resources. Our ingenuity has served us brilliantly and will be the basis of constant satisfaction and success as we come out and come home to more towns and cities in this next era.

Support and build permanent local institutions to house our services and community spirit. The key to future political power lies in institutionalizing our resources. We will need to construct permanent and powerful institutions capable of taking on the formidable forces arrayed against us. Culture and affinity groups are crucial to our lives and form our proud home base, but the cornerstone of our long-term success in building political power—and therefore permanent social change—will be solid, stable local institutions that can weather the rise and fall of trends, individual leaders, and phases of our movement. Ultimately, our national political movement will be as strong as the local foundation that supports it.

We must take a page from the right's book and begin to systematically build our own infrastructure from the grass roots up. "It's the grass roots, stupid!" in the 1990s, as the right well knows; and, as the late longtime Speaker of the House Tip O'Neill always said, "All politics is local." Local community centers can be the building blocks of future political clout, by providing a place to consolidate resources, plan for the long term, and develop real power. Power derives from money and from people—membership lists, donor lists, human skills and competencies carefully and strategically built, maintained, and nurtured over time. With lots of hard work and a long view, community centers can become significant nonpartisan institutions that feed our growing political movement. Members of the center can become mobilized constituents; voter registration and education can become established community tradition through centers; leadership development programs can be created; linkages can be made among our own internal communities; meaningful coalitions with others outside our community can be crafted, donor lists can be built and fund-raising leadership cultivated. The word "center" can be actualized.

We are entering the vital second wave of a long battle for gay and lesbian equality. The radical right has brilliantly and doggedly organized, targeting us in their crosshairs; their influence in this country grows daily. By any measure, we still have a long way to go to reach the people of middle America. About a third of Americans fully support our fight for equality. Another third probably never will. The key battle is for the last third—the middle group who don't yet know someone gay or lesbian (or don't know that they do) and haven't yet grappled with their own homophobia. The struggle for the hearts and minds of that vital middle group of this country's people will be waged on every front over the decades to come. Every local gay and lesbian community will need to establish a hub for its organizing, with spokes extending into every corner of its diverse world—and then out into the wider world as well. A local community center can provide this hub.

This is not an exclusive strategy; we need all kinds of groups to spread their wings across America. We need P-FLAG chapters in every town; we need GLAAD chapters all around; we need state lobbies in every state capital. We need NGLTF, Victory Fund, and Human Rights Campaign organizers everywhere possible. We need our lesbian resource centers, our independent youth groups, our single-issue advocacy coalitions. But ultimately, our long-term ability to create and maintain power will flow upward only from the strongest possible, furthest-reaching foundation of permanent grassroots institutions that can grow to incorporate the widest range of missions. Only then will our national political groups and power reach their greatest potential. I would argue that the most adaptable, best model to develop is the multipurpose community center.

A Community Center in Every Town

Currently, there are about sixty-five lesbian and gay community centers of various sizes and shapes in existence around the country. Fifteen of those have formed since 1992. Another fifteen are coming along. They are nurtured and represented by a new group, the two-year-old National Association of Lesbian and Gay Community Centers, founded by center directors from Dallas, Denver, Minneapolis, New York, and Los Angeles. This is evolving into a significant national movement, particularly because it represents smaller cities such as Scottsbluff, Nebraska; Cedar Rapids, Iowa; Salt Lake City, Utah; and Lubbock, Texas. Cleveland, Ohio, has a long-standing, successful center; San Francisco, interestingly enough, does not—although there are now plans in the works. There is no reason in the world why our huge local pools of talent, funds, and energies could not translate into five hundred or more thriving centers by the year 2020. Our national movement for equality would be catapulted to a new level of power with the groundwork laid by such permanent local centers across the country.

These centers should not take the place of other kinds of local or regional organizations, and they should not be seen as competition. In fact, history teaches that everywhere a local center is established, local organizing of all kinds multiplies and flourishes. New York Center director Richard Burns calls centers "the engines of community organizing." Nor should the center model be seen as inflexible; in some places a community health center may grow to serve the same purpose. HRC's field director, Cathy Woolard, advocates combining a community center with a state lobbying group in smaller states where legislatures meet for only a couple of months. I suspect that creative hybrids will evolve as time goes on, adapting to diverse local conditions.

Regardless of the specific form, however, long-term power can ultimately be best built on a solid foundation of local institutional strength that incorporates advocacy, organizing, education, *and* human services. The burgeoning national community-center movement should be supported for the reasons that follow.

Community centers are our own grassroots, democratic organizations. Centers are vital "free spaces" that develop ideas, leadership, activism, values, and vision. Not only can they nurture diversity and inclusiveness, but they can provide a natural locus for building unity and a sense of common purpose, community-wide.

Having an autonomous place of our own in which to discuss and debate issues generates a constant percolation of new ideas, as well as critiques and evaluations of community thinking and activities. The result is a continuous, thriving town hall, a collective context for our work. And often, we have actual town hall meetings in centers: they are the hub of the community, where emergencies are responded to and hot issues debated, where needs for intervention or clearing the air or facilitation among and between groups and individuals can be met. Centers are where we nurture a set of values, consciously and unconsciously.

Centers are those public spaces that create community, that combat anomie and alienation and build collective self-esteem. New trends or needs or internal issues constantly emerge, find a context to evolve, are channeled into action. For example, I've seen passionate debates on the issue of "nature versus nurture," as biological research into the origins of homosexuality has expanded. In these debates the differences between lesbian and gay male thinking and experience on this issue emerges and an interesting dialogue ensues: lesbians often experience sexuality as a choice; gay men experience it as a biological fact.

Another example: a few years ago, reports came separately from several colleges to the L.A. Center's antiviolence hotline that several out lesbians had been raped. I was amazed at how quickly the information was channeled into warnings in the press and organizing on the campuses. There are countless occasions when centers have organized against police raids on gay bars, or against our own community's racism—the triple carding of men of color at white-majority gay men's bars, for instance. In Cleveland, L.A., and New York, the local centers led this fight, spurred on by groups such as Black and White Men Together and Men of All Colors Together. Or, consider how centers helped identify the "gayby boom" as an up-and-coming issue, and then provided the necessary services for those considering parenting and for those with kids. The New York City Lesbian and Gay Community Services Center now serves over 1,300 gay and lesbian families with their "CenterKids" program.

Centers encourage a community-wide culture of activism and provide a magnet and an inspiration for organizing of all kinds. In 1996, Salt Lake City's Stonewall Community Center served as the organizing hub for community protest against the school board's decision to terminate all high school clubs in order to get rid of the Gay/Straight Alliance. In L.A., the Gay and Lesbian Latinos Unidos and other autonomous groups for people of color hold regular meetings at the Center. Most large local AIDS organizations and many activist groups were founded at meetings in gay and lesbian community centers: in New York it was ACT UP, GLAAD, and Queer Nation; in Los Angeles, the Police Advisory Task Force,

AIDS Project–L.A., the Alcoholism Center for Women, and many others. Today, New York's Center welcomes five thousand people a week through its doors to participate in over four hundred different groups, among them the Gay Sierrans, Bisexual Women of Color, the Gay Men's Opera Club, Clann An Uabhair (a gay Scottish social group), and the Lesbian and Gay Immigration Task Force. Centers are "free spaces," where anything is possible. Give us a lever and a place to meet and we can move the world.

Permanent community centers nurture a vision of diversity. Multifocus community centers naturally bridge race, age, class, political, and gender lines. Diverse services can and should involve people from every corner of the local community and build a much richer, fuller constituency of clients, volunteers, donors, staff, and community supporters. This is one of the key strengths of the center notion.

Many of our centers begin as the dream of a few white middle-class gay men (and perhaps a handful of lesbians) yearning for a "home of our own," a place to meet and nurture community. In order to do justice to the centers' greatest potential, however, we need to plan for and guarantee that the broadest possible cross section of our people gets services, gets empowered, and gets involved. This is why human services and support for coming out should be incorporated as early as possible into the mission of the center, along with community activities.

Why is it critical to plan for and insist on diversity? Because we stunt our potential as a community if only one sector is served. One of the most exciting aspects of the gay and lesbian community is that we are everywhere—that we are a microcosm of the rich diversity of America. We often pay lip service to the idea of inclusion; community centers are actually capable of making real that vision. Bisexuals and transgendered members of our community are welcome and nurture their independent and growing voices; ethnic and gender diversity is nourished. In 1986, for example, only 22 percent of the L.A. Center's staffers were women and 17 percent were people of color. Today the staff is fifty–fifty men and women, and 55 percent are people of color. Institutionalized sexism and racism are all but rooted out. And that's more than a simple matter of numbers. The spirit of the organization has been transformed. Diversity is not feared or viewed as a necessary burden; it is valued. It *is* possible to change our organizations, to create successful models of lesbian and gay multicultural institutions that fully involve our richly varied communities. But in order to accomplish this vital task, we must have permanent places, "centers" in the truest sense, that carry this vision in their organization culture. Centers can create and foster real pluralism.

Centers help develop professional and political skills for successful mainstreaming. Multipurpose centers encourage and support the development of important professional skills: management, fund-raising, finance, and administration; medical and social service delivery; policy-making and planning; political lobbying and advocacy. Development of these skills increases our community's clout. In addition, building and running an organization such as a center forces us to "de-ghettoize." A professional track record gives us the foundation for entering new nongay territories with confidence and real skills to bring to the table.

AIDS has perhaps provided the best example of this, as gay people became major players in service and policy development, legislative response, and citizen activism on AIDS, and then on other health care issues. The burgeoning lesbian health movement has been cultivated in many centers across the country. There are countless examples of gay and lesbian staff or volunteers at community institutions bringing to various policy tables our grassroots organizing expertise as well as skill and data in the fields of mental health, addiction recovery, youth organizing, antiviolence work, civil rights advocacy, and much more. At one time in 1990, representatives of the L.A. Center staff and board sat on over two hundred county, federal, and state commissions, working groups, and planning and policy consortia ranging from the United Way to a U.S. Health and Human Services Agency advisory council.

At a permanent center, working in such a broad range of coalitions develops critical lobbying and political skills and powerful connections. Along the way, doing our own work, we also become key players at city halls, in our state capitals, and in Washington. The

Cleveland lesbian and gay center, for example, has an antihomophobia training program that annually reaches every single graduate of the police academy, every new city bus driver, and every new Emergency Medical Services trainee.

Another benefit of service-oriented centers is that they anchor our legislative and political strategies in real people's needs and provide real-life examples of that need. This concept finds a powerful analogy in the feminist movement against domestic violence. It began with victims' needs simply to flee to safety, so shelters were built for women battered by their husbands. Over time, a coherent policy and legislative agenda developed at the city, then county, then state level, emanating from coalitions of service providers led by the women who ran those shelters (often formerly battered women themselves), or sat on shelter boards, or provided pro bono legal counsel or psychological help. Those laws and policies were based on women's real lives and experiences. They were built from the ground up. Now almost every state has passed legislation to protect battered women, relevant federal laws have changed, and important ancillary education and organizing work are steadily being institutionalized, for example in programs to combat male violence and in widespread training for law enforcement officers and judges.

The grassroots anti-domestic-violence infrastructure was already in place when a mass consciousness-raising occurred over the battering and then murder of Nicole Brown Simpson. The movement responded. As with the Anita Hill–Clarence Thomas hearings on the issue of sexual harassment, groundwork laid quietly over two decades of grassroots organizing by feminists led for a while to an unprecedented level of national consciousness-raising. Had the gay movement developed a similarly coordinated, effective, widespread local infrastructure that could be mobilized, we might have won in 1993 on the military issue as well.

I want to take special note of the issue of fund-raising. While only a tiny sector of the gay community is now well socialized in donating money to candidates or issues, I think it's vital to recognize that this is not an immutable fixed situation. We can expand the reach of the lesbian and gay "culture of giving." I have seen it happen. A strategic focus by an institution can nurture, over time, the development of networks of people not used to "tithing" to their community. At the L.A. Center, in the mid-1980s, we targeted women, recognizing that—whether gay or straight—women traditionally tend to give lots of time but little money in proportion to their financial capability. Over a period of five years, because of our hard work and clear, focused strategy, hundreds of women became new donors to the Center; today, the annual "women's night" lesbian prom draws nearly a thousand women every year. The Center's lesbian donor base, newly acculturated to giving funds, is the largest in the country. Other examples include the pioneering Astraea Foundation, the nation's only national lesbian foundation, and the Legacy Fund, which raises over $100,000 every year from lesbians for lesbian projects in one night's chic party in the Hamptons. In 1994, the National Center for Lesbian Rights hosted an unprecedented $500-a-plate dinner party that drew fifty lesbians. Only a few years ago, gender-biased queer conventional wisdom deemed these events utterly impossible.

Contrary to our own popular wisdom, our institutions *can* consciously develop strategies for widening the base of donors to our movement. Money is one significant form of collective and individual power, and our visibility, political clout, and long-term efficacy increase substantially as we involve more and more people from broad cross sections of our national community in "giving back."

Community centers project moral credibility. In the tradition of minority mutual-aid societies, community centers send a powerful message to the world, both to our own people and to the nongay world: "We take care of our own." This message establishes moral authority and ethical credibility that should not be undervalued. We demonstrated this in our response to AIDS in the 1980s; our credibility on health care issues and our humanity shone forth as never before. By taking seriously the task of building and developing agencies that offer human services, we help counteract the vicious lies propagated against us by the right. Contrary to their false message, we show that we are a highly moral people because we take care of our own. Shouldering this responsibility is a positive and ethical act, and when nongay Americans learn about it, they respond to its humanity. From this base, we move forward on firmer moral ground when we fight for even tougher political and social change, such as recognition of our families.

New York City Lesbian and Gay Community Services Center director Richard Burns sees gay centers as the newest version of settlement houses, which not only provided services for immigrant populations but acculturated them, through education, to their new life in the United States. Like the settlement houses that grew in immigrant communities of urban America, lesbian and gay centers are very important gateways into our community.

We need permanence in the face of AIDS. It is vital—both morally and practically—that we consciously plan for permanence in the face of the ongoing toll of AIDS on our community. One reality of the epidemic is that it is not a short-term battle but a long-term catastrophe. AIDS will be with us long into the future.

Even assuming that we have a discrete network of AIDS-specific education, advocacy, treatment, and social service agencies, we have no choice but to plan for continuity and succession in the gay and lesbian community. No group can sustain the degree of loss of life—of loss of tens of thousands of people, their leadership, their talent, their history, their skills—without trauma to its emotional cohesion. After more than fifteen years of AIDS, our community is suffering from something like collective post-traumatic stress syndrome.

In the face of that "AIDS trauma syndrome," we must take positive, creative steps to help knit together some coherence, some continuity, some cultural permanence in our community. We must build institutional memory and remember our own. More than any American community in recent history, we are losing scores of our best and brightest, our movers and shakers, our artists and visionaries, in the prime of their lives. We must work at double (or even triple) speed to learn from one another, to share our knowledge, to record our stories and strategies for those who will follow. Permanent institutions will not make up for the loss, but they can become catalysts for healing our endless grief, for forging positive responses out of our despair and anger, and for capturing precious resources destined to die with each individual unless we plan otherwise.

At a permanent community center, institutional memory is captured, preserved, and passed on, along with the ideas, energies, and resources of those facing death or fighting HIV. At a permanent center, our individual gay heroes can share their core experience with others and pass on their life's lessons to our collective memory by living example and through video-documented lectures and interviews. Centers can be vehicles for role modeling and leadership development for our youth. They can work out collective ways of dealing with the impact of the epidemic as well as provide direct emotional support and medical care.

Centers are also spaces for memorializing individuals. They are a legacy that is specifically and openly gay, and that is immortal—a solid brick-and-mortar monument to people. Programs, awards, or scholarships; rooms, walls, or chairs-in-residence can be named by, or in honor of, those who are dead or sick, or their friends or families. We could never have completed the new L.A. Center in 1992 without bequests and gifts given in honor of those who have died of AIDS, or without the incredible work and commitment of people who are themselves living with HIV and were deeply committed to the vision of that permanent legacy.

For example, Ed Gould, a Center board member and retired banker who chaired our capital campaign, worked full-time for three years to make that building happen. In order to secure a $500,000 gift, Ed came out both as gay and as HIV-positive to his family's foundation. Ed donated the money for the Center's lobby and big community meeting room—not only for himself, as a gay man with HIV, but also in the name of his gay twin brother, who had died a few years earlier of a drug overdose, a victim of homophobia's devastation of our self-esteem.

Get Involved: Build Your Local Center

This is our golden moment in history to move forward in our struggle for equality and freedom. Each of us must be part of this effort on every level. More than a quarter century after Stonewall, something additional is now required of us. We need to be active on three fronts simultaneously. We must continue to come out, and reach to the edges of our entire sphere of influence. We must maintain, preserve, and expand the autonomous community groups that empower and enliven our world. Simultaneously, we must also move ourselves ever more into the mainstream, to become respected players in the world of community service and of politics, while constantly affirming our basic community pride. Our permanent community-based institutions are best positioned to support this triple approach in our local towns and cities.

Individually, we may already be part of a gay community affiliation group—a gay chorus or bowling league, a lesbian moms' or gay dads' group, a neighborhood or social club, a synagogue or a church. That's great; it's a necessary and important step, and if we can't find the group that fills the bill, we can always start it. But collectively and individually, we will be unable to move beyond simple survival to reach our full potential as a people unless each one of us takes the next step in building community institutions such as community centers. Such a commitment will lead us into the next phase of our movement, consolidating our national resources into a powerful movement for political change.

Every time we bring our hand—and voice, and heart—to the task of crafting community, we reinvigorate the possibilities for human freedom, for ourselves, our people, and the broader world.

4

TURNING HOME TOWARD
FREEDOM: EMBRACING
THE POLITICS OF HOPE

1. INTRODUCTION: A TIME OF
OPPORTUNITY AND DANGER

Over the past thirty years, lesbians and gay men have made miracles happen. Against staggering odds, we have survived bigotry beyond belief, embittering exile from our families of origin, and the "coffin world of the closet." We have healed ourselves, created loving families of choice and friendship circles to sustain us, and built that glory of community—our own home base of resistance against the continuing daily indignities of shame, violence, and hatred. We have fought for our very lives against AIDS, beaten back waves of organized assaults by the homophobic right, and, in the course of those battles, forged a fierce spirit of determination that will never again go back into hiding or dissolve in self-hatred.

Over the past few years in particular, we have not only survived but thrived, moving forward in significant ways. Because we have come out in such great numbers, new social and political territory has opened up, giving us greater opportunities than ever before. We are changing hearts and minds within our widening spheres of influence, and, finally, our issues are squarely—and permanently—on America's social agenda. Virtually every institution in this country is now grappling with homosexuality: religion, the media, the courts, schools, government, business, Hollywood. As never before, discrimination against us and understanding of our lives have become questions of concern for this country's heterosexual majority.

As this situation evolves, as we stream out of closets and gay ghettoes into broader channels, we must take our next step: we must effectively mobilize our individual and community resources to build a powerful political movement at the grassroots, state, and national levels to permanently change policies, laws, and public opinion on our issues. For the first time in human history, we are achieving the critical mix of "out" numbers, crystallized determination, and general social tolerance that allows us to take our place in the body politic. But as we begin to mount our political offensive, we do so in an era of grave danger as well as enormous opportunity.

Facing Barriers, Within and Without

The times couldn't be tougher for our task—a task already made difficult by a puritanical America uncomfortable with any sexuality, let alone homosexuality. We move into this public and political phase of our struggle for equality at the very time that right-wing religious political extremists—whose core worldview institutionalizes contempt of us—have more power and control in America than ever before. The November 1994 elections saw a seismic jolt to the right that altered the political landscape, fulfilling radical rightist Pat Robertson's dream of a virtual takeover of Congress and many statehouses across the land. The ultra-right's ability to set the terms of the national social-agenda debate in this country was consolidated. As part of its broader agenda, the right now has the capability to propagandize widely against gay people and to keep us on the defensive at the very time we are developing the ability to begin the long, arduous job of widespread public education about the truth of our lives.

———

Sheila James Kuehl was elected California's first openly gay state assemblymember in November 1994, at the same time as "the evil Cardassians swept into power in Washington and Sacramento," as the die-hard Trekkie puts it. She assesses our overall political situation this way:

"We're in a new world, a world in which the right is trying to shove their 'revolution' down our throats. In my second year in office, I was appointed the first-ever freshman chair of the Judiciary Committee of the California Assembly, only to have the brand-new conservative Republican one-vote majority eliminate all Democrats from positions of power. So I was removed from the committee. I had two choices: I could act like a bitter, angry loser or I could plan for the next step.

"Our movement is in the same situation: we have to leap to the next level. We have to settle in for the long, long haul. We need to add new tactics to our short-term guerrilla warfare where we've been organizing here and there to defeat a ballot initiative, or hitting the streets. We need to keep fighting, but we have to radically retool our thinking, focusing more on electoral politics, legislative strategy, and long-range movement-building.

"History has thrown down its gauntlet to this community. Do we have what it takes to build for the long term, to get serious about real political power—and the organizational work it takes to achieve it? Because our enemies are deadly serious. They want to make sure that our young gay men and lesbians lose whatever freedom we have gained. They want us back in the closet or dead. It's that simple. The stakes are higher than ever, and it's time to be serious and strategic— it's time to become our most magnificent selves."

———

Getting real—the Clinton conundrum. Not only are we coming into our own in a right-wing era but sometimes we forget that we are a young movement still in formation and unsure of its relationship to power. Nothing has brought this into sharper relief than the volatile relationship of the gay and lesbian community to President Bill Clinton. An emerging social-change movement, particularly one unmoored from its blood family, can easily fall victim to its own hunger for appreciation by authority figures. Although we're a scrappy, rebellious, independent lot, our anguished need for acceptance has sometimes become a political Achilles' heel. The gay and lesbian community has had a uniquely emotional, oddly codependent, and profoundly ambivalent relationship to President Bill Clinton, which we must sort out in order to mature politically.

Luke's eyes flashed with pain. A longtime AIDS and youth activist, he was discussing the convulsive transition that the gay movement had made from anger at President Bush to hope and then quick disillusionment with the Clinton 1992 campaign and early presidency. "Who can ever forget Inauguration Day, January 1993? A political depression I'd felt my entire life lifted like a dark cloud just evaporating. Optimism was contagious; we thought that this day would bring an end to AIDS and instant gay rights. Then, with Clinton's capitulation to the right on gays in the military, it died, and we were even more angry and disappointed than before. For months I was livid at Clinton for caving in, for not sticking with what we all knew *he* knew was right. I still get angry about it, but now I grasp the situation more fully. A big piece of it was our own fault: we gave our power away too easily. We were so hungry for hope after a decade of AIDS that we handed it to him on a silver platter. We went from ACT UP street activism to presidential power practically overnight. We were all too ready to let Big Daddy Bill save us. When he didn't, we freaked out, big time."

In my opinion, Luke is right. In the first year of the Clinton administration, our expectations were far too high. We had trouble seeing clearly the real-world limits of a president facing a powerful right without a strong progressive movement on the outside to back him up. To succeed politically, we have to take things less personally, be more resilient, and work like crazy to build real power by strengthening our movement so our pressure has some clout behind it.

Of course, we must hold the President accountable for his actions when we disagree. We were right to be angry, for example, at Clinton's rapid-fire indication that he would sign the antigay Defense of Marriage Act of 1996. His homophobia—or "homo-stupidity," as gay activist Bob Hattoy called it—seemed particularly insulting because the White House announced the President's position less than forty-eight hours after the pro-gay-rights Supreme Court decision on the Colorado case. The White House announcement seemed purposefully timed to blunt our euphoria on a well-deserved and historic victory—which it certainly did.

But we must be doggedly strategic at every turn, "keeping our eyes on the prize." Despite disappointment at a flawed record on our issues, we need to recognize one bottom-line fact: it is no coincidence that our issues have moved forward at an accelerated pace during the Clinton era. President Clinton's strong support—intermittent as it has been—during a right-wing power surge has opened up unprecedented political space in which to present our case to the American public. Other Clinton pluses, not to be undervalued, include over a hundred appointments of openly lesbian and gay persons to the administration; decisive action against job discrimination in all federal agencies and departments except the Defense Department; support for ENDA; significant increases in AIDS funding; and unprecedented support for lesbian health and gay youth measures.

The right knows President Clinton is the most gay-friendly president in history; they regularly demonize him for his gay rights support. Getting a little more balance into our view of this man—who will be linked for posterity with our community in the public's mind—can only help us move to the next level of our own political maturity.

Additional barriers to political success. There are other barriers to our success in creating a powerful political movement, barriers shared by other marginalized communities. The right wing has successfully manipulated the general public's fear about economic dislocation and rapid social change, and, as a result, we are facing an epidemic of cynicism, voter apathy, confusion, and even despair about the possibilities of positive political change. There is also a strong anti-activist bias working against us, at the same time as AIDS is taking its relentless toll. Perhaps worst of all, gay men and lesbians simultaneously face the great enemy that resides within: an internalized homophobia, or a self-hatred, that blocks our potential. The successful construction of a national movement to achieve real political power and widespread social change requires us to tackle every one of these issues, forcefully and creatively.

2. RECLAIMING "OUR RIGHT TO HOPE"

LaShawn, a shy young African-American college student from Detroit, expressed widely held sentiments about the gay movement: "I know I want things to get better, but I'm not sure where I fit in. I don't really know if I can be an 'activist'—the ones I know are so cynical about everything. They complain that Gay Pride festivals are just big parties and spending sprees, assimilationist bullshit. They trash national groups and anyone who is a leader; they complain that the sixties generation failed to bring permanent change and proved there's no real way to change the system. They seem hip, but hopeless. In my heart I don't believe those things, but where's the vision for the future? Where's the direction? I admit, I'm confused."

LaShawn is not alone. Recently, I took an informal survey of my audiences at a number of college lectures—a total of about a thousand people, of whom 90 percent were probably gay, lesbian, or bisexual. I asked how many of them thought there had been "sweeping positive change" for lesbians and gay men over the past twenty-five years and virtually everyone raised his or her hand. I asked how many people thought we needed *more* "sweeping change" over the *next* twenty-five years and, again, 99 percent raised their hands. I then asked how many thought we actually would achieve those changes. Only one or two per audience, about ten people total, raised their hands.

I was stunned. I asked specifics: would we see a substantial decrease in gay-bashing violence? No. Fewer suicide attempts by our gay youth? No. Would we see a federal employment antidiscrimination bill? No. Would we see gay marriage legalized? No.

Over and over and over again, I have seen this sense of political hopelessness. It's distressing how few people—particularly young people—actually believe that things will get substantially better in the coming years. Despite the great changes that have already occurred, people feel profoundly pessimistic. A young Latina lesbian in San Antonio complained to me: "I'm twenty-six and I'm the only young person I know who is active. I feel so lonely." A young man in Lincoln, Nebraska, almost couldn't speak, he was so upset. "I used to want to be a gay civil rights lawyer, a professional advocate," he said, with pain in his eyes. "But I've come to realize that the hatred is too ingrained. All institutions are corrupt, including government. Maybe queers can resist personally or culturally, or be in-your-face radicals, but we can't change the system."

When I listen to this despair and bitterness, particularly from young people, I feel deeply outraged at a world that is sucking hope from the very people who should harbor the most. In order to get anywhere at all, we are going to have to change "the system." To do that, as a gay community we're going to have to somehow confront and mobilize our people to overcome the defeatism and hopelessness that too often roil under the surface of even our active communities.

The possibilities for the future exist in the exact measure in which we are able to envision them. We must begin—begin again, for many of us—to believe in the collective power of our will and our determination to work together to turn things around on a large scale. Only then will we win over, for example, at least half of the 75 percent of Americans who oppose gay and lesbian marriage. If *we* don't believe we can change their minds, we simply will never be able to do it. If *we* don't believe that decency and a basic belief in fairness and equal opportunity predominate in the American character, we will never prevail against the radical right. If *we* don't believe we can reverse the increasing feelings of alienation and isolation in our own neighborhoods, then our community-building and leadership skills will stay sidelined within the few gay ghettoes.

If we don't believe we can collectively change the conditions of our lives the way we have each already done individually through the courageous act of leaving the closet, fighting AIDS, and building community, then we will remain at the margins forever.

The fact is, as recent history teaches us, that we live in startling times. Historical change can happen virtually overnight; mass movements can erupt with a single spark. In 1995 in France, a general strike over government funding cuts engaged millions of people in organizing and street demonstrations during a quiet and conservative era. In South Africa, apartheid fell and a political prisoner emerged to become the country's first black president—an event absolutely unimaginable only a few years earlier. To pile miracle upon miracle, Nelson Mandela's is the first national constitution in human history to specifically prohibit sexual-orientation discrimination.

Yet somehow, such electrifying changes aren't perceived as possible here in America. Despite ample evidence to the contrary in other countries and in our own American history, we still don't yet believe in our own ability—as Americans or as lesbian and gay people—to get together with like-minded folks and change the world. There is a deep chasm between personal perceptions about injustice, which are widespread, and the sense that political organizing could do anything about it. Perhaps it's because we give up when the quick fix doesn't work. It certainly is partially because we are a country with little sense of history.

With my sixties-inspired heart, and my long view from over thirty years of activism, I'm entirely convinced that things *can* change dramatically in the next five, ten, and twenty years. I feel it in the deepest part of my bones. As Holly Near's song "Wrap the Sun Around You Like a Rainbow" says: "We can make it if we try / I've seen it done before / Where we all opened up our hearts / And that opened up the door / Don't you remember? / It wasn't so long ago."

But it *can't* happen unless more of us begin to believe in it. It's like wearing a miner's hat: we can only move toward a goal when we shine the light to illuminate the path ahead. Vision precedes action, and hope precedes vision. Eradicating a bigotry as irrational and deep-seated as homophobia is a massive, long-term job. In order to do it, we must believe, in our deepest collective soul, that we can do it.

Why should we have hope in these tough times? Because we've seen over and over again that we *can* make a difference. As Lily Tomlin would say, "We have evidence." And that evidence is in what we've each done so many times in so many ways, in our daily lives. We've seen it in the act of falling in love in the midst of hatred all around us. We've seen it through the building of our beautiful families while we ourselves are supposed to be immoral. We've seen it in the creation of exciting, compassionate, and caring community organizations in the face of lies beyond measure about our very beings. We've seen flashes of it when a longtime lesbian couple dances, openly and lovingly, at a presidential inaugural ball. We've seen it when Roberta Achtenberg, one of our best and brightest, survives vicious assaults by Jesse Helms to take a top position in the Clinton administration—and then almost becomes mayor of San Francisco. We've seen it when one thousand students—led by self-proclaimed "accidental activist" lesbian youth leaders—walk out of Salt Lake City high schools and middle schools, demanding their clubs back. Over and over again, we've seen courage create sparks of hope in the rich drama of our daily lives. But we haven't yet managed to parlay those catalytic sparks into a pervasive and guiding activist culture of hope.

I think of my friend the black gay leader and PWA Phill Wilson, a visionary who cofounded the Black Gay and Lesbian Leadership Forum in 1988 with black lesbian-feminist Ruth Waters. He remembers the lack of faith that had to be overcome. "Everyone said it couldn't be done. Black lesbians and gay men were putting their energies into the straight black community or the mostly white gay community but felt angry and defeated by the prejudice we faced in each. Everyone said that there simply couldn't be a viable organization that linked the two. But I believed in it. I knew it could happen because I knew it *had* to happen. We needed a force of our own." Surrounded by nay-sayers from all sides, Phill used his own buoyant hope to pull early supporters along with him. Sure enough, the organization is now seven years old, has become the *National Black Gay and Lesbian Leadership Forum*, has affiliates in twelve cities, and is growing rapidly. The Forum attracts over a thousand people to its annual leadership-building convention, and has become a key player in forging a powerful presence, both black and gay, in broad civil rights circles. In August 1993, at the thirtieth anniversary of Dr. Martin Luther King's 1963 March on Washington, Phill was the first openly gay black man to address the crowd in the name of both struggles for freedom. I believe that the spirit of Bayard Rustin, the black gay man who organized the 1963 march, and whose gayness was very controversial at the time, smiled brightly down at Phill that hot dusty day thirty years later. Phill sums it up for all of us: "My lesson as a black man, a gay man, and a black gay man living with AIDS is: If we give up our right to hope, we're doomed." Sheila Kuehl says it another way: "I feel deeply certain that this harsh and visionless time is what some have called 'the hour of the wolf'—that bleakest darkest time of night just before the dawn. We are in our 'hour of the wolf,' and the sunrise can be just ahead."

"Activism" Is Not a Dirty Word

As if the cloud of cynicism about progressive change that hangs over our hope these days were not enough of a problem, many in our gay and lesbian community exacerbate the problem by rejecting and discrediting the whole concept of activism. Although AIDS activism engaged widespread passions for a few years, in many places it has subsided into apathy and burnout, even as the AIDS epidemic rages unabated.

In this politically and socially conservative era, all dissent and protest not part of the right-wing revolution under way have been effectively marginalized and a fierce anti-activist bias has found its way into our culture and community. Too often, even on college campuses, I hear that anti-activist bias that LaShawn alluded to: "I'm not really an activist, but . . ." Or, "I'm afraid I'm becoming one of those activist types," as if activists were an alien life form. Undermining people's faith in activism is an effective tool for stopping progress; there is a direct relationship between hope and activism, and one of the most effective ways to kill hope, or block its actualization, is to discredit the notion that ordinary people can band together to change the conditions of our lives. Look at the ferocious well-organized backlash against feminism in the 1980s, which resulted in huge numbers of women's rights supporters feeling they had to disavow feminism. A big part of that backlash against feminism was dyke-baiting, a constant attempt to associate feminism with lesbianism, to use us to scare strong young straight women away from activism. The logical next step was to make all forms of activism suspect.

The media love to portray dissent as a quaint throwback to the sixties, as if all social problems have either been taken care of or are permanent fixtures. Whether it was hunger strikes against South African apartheid in the early 1980s, mass rallies against the 1991 war with Iraq, or the Teamsters strike of 1994, protest is widely discredited, ignored, or patronized as quirky and exceptional. Seen as "sixties-style flashbacks," protesters are "granolas" and demonstrations are dismissed as "just nostalgia."

In the 1960s and early 1970s, life was charged with hope for broad societal transformation. Activism was an energetic, exuberant grassroots social force that pervaded virtually every corner of society. Students and teachers were changing education. Churches and synagogues, civic clubs, unions—virtually all our mainstream institutions—were deeply involved in a vibrant, excited, noisy national conversation about the Vietnam War and domestic social policy. There was a hum of possibility in the air, and an optimism that the future could be different. We felt that we could not only end the war in Vietnam but also diminish poverty and racism at home and expand the boundaries of democratic participation to truly include everyone. The women's and environmental movements stretched the horizons of our thinking as we began to explore the idea of global interconnectedness and the connection between the personal and the political. Changing the world became an accessible, dynamic process that engaged the passions of masses of people. Activist impulses were everywhere. And onto this throbbing stage of social turmoil burst those brave drag queens, gay youths, and working-class lesbians who fought the police at New York's Stonewall bar in 1969.

But in the past two decades, the spirit of those protests by millions of people has been lost. It has been replaced by a generalized distrust and dislike of dissenters, including those who are gay or lesbian, along with a popular sense of pessimism about government and about change in general. It's a grim picture.

To an extent, I think it's true that activism has become cliquish and workaholic, regardless of the cause or movement. The activist life is often all-consuming and out of balance, so absorbing and unhealthy as to be unattractive to many, if not most, people. Activist culture too often means endless meetings (and sometimes endless "process"), few friends outside the activist circle, a narrow approach to the world, and peer pressure to work nonstop or be thought of as failing to measure up. Sometimes, there is a self-righteousness that is thoroughly unpleasant. Activist culture often feels exclusive to newcomers. There is sometimes an unspoken but obvious dress code ("activist attire" or "activist drag") and a shared way of talking, and even a way of thinking. My friend Luke, a longtime gay youth organizer, muses that, fearing ostracism from a dogmatic gay activist subculture in San Francisco, he used to make lists of "Politically Incorrect Buzzwords to Avoid at All Costs." One thirtysomething corporate manager in Boston who had tremendous leadership skills but was new to a citywide gay political group told me that she felt required to change out of her business attire into "torn blue jeans and a dyke rugby shirt" in order to feel comfortable at the group's meetings. "There seemed to be rules about what to wear and how to look, and I wanted to do it right," she said.

We must not let our culture of activism devolve into an exclusive, perfectionist, "politically correct" workaholic club. Getting together with like-minded folks to help change the world, or even our little piece of it, is one of the most gratifying of human endeavors. Reclaiming our right to hope will require recharging the batteries of activism with that knowledge, and with some fundamental faith in ourselves as agents of change and in the possibility of changing "the system" at large. Activism is a mighty force indeed, if powered with vision and faith. Activism takes the glory of community to its next stage, broadening its reach to effect permanent change in the world in which we live. This is true whether we are engaging in electoral-political work for a gay or gay-friendly congressional candidate or fighting an antigay referendum or writing a letter of thanks to the editor of the local newspaper for a progay editorial.

To re-energize our activism, to rebuild our capacity to hope— and to sustain these over the long term—we must decide to confront and overcome some of our internal demons, so that we can become, in Sheila Kuehl's words, "our most magnificent selves," capable of building a truly powerful political movement to eradicate homophobia forever.

3. CONFRONTING "OPPRESSION SICKNESS"

A survey taken a few years ago at a conference of two hundred lesbian and gay activists from around the country revealed an extraordinary consensus. Out of over a hundred "weaknesses of our movement" cited by participants in an open-ended questionnaire (which included everything from our relatively small numbers, to the closet, to racism and sexism), three problems were identified by the overwhelming majority as the most important: infighting, lack of support for leaders, and internalized homophobia.

The renowned diversity trainer and management consultant Deborah Johnson, a lesbian who has worked extensively with the community organizations of people of color and with women's and lesbian and gay groups, says that the single quality that most distinguishes gay groups from other groups of Americans struggling against discrimination is "a deep-rooted disrespect and mistrust of each other." Deborah has said, I think wisely, that this is the result of being taught that our love for each other is morally wrong. How can we feel good about each other as political colleagues if somewhere inside we mistrust even our own love's worth?

One of the toxic effects of society's ingrained and pervasive homophobia is that we, as gays and lesbians, internalize it ourselves. It becomes internalized oppression. That is, we cannot help *but* internalize the negative and hateful messages of this heterosexist society. Unfortunately, unless we are careful, we bring that baggage of internalized oppression, that homophobic self-hatred, into our

lives, and into our gay and lesbian community and political movement. There, it can poison our work. This is what I call oppression
sickness.

We are, as one young man I met at a conference said, an "amphibious" people, still evolving from the mud of oppression to the
expansive land of freedom. We aren't there yet, certainly not as a
collective whole, and we are held back by those members of our community trapped in low self-esteem and self-hatred or by those qualities in ourselves. The drowning man pulls down the swimmer trying to save him. Crabs in a bucket claw viciously at the one escaping
and pull her back down. Our very oppression ingrains powerlessness
and fear into us, and fear, because it is the most powerful emotion,
is the most dangerous. We operate from fear when we lack confidence and esteem, and our most crippling fear as a political movement is the fear of power. Fear and distrust of power are natural for
people who have been powerless, and our experience of the dominant culture has taught us that power is usually oppressive—it is
abusive and hurtful. Whether in our parents' rejection or in society's religious, medical, educational, and media institutions that ignore, debase, or dehumanize us, power is directed at us and controls
us. We learn early and learn well that people use power to hurt us;
that's why we hide so deeply in our closets.

Because we have learned this lesson so well—sometimes without even knowing we have done so—many of us carry over that fear
or distrust to other aspects of power: money, success, leadership, and
intellectual or professional skills. These fears may be particularly
strong among lesbians and gay men of color, or poor and working-
class people, whose access to the tools of the powerful has been limited even further, but we all share, in some measure, the outsider's
distrust of power.

Infighting and "Horizontal Hostility"

Our outsider status produces enormous reserves of mistrust that spill
beyond the powerful into widespread defensiveness toward, and
disrespect for, each other. We often see expressions of "horizontal
hostility." That's the term feminists came up with in the 1970s for
attacks misdirected across rooms (or cities, or the movement) at

each other, instead of at our common enemies outside our community. It's much easier to attack each other than it is to figure out
how to unite and conquer our opponents.

This kind of bickering severely limits our effectiveness and is a
powerful disincentive to our youth and to newcomers to activism.
Time and time again, when I speak on campuses or to youth groups,
the first question out of people's mouths is "Why is there so much
infighting? Why can't people get along enough to work together effectively?"

Of course, queers didn't invent infighting. All movements for
social change experience some amount of it. Infighting is, unfortunately, the luxury of the powerless; it is what the powerless too often
do to avoid the hard work of shouldering responsibility for uniting
and taking power. But it is a destructive force. The 1960s student
movement was tattered by internal dissension. Rivalry between leaders and factions of the civil rights movement was legendary, and feminist infighting in the early days included horrendous squabbles. But
at least in the 1960s and 1970s, much of the infighting revolved
around political differences (often arcane and irrelevant ideological
hairsplitting, to be sure). In the lesbian and gay movement, however, ego and turf wars, not political ideology or principles, predominate. There are some real political differences involved but they
tend to be exaggerated beyond reality. To me, as a veteran of prior
movements, lesbian and gay internal fighting seems particularly vicious and arbitrary. Perhaps it's because we have more money than
most social and political movements, and can afford what one friend
calls the luxury of a "boutique approach": if I don't like your group,
I'll just go out and start my own, as one might start a new small business in the next neighborhood. Perhaps it's just an unfortunate pe-
culiarity of gay culture, which loves "dish" and gossip. But the fact
is that the bitter intensity and the tremendous scope of gay and lesbian infighting have been extremely counterproductive and ren-
dered too much strategic work all but dysfunctional.

At one retreat I attended for sixty leaders from across the demographic and political spectrum, we spent hours discussing this
issue. One person after another testified about the painfulness and
pointlessness of the endless squabbling, and the way every new idea
or initiative was deflated, or crashed against a wall of automatic

mistrust. Connie Norman, the eloquent California transsexual activist, pleaded: "When will we start to operate from what we trannies call the spirit of the skirt? I'm so tired of carping and fighting
with my supposed gay family. It's worse than the crazy huge dysfunctional Midwest farm family I grew up in." A Latino gay man
said: "The glass is always half empty in gay community politics. We
knock each other down constantly. Instead of assuming the best in
someone, we automatically assume the worst—they are on a power
trip, their idea is politically wrong, or whatever. We act like we are
permanently powerless, like we're the eternal victims of life. Why
do we have three separate rival groups in this city all advising the
police department on lesbian and gay matters? It's ridiculous."

Like the smog in our air, unseen but lethal, our oppression sickness has generated enormous negativity—unhealthy competition
and rivalry, the undermining of new ideas, and endless infighting.
We can't succeed if our internal squabbling continues to swamp our
ability to operate efficiently and effectively.

Leadership-Bashing

Appropriately called cannibalizing our leaders, or eating our own, the
widespread sport of hammering our leaders back into the ground is
one of the most painful manifestations of oppression sickness. Perhaps we can be forgiven for questioning the value of leadership; after
all, this nation's leaders have done little but ignore, abuse, and op-
press us. But nothing is more destructive to the forward motion of
our movement than tripping up our *own* leaders as they make their
way down an already treacherous path. When you're leading an assault against the enemy, you don't want to have to watch your back.

Principled critique and criticism is vital to good leadership, but
leader-bashing is a different beast. It takes myriad forms, and its intensity increases with the visibility or success of the leader. Someone working her or his way up the ranks of a gay organization often
sees a steady erosion of support, finding herself or himself increasingly isolated and the subject of innuendo and gossip. Nasty carping letters appear in the gay press, elevating minor mistakes to the
status of mortal sins. The gay press itself engages in all-too-frequent
sensationalistic attacks that destroy reputations; even organizations

have been destroyed, as was the National Gay Rights Advocates. Often rumors about our leaders with no basis in fact spread like an out-of-control blaze through the community. These rumors are personally destructive and impede one's ability to get things done. Often criticism about a political point becomes a screaming ad hominem attack during a community meeting that leaves meaningful debate lost among the vicious finger-pointing and negativity.

I don't know a successful local or national lesbian or gay leader who has not suffered quite amazingly brutal attacks: David Mixner, Sean Strub, Tom Stoddard, Melinda Paras, Eric Rofes, Jean O'Leary, Tim Sweeney—you name the leader, he or she has suffered. If a leader was visible, successful, and powerful, he or she was cannibalized, often by the gay press. I certainly was, in my time as director of the National Gay and Lesbian Task Force. There was a two-month period when I received an average of fifteen e-mails, letters, voice-mail messages, or faxes every single workday that criticized me, usually quite viciously. It was relentless. My friend Sean Strub, who experienced something similar, joked about writing a book entitled *People Who Hate Me Who Don't Even Know Me.*

In truth, these attacks function no differently than the purposeful disinformation campaigns that have been unleashed by right-wing ideologues on Hillary Rodham Clinton, President Clinton, and other national figures such as former U.S. Surgeon General Joycelyn Elders. These attacks purposefully detract and distract from positive accomplishments, damage leaders' reputations, and poison the political environment, making it tougher to move forward. The gay and lesbian perpetrators of these attacks on our leaders might as well be agents provocateurs, like those that the FBI sent in to damage progressive groups in the 1960s and 1970s and our own Queer Nation and ACT UP in the 1980s and 1990s. Destructiveness and destabilization result from their actions, whether they intend them to or not.

The level of viciousness reached in bashing gay leaders still stuns me. I particularly get angered and saddened by the many pained phone calls I receive from new or young activists, or those who have risen to new leadership positions.

Sheila Kuehl tells this story, with a slightly baffled, slightly wry look on her face:

"I had come out *very* publicly in 1991 on *Entertainment Tonight* and *Geraldo,* and when I was first running for office in 1994, *People* magazine ran a story headlined: 'Zelda [Kuehl's TV character] Jumps Out of the Closet and into a State Government Race.' *Every* newspaper story and TV show about me used the words *lesbian* or *gay* right up front. But, since being gay is not necessarily any kind of qualification for office, my campaign literature (fool that I am!) concentrated on education, crime, the environment, etc. One day I got a phone call saying that the *Advocate* was considering a story criticizing me for not being out enough because every campaign mailer didn't say 'lesbian candidate.' I thought, 'Don't they have anything better to do than hunt for negative angles on the folks who are trying to do something?' "

———

In the 1970s, the women's movement distrusted leadership as deeply as the gay community does now. Local feminist organizing brimmed over with experimental models of group decision-making that overtly rejected or attempted to deny the existence or importance of leadership. Many feminists maintained that all leadership smacked of patriarchal power-taking, and was, therefore, inherently suspect and oppressive. In the mid-1970s, Jo Freeman, a feminist political analyst, wrote a brilliant—and highly controversial—article called "The Tyranny of Structurelessness" outlining the destructiveness and essentially antidemocratic thrust of our anti-leadership bias.

Feminism's challenge to the basic definitions of leadership has been in many ways invigorating and healthy. It has resulted in some visionary democratization of the notion of good leadership—for example, in its emphasis on collaboration, team-building, and empowerment of others. But after thirty years of wrestling with the question of leadership, the collective feminist wisdom has definitely reaffirmed the vital role leadership plays in building and maintaining any community or movement for equality. There should be no need to reinvent this wheel. Why can't we learn from those who have trodden these paths before?

Simply put, good leadership is necessary for the success of every collective form of human endeavor, whether it's running a business, planning a rally, or directing a choir. When we begin to allow our leaders to flourish, then we will be exhibiting the first sign of a healthy and potentially successful movement for equality.

Political Purism

As an "amphibious" people still evolving from our place of powerlessness, we also have a problem with simplistic thinking. Sometimes we just want easy answers; sometimes we want to stay mired in victimization. However, wise strategies are often complicated and require the synthesis of opposing ideas. They require taking power, not staying stuck in powerlessness. Incorporating the principle of diversity—not simplistic "political correctness"—into all our thinking means embracing ambiguity and complexity. It means reaching beyond simple either/or dualism, consensus group-think, or ideological rigidity. Dialogue and debate must always remain open to the fresh air of new thinking and creativity.

Our own experience as a lesbian and gay movement has given us excellent examples of effective and complex strategic problem-solving, such as the tactics of AIDS activism. There, integrating work both inside and outside the system, combining radical street protest effectively with savvy insider lobbying, could lead to powerful results. But all too often our groups, including many ACT UP chapters as time went on, became rigid and doctrinaire, "politically correct" to a fault. Political purism, a kind of self-destructive perfectionism, has been the downfall of many movements and grassroots political groups of every stripe.

A recent divisive polarity within gay activist circles centers on the word "assimilationism." The word literally means support for the notion of a minority being culturally absorbed into the dominant society, something most gay and lesbian people would have mixed feelings about. (We probably want acceptance but not at the risk of losing our special qualities.) But the word "assimilationism" has recently taken on a life of its own, being imbued by activists with a highly negative charge. It is now used as an all-purpose insult to attack anyone with a different point of view. To show just how meaningless the word has become: a friend of mine was accused by an ex-boyfriend of "harboring deep assimilationist tendencies" when he expressed his displeasure with the boyfriend's rampant faithlessness.

In June 1993, as director of the National Gay and Lesbian Task Force, I traveled to Colorado. This was about seven months into the boycott following state voters' passage of the anti-gay-rights Amendment 2, which prohibited protection for us from discrimination. The boycott was highly successful, creating a potent new tool in our antiright fight. It diverted over $100 million from the "hate state," stigmatized Colorado's rightward turn, and galvanized broad nongay support from Hollywood, civil libertarians, civil rights activists, and people of color, among many others.

But from the minute I arrived in Colorado, it was clear to me that the boycott was also beginning to have some unintended negative effects. Support for it was eroding in key nongay sectors. I met with lesbian and gay national and local Latino/Latina activists, for example, who reported that support was fading fast within the economically hard-pressed Latino community, whose initial boycott endorsement had been precedent-setting. In addition, gay activists outside the small boycott leadership group were experiencing weariness with the isolation imposed by the boycott. There was a growing grassroots sentiment that, at the very least, a time limit should be imposed on the boycott—a real time limit and not just the utopian "until we get equal rights" that had been put forward by the boycott's leadership. I suggested, in meetings with activists and to the press, that the boycott tactic should be evaluated in the light of changing conditions.

For simply suggesting that we should constantly reassess our tactics, like good guerrilla warriors in an ever-changing political jungle, I was vigorously attacked by an aggressive handful of lesbian and gay activists while in Colorado. They automatically assumed that I was unilaterally calling off the boycott. Not only did the faxes, phones, and e-mail boxes back at NGLTF's national office go bonkers with angry letters calling me a sellout, but I was met at a speech in Boulder by a hostile gay picket line. Five young white gay male activists paraded up and down on the street in front of the house I was to speak at with picket signs proclaiming "Torie = Uncle Tom," "Assimilationist Pig," and more. When I went up to one guy and introduced myself and asked if he'd like to speak to me directly, he said, "I don't speak to assimilationists," and kept on walking. There was nothing inherently "assimilationist" in what I was doing. I was articulating the changed pulse of the community and its key allies and was just trying to stay ahead of the downward spiral of support for the boycott. Political purism, however, had enshrined the boycott, making criticism heretical and "incorrect." Smart debate was impossible and had been forced underground by single-minded boycott leaders. Dissent—extremely widespread—was being suffocated. This was either/or thinking at its worst. Of course I wasn't calling off the boycott; that never would have occurred to me. But the "you're either with us or against us" thinking relegated to the status of "enemy" anyone who merely suggested examining the situation. My punishment was to be branded "assimilationist," the catch-all bludgeon-word. This had the dual effect of damaging my reputation and demeaning the sense of an important word in our political conversations.

A healthy movement debates tactics, but name-calling is not debate. We need to always be flexible enough to change tactics when conditions require it. Subsequently, in fact, I and others engaged the boycott's key leadership in evaluating the tactic's effectiveness. A deadline was instituted, and the boycott was declared a victory and called off.

The phrase "politically correct" was first used in light-humored, self-deprecating jest by lesbian-feminists in the late 1970s, to mock our own subcultural tendencies toward purism (particularly in our dyke dress code). I remember a button circulating at a women's music festival in 1981 with a picture of Birkenstock sandals and the slogan "P.C. Forever." Warring buttons included: "P.C. Is Humor-Impaired" and "Politically Incorrect and Proud." But this joking phrase has now taken on a deadly serious meaning. Conservatives have expropriated it as a mindless hammer to attack those of us who are building institutions, coalitions, or movements that are in any way diverse. We are the ones trying to expand democracy—to be sure, occasionally stumbling over our own purism along the way—and those who mean-spiritedly batter us with that overused phrase are hell-bent on contracting the meaning of democracy. While we should guard against our own political purism and its tendencies to be rigid and to actually stifle our ideal of diversity, we must not allow the right's attack on "political correctness" to deter us from fighting for real pluralism in this society. We need to honor the richly varied multicultural voices that are too often mute or muffled.

Nurturing diversity does not have to be utopian or self-destructively politically purist. In fact, we need to give ourselves some praise here: There are brilliant, empowering, unifying examples of work done within the lesbian and gay movement to fight racism and sexism within our own ranks, and to build thriving multicultural organizations. At community centers, for example, gay Republicans and Latino socialists work together to fund-raise. A women-only dance rocks one room while an outrageous drag show fills another. The same young man who wears T-shirts and jeans to hand out condoms and bleach on street corners to runaway gay kids one night dons a three-piece suit to lobby in the state capitol the next day. In addition, top national leadership on diversity issues includes lesbians (who began their work in the lesbian and gay community) such as Joan Lester and Betty Powell of the Equity Institute; Suzanne Pharr, formerly of the Arkansas Women's Project; and Deborah Johnson of the Motivational Institute. Their work has been revolutionary and pioneering and is increasingly moving into broader spheres of mainstream influence. These women and other lesbians, and some gay men as well, have led the visionary change from monocultural (usually white male) to multicultural organizations while staving off self-defeating "p.c." purism.

Inclusiveness powers our finest vision. Learning to respect, encourage, and celebrate difference may be among the finest work done by the gay and lesbian movement. That work and know-how will move with us in the coming years, as long as we let them flourish in our political culture and thinking. This means taking responsibility to face down the demons within, the oppression sickness that has poisoned our activist culture with horizontal hostility, leader-bashing, and "political correctness." Those barriers, generated by a homophobic society but perpetuated by ourselves, have undermined our ability to "become our most magnificent selves." It's time to collectively determine to let those barriers go the way of the closet, to reconfigure our underlying activist ethic so that we lead not from our weaknesses but from our strengths. It's time to honor leadership, to revel in vigorous debate, to embrace our differences. We are a people who have, each of us individually in the course of our lives, achieved such personal courage, such fearless love, such fine community spirit that we can certainly make a decision to exhibit those qualities in our political work.

4. MOVING BEYOND OPPRESSION SICKNESS: TRANSFORMATIONAL ACTIVISM

To overcome the enemy within ourselves and bring our best selves and our brightest visions with us as we come home to America, lesbians and gay men must create a national dialogue about changing our activist culture and thinking in order to effect a paradigm shift. To do this will require bravery. It will require creating an environment in which our leaders can lead. Most of all, it will require claiming our right to have power.

Power is not inherently evil or oppressive. Power is simply money or human resources such as talent, creativity, and skills that can be put to good purposes—to help people and to change things. To move from the margins and build real power in this country, we must overcome those psychological barriers that keep us down and divided and powerless. The first step is to celebrate and nurture leadership instead of fighting it. Second, we will need to embrace a new community ethos in our activism. This ethos must be founded on respect for each other and it must embrace the politics of power, rather than powerlessness. I call this transformational activism.

Leadership Is Key to Our Success

Nurturing good leadership is key to our success as a movement. Unfortunately, we don't have many good models of leadership; our thinking about leadership has been badly polluted. All of us have seen far too many mainstream religious or political "leaders" who are greedy, corrupt, phony, timid, autocratic, or hypocritical. In general, leaders in this society are either idolized beyond believability or distrusted, usually for good reason.

It doesn't have to be this way. As a State Department brat born in Copenhagen, Denmark, I learned early on about a powerful example of positive leadership. I vividly remember turning the pages of a Danish children's book when I was three years old, captivated by the story of King Christian's unique courage in standing up to the Nazis. He himself donned the yellow star the Jews were forced to wear, and paraded down Copenhagen's main street for all to see, thereby setting a moral example of resistance that helped unify the country. Virtually all Danish Jews were smuggled to neutral Sweden by Danish fishermen acting in concert with a brave resistance movement.

This positive role model of national leadership was, for me, quickly eclipsed by a negative example. When I was four, we moved to Madrid, Spain, which was then suffering under the repressive Franco government, where "fascism" was not a vanquished force (the Nazis), but a living system. I remember food rallies dispersed by "Franco's guns," the military police in groups on every street corner. Even my young self knew that people feared and hated Franco. By the time we moved to the United States when I was six, the negative example had burned itself into my brain, and I was already cynical about political leadership. The assassinations of President Kennedy when I was thirteen, of Malcolm X when I was fifteen, and, when I was a senior in high school, of Bobby Kennedy and Dr. Martin Luther King, Jr., increased that cynicism.

I've always been fascinated with the notion of leadership, although for most of my life I didn't realize it was because I wanted to learn how to be a leader. Except for a short stint as the only girl in and unacknowledged head of my white, middle-class, suburban gang during my tomboy years, I was never a leader while growing up. Occasionally in high school I was a quiet adviser to those with power, but it never occurred to me that I myself might have the skills or the desire to lead. I never identified with the term and, in fact, rejected it. I fully bought into the sixties countercultural—and, later, women's liberationist—rejection of leadership as an oppressive concept. Too much of it was. I remember how alienated I was as a freshman at Barnard College in 1968, desperately wanting to be organized, educated, led. Instead, I was subjected to macho diatribes by a steady stream of male radicals screaming rhetoric at the rest of us and jockeying for the best position in front of the cameras.

For years I was a rebel, an organizer, a member of many collectives, and, later, a great second in command. Over time I began to regain respect for the idea of leadership, although it was contrary to the grassroots culture in which I was involved. Influenced by the democratic and feminist principles that emerged in the 1970s, I started seeing leadership as positive and indispensable. I felt, rising in myself, a new and awkward desire to take a leadership role, and I began watching, listening, apprenticing, and seeking out mentors. Not until my late thirties did I develop the necessary self-confidence to become a leader, to act personally on the ideas and visions I had usually passed on to others to implement. I was thirty-eight when I came into my own as a leader, as director of the Los Angeles Gay and Lesbian Community Services Center.

In the past decade, the decimation by AIDS of our established male leadership has jeopardized the very survival of the community and shoved the issue of leadership to the forefront. There is growing sentiment that better support for leaders, and the institutionalization of leadership development, will be indispensable to our success as a movement for social change. Organizations such as the Human Rights Campaign and the National Gay and Lesbian Task Force have finally instituted youth leadership-training programs. Following are a few of my own key conclusions about leadership, developed through my own experience as well as through much conversation with others. (In particular, I want to acknowledge the great Ken Dawson, a brilliant New York student and teacher of leadership who died of AIDS in 1992.)

First, the leader of a group (or project or department or institution or campaign, or . . .) is the one who thinks about the group as a whole, the big picture. The leader organizes the group's input so as to develop and reflect back a vision for the group. The leader then moves to actualize that vision, and is able to motivate other people to join together to pursue it.

Second, strong leadership is absolutely necessary; no group activity succeeds without it. Leadership is a good thing!

Third, everybody can develop leadership skills. Leaders are made, not born. Moreover, most people harbor a deep, often repressed, desire to learn how to be leader.

Fourth, leaders come in many styles, influenced by lots of factors, including personality and cultural background. There are quiet leaders and extroverted leaders.

Fifth, a good leader recognizes the leadership abilities of others and works to develop them.

Here are two examples of top-notch but very different leaders and leadership styles:

———

I first met Mark Kostopoulos in the dark basement of the West Los Angeles Federal Building in October 1988, where ninety of us who had been arrested during ACT UP/L.A.'s first major protest were being detained. We were jammed together in the hallway, stacked up against the walls like so many rag dolls, our hands cuffed behind our backs with those nasty, sharp plastic handcuffs cops use in mass arrests. Many there had never been arrested before, and there was an undercurrent of anxiety coursing through the crowd.

One man, who had managed to wriggle out of his handcuffs almost instantly, was threading his way through the small sea of bodies, moving quietly and deliberately, talking softly with people. As he got closer to me, I could see he was making eye contact with each and every person. He was checking in with the people with AIDS about their medication supplies, their need for food or water. He touched people with a gentle arm or asked quietly, "How ya doing?" Periodically, he would softly remind a small cluster of people that this was the largest mass arrest in L.A. history, or that others were being arrested in other cities across the country—that we were part of something bigger than us. I mused to my next-door-neighbor arrestee that this man reminded me of Jesus, moving with remarkable serenity, a powerfully calming presence among the people. I later learned this was an analogy totally unacceptable to my soon-to-be-friend Mark, a leftist atheist until the end.

Over the next four years, until Mark died, I had the honor of working with him often and of studying his leadership style. He was a truly brilliant leader, though he was understated and even self-effacing. His power derived from his compassion, his twenty-year experience as a grassroots organizer, and his clarity of vision about ACT UP. His steady, wise style constantly empowered and replenished people. I remember being stunned at how Mark, the radical leftist, was able to garner widespread and significant support among wealthy gay doctors in L.A. for single-payer health-care reform. His clarity of purpose and calm confidence were so effective that few could resist it.

Jehan Agrama is a passionate and dynamic extrovert, whose natural warmth and charisma made her a key leader and builder of the Gay and Lesbian Alliance Against Defamation, both in L.A. and nationally. When Jehan walks into a room, it brightens. Jehan is outspoken and forceful in style, but not domineering. Her energy invites others to open up. A skilled facilitator, she's led many meetings out of contention and chaos into fruitful unity.

During the three weeks of militant protest by the L.A. gay community against Governor Pete Wilson's 1991 veto of AB 101, there were two ugly police riots against demonstrators who gathered at the Century Plaza Hotel. At one tense moment, as over a hundred mounted police moved aggressively toward about the same number of demonstrators, panic began to spread through the small crowd. It looked as if they would bolt or fight; clearly people could be hurt. Without a moment's hesitation, Jehan jumped up on a media sound truck, grabbed a bullhorn and started singing "We Are a Gentle, Angry People." This is one of our anthems, the song Holly Near wrote for the candlelight demonstration the night Harvey Milk was assassinated in San Francisco in 1978. Jehan's rich, strong voice calmed the crowd, which then began to sing with her. The media cameras all shifted to Jehan, the police were confused, and the demonstrators got the opportunity to regroup.

We need to celebrate a broad variety of styles of leadership, from Jehan's outgoing charisma to Mark's quiet forcefulness, with plenty in between. A leader is the one wearing that miner's hat, lighting the way with her or his vision and courage to act, sometimes in the darkest of days.

Leaders always take the first step, and developing leadership is key to our progress. Particularly with the continuing devastation of AIDS, and with a new generation of openly gay and lesbian youth coming out in our wake, it will be vital to pass the torch. Leadership training and mentoring programs must be incorporated into all our organizing, our conferences, and our institutional structures. While we do these things, we must constantly reinforce the fact that *everybody can be a leader*. Acknowledging the latent and hidden leadership skills in our midst and consciously nurturing them will dramatically change for the better our movement for equality. (We might also do well to develop a conversation about the art of followership. While each of us can be a leader, at times we all must be followers, and how to do that effectively is worthy of an additional community dialogue over the coming years.)

Transformational Activism: Leading from Respect

In addition to valuing and building leadership in our movement for equality, I think it's time to engage in a community-wide conversation about adopting a set of values that can counteract our oppression sickness. At a 1990 Los Angeles leadership retreat, sixty of us representing every major group from ACT UP and the Imperial Courts to gay religious groups and gay Republicans, spent several hours one morning drafting a "community code of ethics" for dealing with each other. It was unanimously approved as a guide to our actions. Consider this a work in progress.

LESBIAN AND GAY COMMUNITY CODE OF ETHICS, LOS ANGELES, 1990

1. *Begin with respect.* In all our dealings with each other, we must lead from a place of respect at all times. Only within an atmosphere of respect can leadership, creativity, diversity— and fun—truly flourish.

2. *No more trashing.* We affirm the need for constructive debate and criticism, but criticism is not the same as trashing. We must all begin to speak out against the trashing of individuals or groups as unethical. (We referred to the "25 percent rule." If a conversation—or article, or diatribe, or whatever—passes 25 percent negativity, then it's not criticism, it's trashing.)

3. *No "triangling."* Criticism should be communicated directly to the person involved, not via the gay press or the rumor mill. Criticism should also be directed to those who can do something about it, and be accompanied whenever possible by positive suggestions for how to change the problem.

4. *Support our leaders.* Leadership support and development are vital to our success. Let's celebrate our leaders.

5. *Acknowledge our victories,* not just our defeats and mistakes. Affirm and celebrate the positive steps we make as much as possible. The glass is half full.

6. *Our diversity is our greatest strength.* Creatively nurturing diversity builds our movement. Of particular importance is community support for independent organizing by lesbians and people of color to increase leadership skills and strengthen confidence, as well as supporting the goal of building multicultural organizations wherever possible.

7. *Collaboration is a vital, unifying principle.* Decreasing competition and increasing cooperation at every level of our work fundamentally strengthens and empowers us, and generates synergy and unity.

Imagine what we could accomplish if even half the knee-jerk resentment and mistrust we have for each other were eliminated, and we had an activist culture that assumed and aimed for the best instead of the worst. Imagine what we could accomplish if, instead of the fear that traps us in our oppression sickness, we could collectively gain access to our total unfettered courage and respect. So many individuals have been transformed and empowered by coming out or by facing life fully with HIV; this is because they have walked through their fear to the other side and discovered strength beyond their previous imagining. Now we must also walk through our collective community fear of power—a product of our internalized powerlessness—and transform that fear into an empowering and positive impetus for our freedom.

———

Sheila Kuehl talks about her experience with "transformational activism":

"Thirty-seven of the forty-one Republicans up here in the California Assembly are antigay, antichoice right-wingers, part of a concerted effort by the radical right to take power. For a while I found it incredibly hard to protect my heart from taking in the stuff they say about us—I felt these flashes of shame when they would casually hurl those lies about us, those ugly words like *sick* and *immoral*. But the whole experience has forced me to a new place of strength—more than I ever knew I had—and a different approach. Now I look these guys straight in the eye every single time I see them, in the hallways, on the assembly floor. I treat them with utter respect and dignity, no matter what. Slowly but surely, they either treat me the same way, or they just can't look me in the eye. That's when I know I have them, because that's when they know inside they're wrong, that discrimination and devaluing us is wrong—and I can see their moral power is weakened, and ours strengthened. My shift in attitude has transformed me, empowered me—and in an unexpected way, it's slowly transforming them as well: one by one, slowly but steadily, a few votes are turning my way."

———

Power Is Infinite:
Beyond the Scarcity Model

Economic scarcity is very real in this society, but the economic-scarcity model does not apply to everything. One of feminism's most revolutionary insights is that power does not have to be a scarce commodity, a zero-sum game. In order to move most successfully to our next stage of building political power, we must move beyond the scarcity model, which teaches us to believe that we must compete for a finite amount of power, money, leadership, or whatever resources there are.

Power, if it is used democratically and not oppressively, generates more power. Resources well utilized attract or create more resources, whether of money or talent. Good leadership generates more, not less, leadership. Fund-raisers will tell you that donors give more money over time, not the same fixed amount simply split among more causes. Organizing generates more organizing. Activist energies multiply and inspire more activist energies, if they are fueled by love and vision or righteous anger, not by rage and fear and negativity.

At this crucial juncture in our movement we need to approach political activism in this new way, particularly at the grassroots level. We need to move from a scarcity model to an abundance model and to operate not from fear but from an empowered belief that we can win. If we get over our fear of power and success and recognize that money, leadership, skills, and other forms of power are positive, not negative—that they are simply resources to be tapped so as to improve life for lesbians and gay men—we can accomplish just about anything. That is transformational activism.

As we move through our terror of coming out, queer daily life constantly teaches the liberating power of courage. Lesbian and gay heroes and heroines are everywhere in our midst. It is our richest paradox that we need look only to ourselves and our own community for models of how to become activists who can defeat the greatest odds possible and inspire others toward the same.

Life during the AIDS epidemic sparkles with examples of people who have grabbed life by the throat and accomplished in a few years or even a few months what could well have taken decades or might never have happened. Look at Sean Strub's genius: a direct-mail pioneer, he created a million-plus-person gay and lesbian mailing list and then went on to found *POZ*, a unique, visionary, slick yet accessible magazine that is an emotionally powerful tool for HIV-affected people. Take the late writer Paul Monette. He was an obscure Hollywood screenwriter and poet; his fierce literary genius and gripping passion were unleashed by his confrontation with AIDS. Who can imagine American literature today—let alone gay literature—without his *Borrowed Time* or *Becoming a Man*, to name only his best-known works? Then there's Bill T. Jones, gay black dancer and choreographer whose daring work was inspired by his love for and collaboration with his lover Arnie Zane, who died of AIDS. Jones is a visionary on the cutting edge of America's artistic scene, the first openly gay black man to grace the cover of *Time*.

There are countless other examples, famous and not, of the lust for life unleashed by the presence of death. Transformational activism requires bringing to our political work the personal courage each and every one of us has summoned in our journey of coming out, fighting AIDS, and building family and community. There is nothing magical here, except the magic we have already created, in huge quantities, in our everyday lives during tumultuous times. We know how to operate from faith and love, not fear. We know the empowering results of deciding to tell the truth and not to cave in to others' denial or lies. We know in our deepest souls how to speak and act from our higher selves. It's time to take a leap of faith in our political life together, a leap similar to the many we've each taken in our personal lives. It's time we simply make the moral decision to act on this courage, truth, and love as the basis for our nascent political movement. Transformational activism can change the course of history. Fighting the pernicious enemies who currently have the upper hand requires that we give it our best try. And taking responsibility for those who come after us on this earth—and those who have gone before us—requires nothing less than that we succeed.

5. FIGHTING PUBLIC ENEMY NUMBER ONE: THE RADICAL RELIGIOUS RIGHT

With leadership, a little patience, and an unblurred vision, we can achieve just about anything. At the top of our list of goals must be exposing the lies of right-wing Christian political extremists, aka the "radical right"—a fast-growing menace to American democracy. While ultra-rightists have always been a part of America, over the past thirty years they have steadily emerged from the margins of the political landscape, and within the past decade have taken a place of frightening influence on the mainstream. As of 1996, they form a major or dominant force in thirty-one state Republican party operations and have effected a virtual takeover of Congress, as well as many statehouses across the country.

Perhaps even worse, they have succeeded in capturing control of, and skewing rightward, the entire national public discussion about this country's present and future values. Through timidity and underestimating the enemy, moderates and liberals have ceded virtually the entire territory of family and community values, the role of government, and far too much public-policy thinking to a radical right offering only regressive and dangerous answers that benefit the few at the expense of the many.

The radical right comprises a network of state and national (and affiliated local) organizations such as the Council on National Policy, a powerful think tank that holds clandestine meetings; the Family Research Council; Concerned Women of America; Coalition for Traditional Values; and Focus on the Family. The latter is perhaps the most important and influential social-policy organization in the country. It is a mammoth antigay, antifeminist, so-called pro-family social and political propaganda vehicle with an annual budget of $150 million, a two-million-person mailing list, daily talk radio shows that air 60,000 times a week on 1,500 stations in 58 countries, and daily distribution of 13,000 cassette tapes, pamphlets, books, or magazines with practical advice on all sorts of topics ranging from pornography to teenage problems. Focus on the Family is "Dear Abby" with a right-wing agenda, and it's growing by leaps and bounds.

The right's political arm is the Christian Coalition, which incorporates fanatical anti-abortionists, militia members, and other radicals alongside the major groups into a highly effective, fast-growing electoral machine. The Christian Coalition has amassed enormous power since its founding in 1989 out of the ashes of Pat Robertson's failed 1988 presidential bid. Its mission, says founder Robertson, is "simple: to mobilize Christians—one precinct at a time, one community at a time—until once again we are the head and not the tail, and at the top rather than the bottom of our political system. . . . The Christian Coalition will be the most powerful political force in America by the end of this decade. We have enough votes to run this country . . . and we're going to take over!" As Ralph Reed, its director, puts it: "Our priority is to organize, to build a permanent infrastructure. We're looking ahead twenty years, not two years."

The Christian Coalition now has 1.7 million supporters and almost 1,500 chapters, some in every state; thirty full-time-staffed statewide field operations; 50,000 precinct captains; and a $25 million national budget. It has a huge alternative culture of schools, training institutes, newspapers, magazines, think tanks, and radio and TV stations, and a local base of 27,000 churches, with another 35,000 at least loosely affiliated. By the end of this decade, it hopes to have a paid staff in seven out of ten congressional districts, 500 trained leaders in every state, and 4 million readers per issue of *Christian American* magazine—as many readers as *Time.*

The Christian Coalition calls its town-by-town, county-by-county grassroots mobilization "the 15 percent solution." The group's leaders know that only 60 percent of the electorate is even registered to vote and that voter apathy is rising. Only 30 percent of the electorate (half of those registered) vote on a regular basis, so it only takes 15 percent of the electorate to win. By the right's calculations, because of low voter turnout it takes only 11 percent of the electorate to win a national House or Senate seat, 9 percent for a governorship, and 7 percent a local city council seat. By mobilizing a highly motivated, organized minority, the radical right can parlay small numbers into substantive electoral wins; it relies on the zealous participation of supporters to beat out an ignorant, disorganized, or apathetic opposition. Such a political operation could control huge sections of the country over the next two decades. It has already demonstrated its prowess: in the 1994 elections, the Christian Coalition distributed 34 million voter guides, and 60 percent of its top-rated candidates won, including forty-four U.S. representatives, eight U.S. senators, and seven governors. Twenty-four million of the 75 million voters that year self-identified as born-again Christians; 17 million—or 70 percent—of those voted Republican.

The core of the right's recent platform has been opposition to abortion rights, gay rights, and affirmative action, as well as to the separation of church and state. Increasingly, as its influence spreads, the radical right markets itself as representative of mainstream ideas, and is, in fact, expanding its platform to include economic issues (such as opposition to the forty-hour work week), as well as antienvironmentalist and anti-immigration stances. But despite the radical right's growing power and clever marketing, its positions do not align with those of mainstream Americans, an enduring majority of whom strongly support individual freedom of religion, choice on abortion, antidiscrimination protections for everyone, some forms of affirmative action, comprehensive sex and AIDS education, the strengthening, not weakening, of public education and environmental laws, and other positions anathema to the right. The radical right is, in fact, a dangerous antidemocratic minority zealously determined to achieve an ambitious goal: to transform the United States into a theocracy, a nation dominated by their distorted notion of Christianity.

By definition, this is an all-out attack on pluralism, religious freedom, and democracy itself. Radical rightists are absolutists, wanting to impose their conservative, strict, patriarchal, authoritarian views on all of us. These religious fundamentalists want a complete merger of church and state. They abhor public education (which they cannot ultimately control) and have determined to undermine its very foundations. They adamantly oppose multiculturalism, favor creationism and mandatory school prayer, want public funding to support private religious education, and launch virulent attacks on science as a godless form of secular humanism that undermines true morality. Criminalizing abortion and homosexuality is part of their agenda; the ultraradical and influential "Christian reconstructionists" favor capital punishment for gays, along with adulterers and abortionists.

The radical right's homophobia is linked to its sexist, absolutist demand to control sexuality, gender roles, and reproduction. Antifeminism and heterosexism are central to their patriarchal worldview. Pat Robertson, who sees himself as a God-chosen prophet, said, in opposing an Equal Rights Amendment to the Iowa state constitution: "The feminist agenda is not about equal rights. . . . It is about a socialist, antifamily political movement that encourages women to leave their husbands, kill their children, practice witchcraft, destroy capitalism, and become lesbians."

Those who disagree with the radical right's particular brand of extremism are written off as second-class citizens. Despite this, the Christian right is busy building strategic links with key Roman Catholic parishes and leaders, conservative African-American churches, and conservative and orthodox Jewish groups and leaders.

This power flows from excellent organizing, a seemingly infinite supply of money, and an unabashed willingness to lie about anything and everything. Radical rightists are fanatics, who believe their cause is so righteous that God has given them the right to violate basic tenets of most religions. They freely admit to lying baldly, to using "stealth tactics": "I want to be invisible," said Ralph Reed. "I paint my face and travel at night. You don't know it's over until you're in a body bag. You don't know until election night." We have well-documented reports of these claims.

———

"Larry" is a gay activist who regularly attends right-wing organization conferences "to stay on top of what the enemy is thinking and doing." In 1996, he was at a midwestern conference of a major radical right group—one of 1,700 so-called leadership schools held in recent years to train the troops:

"Hundreds of white people jammed the hotel. I saw one non-white person the whole weekend. Everyone seemed busy and purposeful; it was a well-orchestrated, happily humming event.

"Homophobia was everywhere; I heard the words *abnormal, unnatural,* and *immoral* applied to our lives literally every few minutes, like never-ending mantras. Every speaker I heard hammered antigay themes, such as the threatening power of 'the gay lobby' in the Clinton administration. Buttons, bumper stickers, and T-shirts sported slogans like 'Sodom and Gomorrah had gays in the military,' 'AIDS, Abortion, Euthanasia: Don't Liberals Just Kill Ya?' and 'Real Men Are Not Called Hillary.' Hatred of our community is a proven commercial success for them, along with hatred of Hillary and Bill Clinton, which was also pervasive. In fact, I was struck by the consistent linkage between the Clintons and the gay community—the impression conveyed was almost that the Clintons were gay, not straight.

"We were told unendingly that the gay issue is a proven money-raiser. They kept repeating that because of AIDS, gay people had singlehandedly caused the huge increase in medical costs. There was a video room in which *The Gay Agenda* and its companion piece, *The Gay Agenda and Public Education* ran in an endless loop. I never heard the word 'lesbian' except to describe *all* abortion-rights feminists.

"I was impressed, however, by the dogged focus on skills and leadership development. The conference had computer training for *everyone,* all two hundred fifty people who attended the conference, all at one time. We were taught how to do direct-mail merges. We learned about interactive on-line software. We were asked ahead of time to bring our Rolodexes, and while we were there we were told to add names from them to the group's data bank. There were videotaping sessions on question-and-answer techniques. It was impressive—thorough, professional, effective.

"I was most surprised at how they made no bones about how important it was to lie. Their 'stealth' strategy was totally out in the open. We were instructed to hide our right-wing affiliations and agenda, to 'lie, if necessary,' and instead to 'appeal to people's fears of change.' "

———

Taking over school boards and county commissions is now a top priority; radical rightists have gained over 3,500 local school board seats in the past few years, now claiming a total of 12,000. Their school-board candidates won 40 percent of their elections in 1992 and 60 percent in 1994. "We have a plan to take our entire education system back and put it in God's hands. And the way we are going to do it is to take control of every school board in America," says Robert Simonds, president of the Christian right group Citizens for Excellence in Education.

Antigay political assaults are central to the right's agenda, particularly since the end of the cold war has deprived the right of its traditional scapegoat, communism. Immigrants are another easy target these days, but "militant homosexuals" appear to be perhaps the most successful fund-raising and constituent-building issue for the radical right. Their antigay propaganda is pernicious and hysterical; preying on people's ignorance, the right depicts lesbians and gay men as demonic and even subhuman. Sometimes the rhetoric sounds scarily similar to Nazi anti-Semitic propaganda—portraying a tiny minority as responsible for a supposed decline in morals while, at the same time, possessing vast and disproportionate wealth and political power. They use well-produced videos (such as *The Gay Agenda*, of which hundreds of thousands of copies are in circulation) and mass-media channels to promote an aggressive disinformation campaign about us as recruiters of children and sex-crazed maniacs. During the 1996 battle in Utah about high school clubs, for example, the Utah State Senate held a secret meeting during which the rabid propaganda film *Gay Rights, Special Rights* was shown. The senators whipped themselves into such a violent frenzy that they literally kicked around, like a football, a copy of the progay children's book *Heather Has Two Mommies*, screaming antigay slurs at the top of their lungs. (And they call *us* degraded and immature?)

The right made antigay ballot initiatives and other organizing an integral part of its strategy for political takeover of this country. Recently, bans on gay marriage were introduced in thirty-four states; over the past two years, twenty-five states have faced antigay discriminatory ballot initiatives. A comprehensive strategy for defeating gay rights was unveiled at a clandestine conference in the spring of 1994, including a detailed plan to take over every legislative body in a given state. The plan is to identify where every elected official stands on gay rights, then to get 25 percent of the voters to sign a pledge not to vote for any candidate who supports gay rights. After only antigay candidates win, the next step is to introduce new laws that ban gay rights. In California, the right has already seized control of the state assembly because of a band of five multimillionaire right-wingers who have financed thirty of forty-one Republican assemblymembers.

People for the American Way, the Washington-based watchdog organization, issued a report in 1996 that documented 180 national, state, or local organized antigay incidents. These were not individual incidents of verbal or physical assault or discrimination—of which there are thousands and thousands every year—but incidents with "broad policy implications or that set significant precedents": ballot measures, federal or state legislative battles, local ordinances, court decisions, and the like. This report proved what gays and lesbians have been saying for years, that the climate is growing more and more hostile, not less, and that this hostility correlates with the political power steadily accruing to the radical right.

Although they publicly deny it, the radical rightists' organized antigay campaigns invariably foster an environment that leads to violence. The National Gay and Lesbian Task Force has documented a dramatic rise in hate crimes against gays and lesbians in areas where the right organizes antigay ballot measures. In September 1992, for example, during the Oregon Citizens Alliance's vicious campaign against gay rights, a group of skinheads murdered Hattie Mae Cohens and Brian Mock, a black lesbian and a disabled gay man living in Salem, Oregon, by throwing Molotov cocktails into their tiny basement apartment. These horrible murders never hit the national press's radar screen, even though they happened during the heated national debate about political gay-bashing unleashed by the frank homophobia of the GOP convention.

Fighting the Radical Right: Everybody's Job

Because we are in the right's crosshairs and the right is growing in influence, it is no longer enough for lesbians and gay men to come out and hope for the best. Exposing the tactics of the right must be integral to our lives and work. We must showcase their distorted and repressive view of the world, their lack of ethics and their tacit support for violence. Patiently and consistently, we must say, "It's a lie. It's a lie. It's a lie," every time they defame us. We must also aggressively and doggedly organize against them—and not just in sporadic reaction to a specific campaign or state ballot drive.

In California, we fought and won big against the 1978 Briggs and the 1986 LaRouche ballot initiatives. The former would have outlawed gay teachers in the public schools, and the latter would have quarantined people with HIV. We also defeated the Oregon Citizens Alliance's Measure 9 in Oregon in 1992, and Maine's threatened initiative in 1995. But we sometimes lose too, and in 1996, twenty states faced these heinous measures. Even though the Colorado Supreme Court struck down Amendment 2 there (and the U.S. Supreme Court ratified the decision), the message of intolerance sent out by the right's electoral victory increased gay-bashing

and discrimination across the state. Educators estimated, for example, that the number of gay and lesbian teens who dropped out
of high schools in Colorado doubled in the year after Amendment
2 passed. It set the movement for equality for lesbians and gay men
back in time, as it was meant to.

To halt the radical right's forward motion, we must organize to
prevent it from getting to the ballot in the first place. We also need
to regain rational control of the discussions on education, AIDS, sex
education, and family values that the right currently dominates. This
will be a protracted effort, but will require turning our electoral organizations, such as the Human Rights Campaign and statewide
lobbying groups, into powerhouses. We will also need to generate
more progressive thinking—such as that done by NGLTF's Policy
Institute—in order to successfully reframe the debate, to seize back
control of the conversation on family and social values as they represent and affect our real lives. We must undefensively and strategically expose the right's anti-American worldview and tactics in a
constant public education campaign. They rely on timidity and tolerance to promote ugly intolerance, so we must make it our business to counter their lies aggressively and effectively at every opportunity.

We will also need models of grassroots organizing that reach out
well beyond the gay and lesbian community. In recent years, we've
seen some highly successful examples. Building on what worked
well in Oregon, and learning from what didn't, lesbian and gay leaders in the state of Washington organized Hands Off Washington in
1993–1994. They brought in the highly effective Oregon Speakout
training program to prepare community speakers and media advocates. HOW paid a lot of attention to rural areas and built strong
local coalitions, bringing together labor, environmentalist, women's
and gay groups, along with the Washington Council of Churches
and organizations of people of color. One important and active
group was Simple Justice, a group of evangelical Christians opposed
to the radical right's doctrines. Similar ideas were adapted in Maine
as part of the hard-fought 1995 victory.

P-FLAG launched a highly creative response to the radical right,
a TV ad campaign targeting middle Americans in Atlanta, Houston,

Seattle, and Tulsa. Veteran progressive media consultants Pacy Markman and Bill Zimmerman created two powerful thirty-second television ads that juxtaposed clips of Pat Robertson and Jesse Helms with dramatizations of a lesbian teen suicide and a gay-bashing murder, clearly showing the linkage. The spots ran in Tulsa for five days before Pat Robertson's Christian Broadcast Network (CBN) slapped P-FLAG and the local TV station with a threatened lawsuit, scaring other TV stations away from running the ads. Undaunted, P-FLAG ran two print ads in *USA Today* to educate the public about CBN's response, and signed on pro bono legal counsel to fight back (it is hoped that the ads will finally air later in 1996). They also launched a media training and community outreach program in their targeted cities, expanding as well to Minneapolis, Pittsburgh, Dallas–Fort Worth, and San Diego. Meanwhile, free media coverage generated by the controversy has educated thousands of people and brought positive visibility to one of our most important allies.

Another example of effective and pioneering organizing against the right is found in Massachusetts.

———

Holly Gunner has lived in Newton, Massachusetts, for twenty years. This "accidental activist" has become an audacious and effective local leader in the fight against the radical right's assault on public education. Before her current career as a corporate management consultant, Holly—who has a master's from Harvard Business School and a master's degree in education—spent twelve years as a teacher, elementary school principal, and assistant superintendent for instruction in the public school system. In 1989, a phone call from a reporter alerted her to the fact that a right-wing group had surfaced in Newton to fight a sex-education curriculum that discussed, among other topics, homosexuality.

"I thought: This is *my* home. I taught in this school system. I'm a taxpayer. I'll be damned if I'm going to let these outsiders come to my town and impose their views here!" Holly got a copy of the curriculum in question and found it to be "reasonable, mature, and responsible, including a focus on teaching little kids how not to be victims of physical abuse." She made a few phone calls to investigate this supposedly independent, spontaneous group of parents objecting to the curriculum. "I discovered that the Newton Citizens for Public Education was actually connected to the radical right group Family First. I went to a school board meeting and picked up their literature. It was garbage. I wasn't about to let this happen in my town, so I organized like an MBA, with 'target marketing.' I worked out a plan, contacted local members of different organizations like the Massachusetts Civil Liberties Union and some local church groups, and sent them letters alerting them that radical-right groups were organizing people against our local school. This was my town; I knew the people here. After so many years as a part of this community, I had credibility.

"I operated on two assumptions. One was that any citizen has a right to speak her or his mind, or run for office, or organize politically. And, two, democracy requires that everyone be truthful and operate without deception or propaganda. Of course, for these right-wing organizations and many local leaders they train, integrity and candor are not important. In fact, they are anathema—inimical to their goals, because it's not about democracy for them, it's about political power. I was glad to discover that when people are presented with the truth, the real facts, about the right, the vast majority want nothing to do with them or their ideas. If American citizens want to sign onto the right's line, it's their right. But my experience has shown me that they don't want to. In this work, I wear my American hat, not my lesbian hat.

"We started the Lighthouse Institute for Public Policy to collect and distribute information, basically to wake people up about the right, its strategy, and its three major national organizations—the Christian Coalition, Focus on the Family, and Concerned Women of America. These groups send operatives into local communities to undermine public schools and promote intolerance.

"In my many years as an educator, I found that the key to basic education is to teach kids to think critically by developing choice, autonomy, and individual initiative as a part of the education process. What's most disturbing to me about the radical right is that they want kids to grow up unthinkingly following orders—being obedient followers, not autonomous thinkers. This is critical to their control, and this is scary stuff. This is the future of our country we're talking about—our kids.

"I was shocked to discover that the right's political arm, the Christian Coalition, had sent a field director into liberal Massachusetts to set up a statewide strategy for taking over local school committees. One of our local right-wing watchers discovered that some of these people were organizing 'prayer meetings' for state legislators in order to avoid trouble with the IRS on charges of lobbying.

"The Lighthouse Institute counters the right by helping people organize locally. Today, we're working in more than forty local towns, operating as a kind of watchdog network. We work with friendly churches, the PTA, local affiliates of the teachers' union, the National Organization for Women, and the American Civil Liberties Union. If you let people hear the right's own words, if you expose their real thinking, most people consider it an outrage. The naked bigotry of the radical right is so horrible that the vast majority of straight people reject it outright. When the right-wingers played *The Gay Agenda* and *The Gay Agenda and Public Education* on one local cable TV show here in Massachusetts, local community people—all straight, including one Catholic woman—were so upset they all pitched in to produce counterprogramming. It was wonderful."

Holly's organization is a model of effective local organizing: diverse and rooted in the communities represented. The leadership group is mostly straight, and includes a fortyish, married United Church of Christ minister who has five kids and sits on her town's school committee. Key supporters include a blue-collar father active in his local Unitarian church; a gay male AIDS educator; and a divorced dentist whose former wife has become an antigay religious right activist.

One effective approach is to "organize organizations." "We're working with such existing coalitions as Citizens for Public Schools, led by the American Jewish Congress and the League of Women Voters. They organized to oppose 'parochiaid,' the school vouchers initiative," says Holly. She also works with the Massachusetts Teachers' Association (with 70,000 members), the Massachusetts Civil

Liberties Union (13,000 members), NOW (15,000 local members), and the League of Women Voters (7,500 members). "We approach them, brief them, and suggest strategies for working together to mobilize their memberships to counter the right. I do this coalition the way I do my professional work as a management consultant, where I work to help corporations become more efficient by increasing collaboration. There are 351 towns in Massachusetts, and we're only 10 percent of the way there, but we're working toward drawing up one big map and dividing up the work, the organizing of the towns, between all the different groups who naturally oppose the right. We have sympathizers in every town."

6. BUILDING FOR LONG-TERM POWER: COALITIONS ARE KEY

Holly's work is an example of one woman's effective leadership. Her success comes from forging alliances with nongay people and with existing organizations with memberships, resources, and constituencies. Our future depends on open lesbian and gay leadership supporting or creating, and maintaining, such alliances.

A couple of years ago, I attended an extraordinary weeklong retreat with twenty-four other activists from a wide range of social-change movements—education reform, union organizing, inner-city gang work, the black women's health movement, AIDS work, environmentalism, global feminism, and more. We were all ages, colors, sexualities, class backgrounds; each of us had been an activist for twenty years or more. At that serene mountain lake retreat in the Adirondacks, we represented, collectively, over six hundred years of activist expertise, astounding accomplishments, dreams and hopes, disillusionments and victories.

For one exercise, we divided ourselves randomly into five groups and were asked to spend an hour identifying our top three issues. After only a half hour, an amazing thing happened: each of the five groups independently identified the exact same top issues— *violence, health,* and *family.* Obviously, the focus brought to each of those issues varied. Health priorities for the Cherokee Indian leader on an impoverished reservation meant something different than they did to the white middle-class lesbian-feminist breast-cancer activist, for example. But the startling level of agreement took the group by surprise.

I tell this story because, as lesbians and gay men work on issues particularly meaningful to us—combating gay-bashing in our neighborhoods, creating a support group for lesbians with disabilities, volunteering at a runaway youth shelter—it's sometimes hard to remember how many millions of others out there who are not gay are themselves struggling with only slight variations on the same themes. We are not as isolated as we think.

It's also critical to recognize that the time can come—although it's not here yet—when all the separate threads of groups and individuals struggling in a million ways to fight problems in this society, will weave together into creative alliances and forge more powerful bonds. It's interesting to me that, even though in the early 1970s there was much more hope that we could change the world than there is today, in fact, there are far more people today who are active, in one way or another, than there were back then. If you add up the numbers of people involved in good works of all kinds— volunteering or doing nonprofit work in civic and religious, environmental, women's, civil rights, and social service groups—they number in the millions. In addition, there are countless tens of thousands of people, including many in evangelical churches, who would be moved to activism by a hopeful and compelling democratic social vision that speaks to their hearts. We simply don't yet talk to each other, across our differences, in any substantial numbers—nor do we reach beyond, to new people harboring hope beneath their cynicism. When we do, there will be a sea change in the political and social possibilities for improving this country.

I'm also convinced that the current migration of lesbians and gay men out of our closets and ghettoes will be key to catalyzing that conversation about shared concerns across different groupings; we appear to be natural bridge-builders because of the many identities we each embody. I for one can't wait until that conversation breaks wide open. Even now, we can see glimmers of how far those bridges can take us.

———

In the spring of 1996, outraged Salt Lake City straight parents and students in unprecedented numbers joined the Citizens Alliance for Hate-Free Schools (launched by lesbian leader Charlene Orchard of the Utah Human Rights Coalition) after the city board of education voted four to three to outlaw *all* high school clubs—such as hiking and knitting clubs—in order to eradicate a new Gay/Straight Alliance. Polls showed two-to-one opposition to that vote, and Salt Lake City had never seen such widespread protest in its history: one thousand high school students staged a walkout, demanding that their clubs be reinstated; some 3,000 people attended the largest-ever rally in the city. In addition, the national Gay, Lesbian, and Straight Teachers Network (GLSTN) was featured on MTV News during the Utah protest, promoting its popular publication "How to Start a Gay-Straight Alliance," which had inspired the club that sparked the revolution—the Gay/Straight Alliance at East High School in Salt Lake City.

The Lavender Project was created in 1994 at Presbyterian/St. Luke's Medical Center in Denver, Colorado, specifically to provide lesbians and gays comfortable access to their services. A referral service to gay-friendly health care providers, it features special targeted programs such as a cancer support group for lesbian women and the Last Drag stop-smoking project. It is so successful that over 30 percent of the medical center's health care providers—from pediatricians to geriatricians—asked to be listed as gay- and lesbian-sensitive.

When a rabidly homophobic African-American minister was appointed to the Human Relations Commission in San Francisco in 1993, straight Latino community leaders stepped forward to object. They were supporting a number of Latina lesbians who had worked with the United Farmworkers, supporting the 1970s and 1980s lettuce and grape boycotts. Because of the bridge-building of these brave lesbians, yet another attempt by the right to create a rift between gays and communities of color was doomed to failure.

In an unprecedented 1994 coalition effort, the California branch (with over 3 million members) of the American Association of Retired Persons (AARP) lobbied heavily for a domestic partnership bill authored by California's lesbian and gay state lobbying group, LIFE Lobby. The bill would have granted domestic partners the rights to hospital visitation, conservatorship, and inheritance. Recognizing that seniors, like lesbians and gay men, create nontraditional family units, the AARP and many similar groups were successful in getting the bill through the legislature. (Unfortunately, Governor Pete Wilson, again pandering to the right wing of his party, vetoed the bill.)

In the late eighties, after lesbians had spent years participating in and leading AIDS activism and service work, gay men began to organize "Brothers for Sisters" campaigns of support for various lesbian issues. New York gay leader Ken Dawson authored a direct-mail appeal to gay men on behalf of the country's only lesbian foundation, Astraea. In many cities, gay male ACT UP members joined women in clinic defense squads protecting abortion clinics from anti-abortion protesters. Gay men consciously supported women by spearheading fund-raising for, or working on boards of directors of, groups such as the Women's Building and Connexxus lesbian center in L.A., EMILY's List and the Women's Campaign Fund in Washington, D.C., and the National Center for Lesbian Rights and Chronic Fatigue Immune Deficiency Syndrome Foundation in San Francisco.

In 1990, the National Black Gay and Lesbian Leadership Forum brokered a historic meeting on gay issues among top officials of every African-American civil rights group, including the Southern Christian Leadership Conference, the NAACP, and the Urban League. In 1995, the Forum organized a contingent of over two hundred black gay men (and a few brave lesbians) to march in the Million Man March. "We felt we had to be a visible presence—and to everyone's surprise, we got a wildly positive response. People yelled and cheered and rushed up to hug us," said Forum director Keith Boykin.

After the ugly 1992 Oregon fight to defeat an antigay initiative that would have deemed homosexuality "abnormal, wrong, unnatural, and perverse," a new organization called LOGIC (Lesbians, Others, and Gays in Community Service) was formed. Two hundred fifty gays and lesbians worked with other citizens on volunteer community projects, such as rebuilding the town's oldest African-American church after a fire and collecting food and blankets for the homeless.

The Leadership Conference on Civil Rights (LCCR), Washington, D.C.'s powerful two-hundred-group civil rights coalition, put gay rights at the top of its agenda for the first time in 1993, beginning with fighting the military ban. LCCR continues to lobby hard for the Employment Non-Discrimination Act, introduced in Congress in 1994. In 1994, LCCR granted a coveted executive committee seat to the Human Rights Campaign.

Republican conservative leader Barry Goldwater and Coretta Scott King joined forces in 1993 to head an advisory committee to help end the military ban on lesbians and gay men. Despite a backlash in both of their camps, they each actively and eloquently opposed discrimination against lesbians and gay men as a natural outgrowth of their respective ideologies.

The Gay and Lesbian Alliance Against Defamation joined the Gay and Lesbian Latinos Unidos, the United Lesbians of African Heritage, and the Black Gay and Lesbian Leadership Forum in organizing gay and lesbian carpools into South Central Los Angeles after the 1992 riots to help clean up the debris.

When she ran for the California State Assembly in 1994, Sheila Kuehl found that many of the prime coalition-builders between the constituent groups she lobbied for support were gay men of color and lesbians. Her liaisons to labor unions and to the powerful environmental movement were both gay Latinos, while the lesbian mayor of Santa Monica was her link to the local renters' group.

Mary Fisher, the Republican mother, author, and socialite with HIV who contributed the only heart to the soulless Republican convention of 1992, credits role models in the gay AIDS community with helping teach her to reach out across differences. She has become a compelling and unifying voice for compassion, speaking regularly across the country at conservative churches, suburban high schools, and southern campuses.

In 1994, gay leader David Mixner inaugurated the first-ever joint effort between the national gay and lesbian community and a major religious group: the Gay and Lesbian Project of the United States Holocaust Memorial Museum, which expects to raise $2 million (exceeding its original goal of $1.5 million) by the end of 1996 for research, scholarship, and education on gays and lesbians in the Holocaust.

Unprecedented alliances are being built geared to elections. As part of an effective coalition with labor, environmental, and women's groups determined to out-organize the opposition, the Human Rights Campaign's intensive 15,000-voter gay and lesbian get-out-the-vote effort in 1995 helped provide Democratic senator Ron Wyden's slim margin of victory over a conservative opponent in Oregon. Also, in the largest ever national electoral-political effort by a gay group to defeat a political enemy, HRC initiated an unprecedented $250,000 independent expenditure against North Carolina's senator Jesse Helms in 1996—targeting middle-of-the-road voters with an aggressive mail and phone campaign to educate them.

The Centers for Disease Control (CDC) Breast and Cervical Cancer Early Detection Project, which provides free Pap smears and mammograms for low-income women in all fifty states, has entered a unique partnership with the YWCA in four cities (Tucson, Seattle, Minneapolis, Dallas) to develop pilot-project lesbian-outreach initiatives. This is unprecedented collaboration between the federal government, a large national mainstream women's organization, and the lesbian health movement.

Despite widespread voter alienation and cynicism about political change, thousands of disparate people are quietly linking together their battles as we approach the millennium.

Lesbians and gay men already possess all the tools it will take to build a vigorous movement over the next decade, for our own rights and for the rights of those with whom we share goals. If we can successfully move from hopelessness to hope, support our leaders, and shift our thinking about power from fear to eager acceptance of the tasks before us, we will be well on our way to a successful new era in our struggle for freedom.

The specific issues that bring us together locally or nationally are less important than our determination to build and organize for the long term, with faith in our freedom and a determination to succeed. There are also multiple forms of activism that can engage us: single-issue advocacy such as work against antigay violence or for lesbian health projects; raising funds or volunteering for lesbian and gay candidates or progay allies; slow but steady building of grassroots organizations, such as our centers or other state and local institutions. All of us should share a coalition approach, a vigilance about the dangers of the radical right, and a sense of clear purpose about our work. There is no quick fix on this freedom ride; this is a lifelong project, whether we are occasional check writers, active volunteers, or full-time paid activists. Each of us must get involved in community and political work at whatever level feels great, feeds our spirit, and nurtures our hope. Whatever role each of us chooses, we are transformational activists engaged in the greatest project imaginable: enabling the brightest vision of American democratic pluralism once again to break through the current cloud of political defeatism and, finally, to truly flourish.

5

COMING HOME TO
AMERICA WITH NEW
VALUES AND VISIONS

I n deference to all those lesbians on all those softball teams all over
America, playing on New England town greens or inner-city parking lots, let me use a sports analogy: you can't come home until you
step up to the plate, connect, and touch all the bases.

By coming out, gays and lesbians declare our existence: we step
up to the plate. We connect by explaining and defining that existence to ourselves and to others. We touch all the bases by organizing, by linking our lives to ever greater circles of people.

All that remains is bringing home all the lessons of our lives,
bringing home our fullest selves. Lesbians and gay men, like every
other disfavored group, have been defined by our *difference* from
others. Being different has taught us distinct lessons, nurtured special qualities, and allowed us—sometimes forced us into—unique
ways of being. Those lessons, those qualities, those different ways
of being, can now be vitally important to this country.

1. AMERICA'S HEART IS HURTING

The 1992 Los Angeles riots were a flashpoint experience for many Angelenos, including myself. For most of America, what was beamed across television sets bore only a dim resemblance to our shockingly vivid reality.

Each and every one of us has glimpsed, at some point in our lives, the ways in which violence or fear of violence can isolate, divide, and frighten us. It can also suddenly exacerbate racial or class divisions, as well as other power differences. But each of us has also witnessed how heroically families and communities can come together in powerful ways when faced with catastrophe. What was most extraordinary about the events in L.A. in the spring of 1992 was that hundreds of thousands of people experienced *both* of those social phenomena, in the same place and time.

Immediately after the acquittal of the Los Angeles police officers who had been videotaped beating Rodney King was announced in the suburb of Simi Valley where the trial took place, outrage, violence, racial fear and division, widespread arson and looting, and then total social anarchy exploded in L.A. It spread to almost every corner of the county and continued for two days. Then, literally overnight, that energy of fear and violence was transformed into a massive outpouring of hope, healing, neighborliness, goodwill, and even sudden social intimacy between strangers.

The day after the riots began, I was afraid to go outside in my friendly, racially mixed neighborhood. The day before, I had witnessed the total breakdown of the normal social contract: I'd watched out-of-control raging youths trash and torch buildings. I'd gotten stuck in a seven-hour traffic jam trying to drive ten miles home to Santa Monica from Hollywood when panic overtook the roadways and nobody obeyed traffic signals. I'd seen people of all colors and ages get swept up in the looting frenzy and descend on a local 7-Eleven, wiping its shelves clean in minutes. I'd seen people suddenly spill out of a city bus and then, as if in some weird, well-choreographed dance, divide into racially segregated groups—Latinos here, Asians over there—and combust into multiple fistfights at once. The whole thing was surreal.

During this forty-eight-hour period, the atmosphere was charged with volatility. Chaos predominated, and the smell of fear and violence was everywhere, pungent and palpable in the air. The next day I walked to my neighborhood store to stock up on basic supplies. Nobody I saw made direct eye contact. Everyone kept looking around nervously. Suspicion and fear were written on people's faces, particularly when someone of a different race approached. That day, a gentle Latino neighbor of mine almost shot a ten-year-old African-American kid who showed up at his door selling magazines for school. My Middle Eastern local store owner told me, with tears in his eyes, that he was suddenly and irrationally frightened of customers he'd known for years.

Then, as if by magic, everything changed. The next morning I was wakened from a fitful sleep by my doorbell ringing. My next-door neighbor, active in a local evangelical Christian church, was organizing people from the neighborhood to carpool to South Central to help clean up the debris. She laughed excitedly as she told me that *everybody* wanted to help, to do something positive. The motley neighborhood mix of people included a single Latina mom and her teenage son, a local gang member; an entire Japanese-American family of four; a white gay artist; and even the crotchety old French lady from down the street.

This kind of thing was happening all over Los Angeles, it turned out. There was a sudden, heartfelt outpouring of goodwill. Everyone started talking to everyone they saw—particularly, it seemed to me, if they were of a different race. A collective spasm of regret formed itself into positive action. That same young African-American boy whom my neighbor nearly shot made a lot of friends and tons of money going door-to-door selling magazines. Neighborhoods organized discussion groups and "town" meetings to talk together about what had happened and how racial intolerance could be averted. I've never seen anything like it. All the buried contradictions of contemporary life burst through to the surface. I remember one conversation with a wealthy white gay man who lives in a gated, guarded complex in mid-L.A. He described buying a gun and organizing his neighbors to help protect their exclusive enclave from the rioters. In the very next breath, he said to me that he fully understood the despair that drove young black men to violence, and said—with no apparent awareness of the contradiction—that he thought it would be more appropriate if the riots and looting "moved out of the ghettoes and into Beverly Hills so that rich people, who have been looting the economy for years, could see the impact of their ways."

In those few days, Los Angelenos learned from bitter firsthand experience how closely this society skirts the edges of utter chaos, and how deep the economic and racial divides are. But we also learned how hungry almost everyone is—rich or poor; white, black, or brown—for healing and community, for vision beyond those divisions.

It's clear to most people that America is not working. The political tumult of these past few years has driven this home. It's just as clear that, despite claims by the right, no compelling and viable social vision has emerged to fix it. There is a widespread sense that the old order is dying or dead and that a new one has yet to be born. As Dexter, my favorite Washington, D.C., taxi driver—chubby, jocular, tattooed, and great at dispensing earthy wisdom—said to me the other day: "Where are the new answers? I know the old ones don't work anymore, but I sure don't know what the new solutions are yet."

For the vast majority of people, the quality of life is steadily deteriorating. As painfully evidenced by the O. J. Simpson trial and verdict, racial divisions cut more sharply than ever. Economic disparity is rapidly widening. The life expectancy of an African-American man in Harlem is lower than that of a person in Bangladesh. The gap between the super-rich and the rest of us is wider than it has been in half a century: one percent of U.S. citizens now control 40 percent of America's wealth—double the amount in 1980—and 10 percent control 70 percent of the wealth. The contemporary economic revolution—from the industrial to the postindustrial information age—is causing serious dislocation and uncertainty; as blue-collar and service-sector jobs evaporate, where exactly will millions of replacement jobs come from? So far, no clear answers exist.

Violence grows more prevalent every day and love seems more scarce. There are a million handguns out there in private hands and yet we've never felt less safe. Even though America is the richest country in the history of the world, it has a higher percentage of the population—an astounding 1.5 million people—in prison than any other nation except Russia. Feminism has lifted the veil of denial about the ugly underside of "traditional" family life: outrageous rates of incest, domestic violence, and other abuse; addictions; oppression. People everywhere mourn the loss of community, economic security, national purpose, clear morality, family ties.

Meanwhile, public esteem of government is at an all-time low. Voters are disgusted with negative campaigning and with demonizing the minority of the month. They are fed up with the paucity of genuine political leadership that speaks to the realities of their lives, so they vote with their feet—by staying home. The U.S. voter turnout in 1994 was 39 percent, compared with nearly 80 percent in France that same year.

These are scary, lonely, tough times for most people, regardless of economic circumstances. There is widespread yearning for change, but no vision of how to accomplish it, other than that offered up by the radical right: reactionary and theocratic public policies, an "old-fashioned" morality based on an absolutist view of God, and a return to a (largely mythical) pre-1960s male-dominated patriarchal "traditional" family with strict, separate—and unequal—gender roles for men and women. The majority of men and women know these are not the answers needed by this great multicultural, multireligious nation in order to move forward, but the right does strike a responsive chord because it touches on issues of deep concern to people—morality, family, community, spirituality—and offers a coherent worldview in the face of confusion. In their uncertainty, more and more people tilt rightward, and a regressive and oppressive vision thus has influence well beyond its minority support.

As a result, hope seems shuttered by fear and cynicism and, increasingly, the ideals of democracy and pluralism seem emptier and emptier. In order to craft viable answers that enhance rather than constrict the meaning of democracy, America needs strong and visionary leadership as well as a collective national willingness to seek solutions in some new places. Great numbers of people will need to coalesce and mobilize their talents, creativity, and faith in change. America can do no better than to look to the hidden minority—to lesbians and gay men—for some answers and innovative models, as well as other gifts to aid in the giant national project of healing and changing this great country for the better.

2. LESBIANS AND GAY MEN CAN HELP HEAL AMERICA

The Los Angeles riots were a brief, powerful lesson. Soon after the magnificent outpouring of healing and love that overtook the city for a bright moment in time, business went back to normal. South Central still has not been rebuilt. The magic faded away into the grim realities of urban life: racism and racial separation, growing poverty and hopelessness, pervasive violence.

For a shining instant, a sense of community spread across Los Angeles, uniting strangers, making neighborhoods neighborly, and obliterating ugly race lines. Anyone who was there remembers that powerful and hopeful moment when people drew together in a rare sense of commonality and shared social purpose. That all too short-lived spirit of community touched a longing that is deeply felt in this country. There is an ache for community, a yearning for connectedness beyond our differences. There is a longing for new values and social vision that brings out the best in us, that emphasizes unity and compassion instead of materialism and individualism. Just as close to the surface as the violence, chaos, and division that can tear us apart is a deeply felt need for collective healing and change. We are poised equidistant from anarchy *and* from hope.

Community, healing, and new values are something we gay men and lesbians know a lot about. Out of our lives in exile and out of the agony of AIDS, we have quietly forged an extraordinary community. We have also developed a new underlying group culture of empathy and compassion for each other. During this coming time, as we become visible at last, as we come home to America and bring our fuller selves to the world we live in, we bring these skills and values with us.

Lesbians and gay men have valiantly struggled to work across wide chasms of difference. We have proudly succeeded in learning to value diversity, and to combine some unity with respect for that diversity. It has not come easy, but this value is brightly emblazoned on our best community vision.

Healing America's soul will be a spiritual process in the broadest, most democratic sense of the term. It will require faith and some transcendent sense of purpose, although that faith must necessarily have myriad names and forms. For that spiritual sensibility to work with and not against democracy, it will have to be expansive and pluralistic. Forging an inclusive spirituality is, again, something we gay men and lesbians know about.

A social vision for the twenty-first century that can invigorate and expand democracy will require the ability to break free of old ways of thinking, particularly this culture's deep-seated either/or dichotomy. The answers for tomorrow must move beyond today's liberal/conservative split, the dichotomy between right and left. It's time for fresh, flexible, multifaceted thinking, for new blends and innovative models. Again, lesbians and gay men are well equipped to provide some leadership and brainpower in generating creative solutions that can help this nation get moving forward again.

Finally, gay men and lesbians bring home to America some helpful and zestful cultural traits that add sparkle to life and the process of social change. We bring our unlimited creativity, an affirmation of sexuality as joyful and positive, a deep empathy for "otherness." We bring our insistence on blending and bending gender roles, and on laughing in the face of anything that comes along. If there's a gay gene, as lesbian leader Joan Lester has said, it's the gene for fun; and, I would add, if there's a lesbian gene, it's probably a passion for justice. So if there is a jointly gay-and-lesbian queer spirit, it's a fun *and* transformational one.

Lesbians and gay men have always been cultural agents of change. As nongay social critic Robert Anton Wilson says, throughout history, gay people have performed "quasi-shamanic functions of making, breaking, or transforming cultural signals." We are the artists and poets, social reformers and even visionaries, warriors, spiritual or medical healers, mediators, teachers, and, of course, genderbenders across cultures and across time. Together, gay men and lesbians have camp, creativity, gentleness, great courage, and a passion for social reform. From the "two-spirited ones" of Native cultures, through our long history of artistic genius in every branch of the arts and literature, to our leadership in every social justice movement in history and our unrecognized professional overrepresentation in today's schools and hospitals, gay people have a rich tradition of challenging and helping improve the world.

While gay men and lesbians today go about healing ourselves and our community, America needs to heed our example and learn from us if this country is truly to begin a much-needed, widespread process of repairing its broken spirit. With any luck—or justice— over the coming few decades, our proud work will help build a brighter world for everybody, will resonate ever more visibly, ever more forcefully—and will be ever more appreciated.

3. What Lesbians and Gay Men Can Teach America: Our Community Ethic of Caring

More and more, people are searching for ethical guidelines beyond the marketplace-generated celebration of consumerism and me-firstism that currently dominate this country's culture. People increasingly decry the growing violence, the breakdown of community, and the strains of economic pressures that crowd private time. Hundreds of thousands of people flock to self-help groups or buy books designed to improve their ability to have love and intimacy in their lives and to fill the spiritual void that they feel. This society is hungry for a revolution in values.

Quietly, at the margins of society, gay and lesbian people, those current scapegoats of the right, have been fashioning new community values that can serve as helpful models. Attacked as immoral by the right and commonly characterized as hedonistic individualists disconnected from family responsibilities (or, worse, actually responsible for families' destruction), we have slowly but steadily transformed our own society into one that emphasizes connectedness to and responsibility for family and community. We have created a culture of empathy that I call our community ethic of caring. The value we collectively place on community-building emerged from our role as exiles, and has been interwoven with our cultural and political survival as well as our emergence into visibility. Pioneered by gay liberationists and then expanded by lesbian-feminists in the 1970s, community-building has reached a new maturity in the 1990s. AIDS tied together the multiple strands into a more unified and coherent fabric with some widespread cultural commonality.

As we watch the fragile ecology of our community be disrupted and destroyed by endless death from AIDS, we have developed a heightened respect for that ecology. We have learned the hard way the hollowness of "rugged individualism," of going it alone, even as we have greatly valued the virtues of self-reliance and individual responsibility in dealing with coming out, homophobic assaults, and AIDS. We have seen and heard of too many of our people dying alone, friendless, homeless, abandoned by blood families. Those experiences have inspired us to redouble our commitment to care for our own, to face the illness and the dying together, in our chosen families and beloved friendship networks. The deepest irony of AIDS is that the ultimate separation and letting go that is death has deepened our ability to love, to connect intimately, and to nurture mutuality and maintain community. America's queer exiles have been quietly learning to institutionalize a community-wide ethic of caring within our daily lives, our organizations, and our relationships. It has changed everything.

———

Lauren, a forty-nine-year-old lesbian college professor, tells this story:

"When my friend Gabe was suddenly and unexpectedly in a coma and dying—from a brain biopsy that set off a hemorrhage—you wouldn't believe how we jumped into action. That hospital hardly knew what hit it. It was transformed. We commandeered a section of the waiting room and created "Dyke Central"—since it was lesbians who formed the nucleus. We had a cellular phone and at least two women there around the clock, calling people, letting them know what was happening, preparing them for Gabe's death, letting them know they'd better get there if they wanted to say good-bye, providing food, meeting and greeting visitors, and caretaking everyone in Gabe's life who was dealing with the shock of his sudden dying. We called in our lesbian rabbi to provide solace and counsel to Gabe's family and friends.

"His parents were deeply touched that so many people cared so much for their son. The hospital staff were quite awed by our dedicated efficiency and our unabashedly open loving and grieving. We hugged. We turned on the radio, and danced wildly all around the waiting room. We cried and cried and cried. We became instant family—even friends of Gabe's who had never met each other, who had traveled hundreds of miles to be there together."

———

The private has met the public with AIDS. Our myriad painful and powerful private moments together at hospitals, at deathbeds, at wakes, or over coffee, talking about the meaning of it all, have collectively imprinted our soul with a communal respect for *real* family values: love, unconditional caring, and affirmation. At the same time, our public, political work building the community response to AIDS and fighting for AIDS awareness, treatment, and funding have woven together a new community unity and an ethos of social responsibility.

Thousands of life-changing variations of scenes like Gabe's death and dying have been enacted in hundreds of towns and cities across this country. It's not that we haven't, as a community, experienced trauma before; certainly lesbians have been struggling with an epidemic of breast cancer for years. But the concentration of death and psychic trauma has been transformative, and the cumulative effect has been a values shift and a sea change in the community's culture. In recent years we've all seen individual lives changed dramatically, in huge numbers.

———

"I know it's a cliché, but this disease has totally changed my priorities," says a Chinese-American gay man from New York. "I love my work as an architect. I'm out at work and I work for a gay-friendly firm that gave me as much time off as I wanted and needed when Alberto got sick. But as the saying goes, no one says on their deathbed, 'Gee, I really wish I'd spent more time at the office.' Death forces you to see what's really important. I particularly remember the last picnic I had with Al and our close friends on a trip to the mountains. It was sheer magic—the simple comfort of being together in a beautiful sunny place, buzzing bees, singing birds, warm companionship. That image of the five of us will live with me forever: a small circle of loving friends, sitting under a tree in the gorgeous Vermont fall, my beloved Al's eyes all lit up, serenity on his face, surrounded by his family of friends. There is nothing more important."

"Money, success, my rising power in the entertainment industry. That's what used to matter to me," says a fiftysomething TV producer in Hollywood. "Not anymore. I swear, I find my work cooking food for PWAs every Wednesday morning with a zany group of folks much more fulfilling. There's the homeless old black man, a recovering heroin addict. There's a Beverly Hills housewife. There's a young college student, a straight guy from a Christian fundamentalist college. Boy, how we've bonded. As a result, I've gotten more and more active in community service."

An older lesbian lawyer from Chicago says: "I find the simple things more meaningful. I've slowed down my life. Would you believe it? Me, the crazed workaholic—I take time now to look at sunsets. And I talk to people more: grocery clerks, gas station guys. I try to connect, to really relate to people. I never did before. And I spend lots more time with friends, time I used to spend working. Workaholism is now something I avoid, instead of aspire to. I'm HIV-negative but definitely AIDS-affected. AIDS has taught me how to live."

An Atlanta lesbian doctor and researcher says: "Working in AIDS has changed me a lot. I take care of myself better. I've gotten healthy and I go to the gym. It's funny—I'm a better fighter, for myself and for my own rights. But it's also softened my edges. I'm less judgmental about people around me. I appreciate my lover more. I call my mother every week now; I spent more time and focus on my patients. A restlessness and rage around my edges is gone."

Each of us in the gay and lesbian communities affected by AIDS has stories like these. Stories about how our lives have changed and about how we and others in our lives have mobilized to participate in the community response to AIDS. Stories of everyday acts of outstanding courage and compassion.

We've created new, communal ways of caretaking the sick, the dying, and their families. We've seen how our values have shifted from material success and individual achievement to community service and helping each other. We've seen over and over and over again the treasure that true friendship is. There has been an intensifying of intimacy, a heightened sense of spirituality. And while love may be scarcer in the rest of the world in these trying times, it has definitely multiplied geometrically in ours.

The Magic of Love

I will never forget visiting my friend Philip a few days before he died. He was at home, in the gentle and patient care of good gay and lesbian home health care nurses and his lover, Michael. Philip was a stoic man, quiet and reserved by nature, not given to verbal or physical expressiveness. He had kept a good deal of his pain and discomfort to himself during the preceding tough months. As he faced the very end, beyond fear or anger or depression, he was transformed into a man who radiated love. He had always been a gentle and compassionate soul, but this was a new and different, more powerful force. It was a palpable love energy that poured out of his eyes, his face, even his hands as, in a most uncharacteristic way, he reached out to touch everyone who visited him.

As his body failed, he became, it seemed, pure loving spirit. It was impossible not to have an intimate connection with Philip during those last couple of weeks he was conscious. And it was impossible not to be touched and even changed by the clarity and directness of the experience. Nothing seemed to matter as much as the power of that healing love. The very force of it bonded together people who were previously strangers, and strengthened ties between friends. It spread grace and forgiveness, warmth and generosity.

This quiet, unassuming, self-contained man became, in dying, a healer emanating love and generating an instant electrifying sense of community in all who came near him.

Though powerful, my experience with Philip was in no way unusual or unique to me. Tens of thousands of us have had similar experiences of learning, from those dying, about love and our yearning to be more connected with each other. It's as if the AIDS-affected gay and lesbian community has had a collective near-death experience that has changed our lives. The force of it has generated a million small, transformative sparks of epiphany—individual, self-healing values shifts that point us to the fundamental connectedness we have with one another if we open up our hearts. This force, powerful and spiritually resuscitating though it is, has not yet fully been articulated in any public or political discourse. But it is the truth of our daily lives. Day in and day out, it is the rich, raw, beauty-in-horror stuff we experience. It has been so for over a decade, and it promises to be so for far too much longer. It is permanently changing those of us touched by it in ways we have yet to even fully grasp.

Our challenge is to translate what we feel individually, and largely in private, into language that is public and ideas that resonate universally beyond our experience. In this inchoate and ineffable truth lies the true politics of hope, the living glory of community that nurtures unity and can help heal the world. In the face of death and hatred, this force of love lives and breathes in our community ethic of caring.

Our determination to bring this healing and hopeful new ethos of compassion and of care with us as we come home to America will cause some ruckus. We are now still the hated ones who fight for the right to be visible, let alone to be seen as examplars of morality or public values. But we have a passion and steely determination that belie our generally gentle natures. I believe this collective force will only grow more potent and more visionary with time. With full confidence, I say: make no mistake about it, we will be leaders in crafting a broader national conversation about social change as this country struggles toward higher ideals to charge its spirit. What could be *more* about genuine family values, more deeply and powerfully moral, than what we have done?

4. WHAT GAY MEN AND LESBIANS CAN TEACH AMERICA: THE AFFIRMATION OF DIVERSITY

A merica must grapple successfully with the issue of diversity. This country is undergoing a profound demographic shift that is already causing seismic social volatility: by the year 2050, according to a 1996 U.S. Census Bureau report, only a slim majority of the nation's population, 52 percent, will be white (a drop from 80 percent in 1980 and 73 percent in 1996). This radical demographic shift has combined with the expanded promise of democracy sparked by the 1960s civil rights movement to generate a defining crisis of social vision for the nation.

We are a country at a crossroads. Heterosexual white men are only 25 percent of the population today, but still hold 90 percent of the power positions in business, media, and government. Basic fairness mandates that this change, although recent history has clearly taught that "political correctness" and white-male-bashing are entirely counterproductive toward that end. A unifying vision that benefits the vast majority of people is required—and is certainly promised by the broad scope of the American dream.

Our growing ethnic diversity and the increased participation of all women, by people with disabilities, and by gays and lesbians in the workplace and in public life, has the potential to enrich and ennoble this nation. America can choose to expand its social vision, embrace its many different peoples, shift its human and economic resources toward greater equality, and end up the world's first major nation that is a true pluralist democracy. America can live up to its finest ideals. Or the fear of growing diversity can continue to lead to increased social and political fragmentation, inequality, divisions, and the demonization of many subgroups. If we as a nation choose to stay the current course of widening economic inequality, increasing racism, immigrant-bashing, and all other forms of bigotry, the future guarantees not only more riots such as L.A.'s, but the obliteration of hope for this country to deliver on its greatest promise to history: democracy.

Gay men and lesbians are in a position to help craft a new social vision of democratic pluralism that affirms difference. This is true in part because we are everywhere—in boatloads of immigrants, in corporate suites, on factory floors, in well-manicured Republican suburbs, and in urban black churches. We are a microcosm of the larger society. We are the one minority group that is becoming increasingly visible within each and every racial and ethnic community. We are urban and rural and suburban; rich, middle-class, and poor; we are women and men and transsexuals. This gives us unique access to bridging different communities and cultures and playing a transformative leadership role in forging alliances between peoples and among communities.

Our internal diversity has also been the genesis of our own intense and proud struggle with this issue of difference. Often the only thing we have in common with each other is that we are gay and have been thrown out of every other community. Very often, we have been thrown together despite very real and painfully obvious differences. Therefore, within the lesbian and gay community, we've had to deal with the challenge of inclusiveness and diversity. From the beginning, we've seen drag and leather folks mingle in gay men's bars, and working-class and middle-class dykes play in lesbian softball leagues together. More recently, as we have consciously built our home-base culture, we've worked at building a respectful movement and community that cross age, class, race, ability, and gender lines, and we have struggled with inclusiveness of sexual minorities within our ranks. Although we have not completed our work by any means, we have covered some new territory, forged leadership, and creatively faced up to the issue of diversity far more than most people or groups in this society.

Not everyone has totally signed on, but affirmation of difference *has* emerged as a lesbian and gay majoritarian value. Sometimes, isolated at the social margins as lesbians and gay men have been, we forget just how lucky we are to have this value imprinted on our community-wide vision. Sometimes we forget how unusual our diverse community is, and how much progress we have made. When my heterosexual younger sister, Ann, attended my two-hundred-person fortieth-birthday bash a few years ago, she was most struck by two things. "Damn," she said, "so this is where all the good-looking men are—in the gay community!" Second, and more seriously, she was flabbergasted at how incredibly diverse the group was.

Ann is a young woman with an open mind and an adventurous spirit. She was married to a Latino man, spent several years as a professional fisherwoman off the coast of Oregon, and worked in a factory in Alaska. As a result, she certainly has had more variety among her own friends over the years than most white middle-class women. Still, she was struck by the fact that the party was a rainbow of women and men of different styles and backgrounds. During the course of the evening, my gregarious sister schmoozed with a millionaire white man whose date was an African-American architect and lawyer; a Filipina social services administrator; a Latino former Marine turned corporate manager; a transsexual AIDS lobbyist and her "husband," an interior designer; a white lesbian carpenter, proud of her working-class background, and her lover, a Native American businesswoman; and a white gay cop wearing an ACT UP T-shirt. "Wow," Ann exclaimed later. "I have *never* been to a straight party with such a mix of people. And everyone seemed to get along."

Almost every nongay person I've ever met who has gone to a sizable gay/lesbian gathering has noticed the same thing: the diversity of the crowd. A friend's mother who attended the 1993 March on Washington said to me: "You guys aren't joking when you say, 'We are everywhere.' In just one afternoon I met a black woman college professor and her white lawyer lover; a Jewish deaf gay teacher; and a Chinese-American single lesbian mom with two straight teenage sons who have become AIDS volunteers. That kind of diversity is unheard-of in my world. We stick with people pretty much like ourselves." Thrown together by our ostracism from the mainstream, gay people have evolved friendship circles and community acquaintanceships that cut across lines of difference that usually separate people. For example, we are more likely than straight people to have partners who differ from us in background, education, or race.

This is not to say that we've achieved a perfectly harmonious multicultural utopia, but we do tend to bridge demographic differences in our personal circles and in our communities more than most people in this society. Over time, through living and working together, primarily during the past decade's war on AIDS, we have learned better than most not only to tolerate difference but to value it deeply.

Fighting AIDS: From Fragmentation to Family

The past decade has seen a profound change in the relationship between lesbians and gay men, and steady progress in fighting racism and other forms of discrimination inside our community. We have also developed a solid track record of building multicultural organizations and have identified some key principles for doing this work successfully. One major principle, "independence first"—recognizing the importance of autonomous organizing by various subgroups—has become a foundation principle, guiding our best work and helping create our most vibrantly diverse groups and institutions.

Forging unity between women and men. Our greatest success to date—and one that has helped us blueprint diversity work for the long term—has been making peace between men and women after the bloody "gender wars" of the 1970s. Until very recently, women and men mostly lived in completely different worlds. AIDS changed all that, because the men's community grew to embrace issues that had long been lesbian concerns: recognition of alternative families, the need for systemic health care reform, the linkage between forms of discrimination.

There was also another important reason that AIDS brought women and men together after all those years of gender separation— a simple, serendipitous reason: there are a disproportionate and very high number of lesbians in the health-care professions—nurses, doctors and researchers, health educators, and social workers. As a result, the disaster that struck gay men swept thousands of lesbians into its front lines. For the most part these were not activist, even out-of-the-closet lesbians. They were ordinary middle-class and working-class women ensconced in their closeted regular lives.

———

Jean was a Nebraska farm girl proud of her college education and nursing degree. Still completely closeted, she joined the Air Force medical corps, where she discovered an entire lesbian subculture. Virtually all the women nurses were lesbian or bisexual, and she had a treasured circle of lesbian friends within the male-dominated army. "There wouldn't be *any* armed forces medical personnel if all of us were kicked out, as far as I can tell," she told me.

When Jean left the Air Force, she moved in with a new lover, joined a lesbian social group, and built an extended family of lesbians. She had no gay male friends until the home health-care company she worked for began to serve more and more AIDS patients. Slowly her world opened up to gay men. She became friends with gay AIDS doctors, with gay patients and their lovers and friends. Her involvement with the AIDS community deepened her own spirituality; she joined the largely gay and lesbian Metropolitan Community Church, where she found even more gay male friends. As she was captured by a sense of mission and urgency in fighting the epidemic, her professional work came to revolve entirely around AIDS. She specialized in setting up AIDS care in private clinics and doctors' practices, and then moved into helping nonprofit clinics. "In a matter of a few years, my life changed from a social circle that was almost exclusively closeted lesbians, and a few straight friends, to one that included as many gay men as lesbians. I never used to be able to relate to gay men, but they are my brothers now. I love their humor and fun, especially in the face of death and daily pain. And I think they appreciate my tough Amazon dyke advocacy on their behalf."

———

Jean's story of undersung heroism has been echoed a thousand times in a hundred cities as lesbian health professionals, volunteers, and activists have fought tirelessly against AIDS (and ended up coming out and getting active in changing the world in the process). A poignant coda to this particular story is that, after ten years of AIDS work, Jean herself was suddenly struck by multiple sclerosis. With loving mutuality, the gay men she had worked with in fighting AIDS immediately rallied: they cooked meals for her and took care of her, just as she had done for so many of their brothers.

The leadership provided from the very beginning of the AIDS epidemic by lesbian health-care workers, quietly, firmly and behind the scenes, has been quite extraordinary. Many a hospital ward, home health-care firm, or community clinic was transformed under lesbian leadership to include specialized care for patients with AIDS. Lesbians have done "Sisters for Brothers" blood drives and run fundraising efforts; performed pro bono legal work; provided laundry services and pet care; and given spiritual and emotional support as caregivers at hospices and individual deathbeds. In addition, lesbians have a rich tradition of social reform and activism, beginning with Jane Addams and Eleanor Roosevelt and continuing through the current feminist movement. Beginning in the mid-1980s, lesbians took leadership roles in many ACT UP chapters and protests and in gay rights groups. Our activism and leadership eventually helped forge political unity across our movements:

———

Ellen Malcolm, founder and president of the Democratic political women's group EMILY's List, remembers she joined the Human Rights Campaign's national board of directors in 1987 as a favor to a friend, planning to stay for a year. She ended up staying five years. Why? "Because of AIDS. I came in as a feminist lesbian skeptical about gay men. I mean, what did I, a longtime feminist advocate, have in common with a closeted, anti-abortion Dallas Republican lawyer and a rich New York party boy who hadn't thought about much of anything before except decorating his own apartment? Not much, before AIDS. AIDS bonded us. In fighting together for funding against the Reagan and Bush administrations' complete insensitivity to this epidemic, channels opened up. Those guys changed, and I changed too. We became comrades in struggle, and then family. Over time, that Dallas lawyer even became prochoice, as he grew to understand the organic link between control over our bodies as women and as gay people."

Steve's political anger had been catalyzed by AIDS. A successful entertainment executive who was fired from his job because he had

HIV, he got angry, joined ACT UP, and was arrested several times. After being arrested in 1987 in Washington, D.C., he found himself shoved by the police into a paddy wagon and jammed right up against June and Bunny, two feisty lesbians in their late fifties, also from Los Angeles. They spent hours sharing their stories while waiting to be processed by the police. Steve learned that both women were fighting cancer in their own lives; one of them, June, had been given less than a year to live. They were active in women's and lesbian social groups, but had decided the time had come for them to show solidarity with gay men in fighting AIDS. By the end of their "jail time" together, the three were fast friends, and Steve had vowed to donate money to their cancer wellness group, as well as to join Bunny and June in an upcoming early-morning defense picket for an abortion clinic targeted by Operation Rescue. As Steve put it: "Older lesbians like June and Bunny were invisible in my world before. AIDS activism sure changed that. I was so moved by their commitment to my issue, I wanted to pay them back."

Expanding the Family Further: Building Racial Diversity

Battling HIV has not only naturally brought together white women and men, but also—and increasingly over the years—men and women of different communities of color. Mirroring the growing tensions of society in general, gays and lesbians have yet to bridge race and class divisions as successfully as we have those posed by gender. We are, however, struggling honorably and directly with fighting racism in our ranks; there is far more commitment to this struggle in our world than in nongay communities, and our community increasingly values its racial diversity.

The L.A. Center is one of our most successful models of a multiracial, co-gender institution. During my five-year tenure as executive director, with the expert guidance of African-American lesbian management consultant Deborah Johnson (whom I describe, with nothing less than awe, as an organization shaman), I was able to help effect a transformation of the Center's organization culture. A few years earlier, the Center staff was 83 percent white and 78 percent male; when I left, the staff was 50 percent women and 45 percent people of color. (Today, that latter statistic is up to 55 percent, fully reflecting the multicultural demographics of Los Angeles.) Staff meetings are a vibrant, wonderful rainbow of diversity.

————

Hugh, a forty-five-year-old gay public health professional with proud Irish roots, began work at the L.A. Center when over 75 percent of the staff were white gay men like him. He weathered the transition to a diverse, multicultural workplace with some trepidation: "I thought I would lose something. I thought I would lose my sense of ownership of this place," he told me. "The Center was built primarily by white gay men, and since we were dying off, I feared we would lose again—lose our own home in the community. But on the contrary, when this place changed, it came alive. Staff energy and morale skyrocketed, and us white guys thrived! I've loved learning about other people's cultures, and getting rid of some of my own walls of prejudice. Now, when I visit an agency that has mostly white faces, I find it boring and bland."

Artrice is a twenty-five-year-old African-American youth services caseworker who also saw the cultural change at the Center. "When I first came here, I was skeptical about this place. But a job is a job, so I figured I'd try it. I worried I was a token, since I was hired during the growth period when lots of new women and people of color were coming on board. Now, I've changed my mind. It's been a trip. I live south of Pico, in the same black neighborhood where I grew up. Now I'm totally out in my neighborhood. That's been a gift the Center gave me.

"The Center paid for me to go to the Black Gay and Lesbian Leadership Forum's conference for several years in a row. I'd certainly never had a workplace support my cultural identity before, and that built trust. Over time, working here has been a healing and positive experience. It's also opened my eyes to what the world can be like if we try."

————

Some Guiding Principles
for Successful Diversity Work

In my work leading the transformation of the Center from a white-male-majority organization to a truly multiracial, co-gender one, core guiding principles emerged as key to successful diversity work. First, there must be a real and determined commitment by top staff and board organization leadership. Avoid tokenism and lip service! Second, the overcoming of learned prejudice requires the building of trust, and building trust takes patience. Successfully embracing diversity on an institution-wide basis is not an overnight event; it is, rather, a process that takes place over several years (three years for the Center). Third, the increasing of cultural sensitivity involves a full-scale organization "audit" of policies and procedures (for example, a reconsideration of where job advertising is done). This audit must be thorough and honest, and must result in systemic changes. Fourth, in developing diversity, include cultural education, and have fun doing it. Administrative leadership on policy should be complemented by overall consciousness-raising and sensitivity training on cultural differences. Corny as it sounds, unlearning racism involves getting to know each other's cultural traditions. Having fun sharing food together or learning about various musical or holiday traditions builds mutual respect and personal connection, the underpinning of successful organization change. Fifth, applying the principles of "transformational activism" is important. Avoid "political correctness"; lead from respect for *everyone*. Leaving anyone out (i.e., white men) undermines the spirit of inclusiveness. Also, don't get trapped in what I call the guilt-rage dance between white people and people of color, where anger at racism (often legitimate) generates reflexive white guilt, and everyone gets stuck there. Both guilt and rage are, ultimately, utterly useless emotions for constructive social-change work. Move beyond them, whatever it takes. Remember, we're all in this together.

In addition, the vital parallel principle of respect for autonomous organizing must be incorporated into all diversity work.

Independence First: The Importance of Autonomous Organizing

We often need separation from the dominant culture in order to empower ourselves and strengthen our independent voices. Only then can we take an equal place at the table. Lesbians have had to find our own solidarity and autonomy first, in separate groups or caucuses or organizations, in order to overcome our own lower self-esteem and grow the confidence necessary to work on an equal basis with men. If it weren't for those women's music festivals, those endless conference caucus meetings, those angry strikes and boycotts and walkouts from male-dominated organizations in the seventies and early eighties, unity with men in the nineties could not have been achieved.

This principle—respect for autonomous organizing—has now become a valued part of our best vision of how we build our movement and nurture community unity. In a sense, that's also exactly what the entire lesbian and gay community has done: by creating and nourishing our rich network of community-based groups separate from nongay society, we have trained and strengthened our own rich voices so that we might sing out loudly and proudly when we reenter the wider world. Within our own gay and lesbian community, we mirror, in multiple ways, this principle of "independence first." At the Center, during our three-year transition period, we had separate women's, men's, PWA, and people of color caucuses at different times, as well as our diverse, representative Multicultural Issues Task Force (to conduct the policy audit), and Multicultural Exchange (to plan educational and fun cultural activities).

Just as lesbians separated to organize ourselves in earlier days, so, too, have other communities within our broader community. There are seniors' groups, pioneered in New York City by SAGE (Senior Action in a Gay Environment). Today there is an explosion of independent lesbian and gay youth organizing across the country, with hundreds of programs springing up in high schools, communities, and colleges. Over and over again, we see that the most effective unity across racial differences is preceded or accompanied by autonomous organizing by people of color. Affinity groups like the

National Black Gay and Lesbian Leadership Forum, Llego—the national Latino gay organization—and local groups such as California's United Lesbians of African Heritage are vital in empowering people of color. Lesbians continue to need independent organizing as well. All of these autonomous groups provide parallel home bases of support for self-esteem and skill-building that enhance people's ability to come together in pluralistic groups and maintain our strongest selves.

Many of us who were around in the sixties learned from our involvement in fighting racism that racial integration in this society has, so far, meant only selective assimilation of the few. This made us suspicious of identifying integration as a sole goal. Too often, integration can mean the washing away of vital differences and the absorption of diversity into a dominant culture that highlights the middle-class values of the straight white male minority. At the same time, though separatism is a necessary and empowering part of building self-esteem, as a sole strategy, it ultimately leads to isolation, sectarianism, and ghettoization. Successful lesbian and gay organizing now makes room for both: unifying integration across difference, *and* autonomous organizing by women, people of color, seniors, the disabled, youth, and any other group that needs to nourish its identity along the way. Both independence and integration are necessary for a real vision of equality with diversity. A salad bowl filled with colorful flavorful different vegetables is a more compelling image to many of us than a melting pot that stirs diversity into one monochromatic majority-culture stew.

The Unfinished Revolution: Sexual Minorities

As we come home to America's mainstream, we also face our own ethical challenge internally: how to keep alive and vital our own best vision of diversity vis à vis the most marginalized, least "acceptable" people, sexual minorities. This is an issue that deserves our attention to learning from our own past. Resistance to partnership with lesbians limited men's access to huge, and necessary, talents the women had to offer. White people's fears of facing down their own racism and embracing people of color have too often narrowed the field of talent and leadership. Today, some gay and lesbian organizations are reluctant to incorporate into visibility the talents of transgendered and bisexual people.

California transsexual activist and PWA Connie Norman says:

"Unfortunately, the struggle too often has centered primarily on language, on incorporating the words *transgendered* and *bisexual* into the names of projects or organizations. It has become bitter over the most superficial issue—and in a right-wing era that's a divisive and a losing proposition. For me, principles and leadership emerging organically from the bottom up are most important. I don't come in fighting first for *transgender* to be added to the name. I fight first for recognition of our needs to empower ourselves. In the early days at the L.A. Center, this meant the right for trannies even to meet— believe me, there were years where we were persona non grata. It was really ugly. First, let us in the door, then watch how marvelous we are, and we will win you over. Once the relationship is there, the human connection is made; then the words will flow naturally out of everyone's lips. This is our unfinished revolution as a gay community—there is still bi-phobia and resistance to sharing power with transgendered folks. But deep inside, even those well-heeled gay suburbanites know we're in their family, too. They're just still too ashamed to admit it. But they'll come around; I have faith."

Diversity is our greatest strength as a people, and we are generally well aware of it. It used to mean men's bars being shared by drag queens and leather men, or women's bars operating under an awkward truce between middle-class and working-class lesbians. All were forced by intolerance into cramped social spaces that, nevertheless, bred slender tendrils of community inclusiveness. Increasingly, we have honorably and creatively built organizations and values that incorporate very different people into the same world. We've met the issue of diversity head-on, and have depth of experience to share with others. We have valuable lessons to share about models for unlearning racism and sexism, for knitting unity out of many cultures, for learning the joy of appreciating difference.

We have come to know and affirm the amazing richness that diverse people working together bring to our lives and the wider world. In our families, our friendship circles, our community organizing and our vision for society, we bring a deep and abiding commitment to the highest principles of a pluralist democracy—cherishing the differences between humans even as we construct the mosaic that binds us together. This has been a healing and hope-inspiring force for our community, and can be for the whole country as well. This country could become the world's first large, successful multicultural democracy, if there's the will and the vision. Lesbians and gay men offer some ways to help.

5. WHAT LESBIANS AND GAY MEN CAN TEACH AMERICA: MOVING BEYOND EITHER/OR THINKING

In this culture, thinking tends to be dualistic, rigidly divided into either/or categories that permeate the way we look at the world. Everything is seen in narrow dichotomies, starting with a heterosexist worldview that divides everything in two, beginning with the fundamental male/female split. ("Is it a boy or a girl?" is the first question on everybody's lips when they encounter a new baby.) Male/female, good/bad, mind/body, "man"/nature, black/white: the world is divided into strict dualisms, with positive qualities usually ascribed to one of them and negative qualities to the other. The underlying assumption is not of egalitarian partnership; rather, we assume that one quality or gender or species or race is better than the other. To paraphrase writer Ursula K. LeGuin: "Same and different are nurturing words, but better and worse are killing words."

Feminism has amply documented the damage done to women and girls by sexism and the strict gender roles it enforces; the growing men's movement attests to the hurt caused to men as well. Environmentalists further document the damage humanity has caused the planet by a hierarchical view that places "man" above nature, giving "him" license to ravage "her" as a result.

Reality is highly complex—and daily growing more so in this postmodern, high-tech, information-explosion world. It cannot often be successfully reduced to either/or paradigms. Nobody knows that better than gay men, bisexuals, lesbians, and transgendered people, who inherently challenge that most basic element of binary thinking, gender division. Feminism and environmentalism have questioned the heterosexist worldview. We take this challenge to the next level. Gay people's same-sex preferences, by their very nature, defy dualistic, heterosexist categorization. We are same/same, not same/other. In addition, our outsider status has forced us to develop and rely on enormous creativity. We are not invested in what everyone else automatically thinks is right. Our ways of thinking often challenge the restrictive and narrow either/or thinking that predominates. Perhaps the young person who pointed out that the emperor had no clothes was gay.

As we enter an intensified national conversation about the future of this country, breaking free of rigid, dualistic, prescribed ways of thinking and constructing the world will be vital to any social and political solutions to our country's problems. The broader society will need to let go of assumptions, and let some fresh air into the process of problem-solving. Connie Norman puts it this way: "The age of simple answers is over. To grapple with today's realities, we need to blow up this dualistic mind-set that heterosexual society bequeaths us. Who better understands the complexities of the postmodern world of multiple identities and challenges than us? Call me 'queer chauvinist' if you want, but I really believe our time has come. Either/or thinking is outmoded. Real democracy to me means allowing multiple truths to coexist at the same time—not just one dominant group's truth. It means the ability to design new social models beyond the status quo, just like we've had to do all along. Who says things have to be as they are?"

Gay and lesbian creative problem-solving transcends the usual polarities in so many ways. I've discussed the "bi-tacticalism" of AIDS activist strategy in combining militant direct-action tactics with effective insider lobbying. Community centers and AIDS organizing have developed visionary holistic models that integrate effective advocacy with human services and community-building. In addition, the traditional conservative ideas of self-reliance and individual responsibility merge in our best community groups with the liberal values of compassion and social responsibility. Blending the best of liberal and conservative might be one good place to start in order to form workable new values.

I can't think of a successful model of community organizing or political strategy as produced by the gay and lesbian community and movement that doesn't explode traditional either/or categories. "Both/and"—or "Yes, and . . ."—thinking has been found in all of them. Although there is a much-publicized split between "assimilationists" and "gay liberationists," it's really an academic and abstract argument. In my experience, the vast majority of us have *both* tendencies. We have a restless, searching need to blend and bend strict categories. We desire both to attain power and stand within the dominant culture, *and* to develop some creative alternatives along the way. In real life, we automatically tend toward embracing both unity and autonomy, both separatism (of various kinds) and integration into different worlds. Gays and lesbians move more fluidly between categories, across worlds. We are the world's great mediators and synthesizers.

————

Mike, an expert and longtime community organizer, says: "I always felt I brought a special gay touch to my Chicago work organizing churches in poor Latino and African-American neighborhoods to fight city hall. It was just the way I thought. I approached situations differently from others. I mediated opposing points of view, and integrate seemingly opposite positions easily."

One midwestern gay businessman, Dwayne, credited his being gay with enabling him to take the risk of revolutionizing management techniques at his parents' business when he took it over. "I believe business can be both profit-oriented and people-oriented. And while I certainly didn't invent quality circles and all those other democratic, team-oriented progressive management techniques I brought in, I fully credit what I call my gay brain with taking the risk to put them to work at this conservative company. As a gay man in the age of AIDS, I was simply willing to go out on a limb. I was willing to institute deep changes in this firm." Dwayne's leadership took the family business from $5 million to $50 million in annual sales in only five years. Part of his management philosophy included paying for the college education of every single employee.

A noted nongay African-American civil rights leader told a friend of mine that he always included gay men and lesbians in his brain trust. "I rely on the gay ability to look at the situation from a totally new angle. Gay people take the crystal and turn it around just enough to find a whole new facet gleaming there."

Marge, a manager climbing the corporate ladder, says: "I don't frankly know if it's my bisexuality, my feminism, or being from a working class background, but I sure don't approach problems the same ways as the straight boys at work. They think win-lose. I think win-win."

A lesbian pediatrician, Dolores, a leader in the black women's health movement, says: "Being gay has given me a tool, the gift of trying new ideas along with old ones. I work on programs to help combat teen pregnancy, and I've learned to blend models from gay men's peer AIDS-education efforts, from the alcohol and drug addiction recovery movement, women's consciousness-raising groups, and various lay and professional counseling techniques. I'm convinced that creative synthesizing is a queer thing."

"I could be engaging in some wishful thinking here," says Geraldine, a political scientist and college professor, "but in my experience, the gay and lesbian students I teach are far more interested in some of the new ideas that are emerging from visionary social scientists about the country's future economy. These students seem to resonate instantly, for example, when we talk about moving beyond the classic split between capitalism and socialism, between big government and big business, and building up the third sector—the civil society of nonprofit and community service groups. Gay people get very excited by new ideas about the future."

The either/or model is so ingrained as to be considered normal. But new challenges in this postmodern world, with its information and technological proliferation, rapidly changing economic realities, and even shifts in contemporary scientific thinking—where physics is increasingly metaphysical in nature—open new doorways. Isn't it possible that the very qualities that have marginalized us, such as bending gender roles, are now needed to help pioneer paths into new territories? We appear to be experts at exploding old paradigms, questioning the status quo, and coming up with some new models, just from our daily life experience. It's a good bet these attributes will be put in service of the wider world over the coming years.

6. WHAT GAY MEN
AND LESBIANS CAN TEACH AMERICA:
SPIRITUALITY IS DIVERSE, TOO

Today's headlines proclaim a resurgence of interest in spirituality and religion: baby boomers are flocking back to churches they haven't attended in decades. In 1995, Black Muslim leader Louis Farrakhan drew a million African-American men to Washington for a rally that was, by all accounts, essentially an experience of spiritual empowerment. This year, a million different men will attend conservative Christian rallies produced by the Promise Keepers in football stadiums across America. Thousands of folks flock to New Age conferences and human-potential seminars. Millions regularly utilize the spiritual program of Twelve-Step and other self-help groups. The vast majority of Americans believe that angels visit them.

God is certainly not dead in these tough times, but the relationship of all this spiritual activity and searching to public life and democratic values is unclear. The deep desire for a more explicitly spiritual sensibility and public morality that can unite Americans while coexisting with the separated church and state seems to be growing in these times. So far the right's narrow Christian-theocratic dogma is the loudest single voice in the discussion. But alternative, progressive ideas are beginning to emerge—for example, *Tikkun* magazine founder Rabbi Michael Lerner's "politics of meaning"— that reaffirm the human need for linking politics with faith without the exclusionary bias of the radical Christian right. For this new national conversation to work with, and not against, America's highest ideals, the underlying spirit and vision must be fully democratic and pluralist, able to encompass faiths of all kinds.

The radical right demonizes gay men and lesbians; it brands us immoral. But the families we have invented and the community we have created—as well as the ethic of care we express through them— belie this bigoted, old-fashioned view of us. As the debate about spiritual and moral values heats up over the coming years, there is no doubt in my mind that gay men and lesbians will be vocal participants and leaders in it. Spirituality is experiencing an AIDS-powered surge throughout the lesbian and gay community, with an even greater intensity than in the rest of the country.

In our own often unorthodox ways we have always been deeply spiritual people. Certainly our forebears were. History is replete with spiritual precursors who, if not always explicitly homosexual, exploded culturally assigned gender roles. In many traditional Native American cultures, "two-spirited ones" (known later by the French term "berdaches") were cross-dressing, often magical persons of both genders who frequently became medicine people and were considered mediators between women and men. In medieval Europe, witches—nontraditional women, at least a few of whom were probably lesbians—were remnant practitioners of pagan religions, folk healers, and often freelance traveling peasant organizers. They were persecuted for their defiance of patriarchal Christian religion and of the male medical establishment's theft of the healing arts from women. Over the centuries, monasteries and convents were clandestine centers of homosexual desire, activity, and culture, despite denial and repression by the Catholic Church.

In contemporary gay and lesbian life, even the act of coming out is identified by some as inherently spiritual. Gay writer Mark Thompson calls it a fundamental "death-rebirth spiritual experience." People often experience their "coming-out click" as a spiritual epiphany that unites them not only with their own true sexual and affectional nature, but with a unifying and harmonious force greater than themselves. One lesbian said to me: "For me, coming out was not only about coming to terms with my sexuality. In connecting with my physical sexuality, I found I also experienced a surge of spirituality, a belief in a Higher Power for the first time. There's God in lesbian sex—I swear it!" A gay Latino man told me: "Coming out and coming into gay pride meant releasing the shame about homosexuality I'd been raised with as a Catholic. I also reconnected with God. He had been dull and distant and dead for me since childhood, but He came alive for me for the first time when I came out to myself." The coming-out process can be very like a shamanic journey of soul retrieval—the reconnection of a divided and lost soul or spirit with the body after a bitter and traumatic separation caused by the force of homophobia. My own final "coming-out click" at age twenty-two felt like a radical reintegration with something I'd been cruelly separated from, as if I'd recovered the spirit of my childhood dyke-self stifled by years of socialization.

The logical trend for gay people has been toward forced separation from traditional organized religion. Institutional homophobia —the religious proscriptions against homosexuality that are found in so many organized religions—drove many gays and lesbians away from traditional religions for years. In fact, a fierce split between political activism and spirituality developed in the early 1970s and has only very recently begun to heal. For the most part in those early years, gay political activists' faith was in liberation, not in God. With the fervor of religious zealots, gay liberationists and lesbian-feminists built 1970s community and organized politically while either adamantly rejecting the spiritual realm or relegating it to the quiet periphery of our political lives. I remember being in a "politics and spirituality" group in San Francisco in 1979 and 1980. We studied and explored a variety of religious and spiritual practices and utilized guided visualization and deep meditation to explore and improve electoral and grassroots political organizing strategies and counter activist problems like burnout. Heretical in those politically charged and definitely secular years, we joked about being outcasts among the outcasts and about trying to bridge the gap between the "heavy revvies" (revolutionary politicos who damned spirituality as an opiate of the people) and the "bliss bunnies" (who searched within themselves and eschewed political activism). We intuitively knew that synthesis between politics and spirituality was possible but there was no widespread discourse on the issue in those days.

In fact, gay activism held spirituality in a closet for the better part of the past twenty-five years. Gay religious pioneers like the Reverend Troy Perry have repeatedly said that it was easier to come out of the closet as a gay person than to come out as a Christian in the sharply biased antireligious culture of modern gay activism. Reverend Perry, a former Pentecostal evangelical minister, committed an act of great courage in defying both mainstream Christianity and the secular gay community and founding the primarily gay and lesbian Metropolitan Community Church in 1968. MCC further defied heterosexual norms not only by ordaining women ministers but by replacing the patriarchal Christian liturgy with nonsexist language. MCC saw its early churches torched and its leaders harassed, but it has had its sweet revenge: there are now over 325 churches with 50,000 members in nineteen countries, and the church is growing at a 10 percent annual rate. Congregations are springing up monthly in places like Eureka Springs, Arkansas, and Paducah, Kentucky. With 3000 members, MCC's Dallas, Texas, congregation is one of America's largest of any denomination. It is expanding so rapidly that it has already outgrown a recently built 34,000-square-foot church. MCC has hired world-renowned architect Philip Johnson to design a new, $15-million Cathedral of Hope that will seat 3,000 people and serve as a major religious center for gay and lesbian Christians from around the world.

In addition to MCC, there are active gay and lesbian groups within every major religion in this country. Roman Catholic priests defy their church by celebrating Communion with gay and lesbian Catholic members of Dignity. There are Buddhist and Hindu groups. There are Evangelicals Concerned, Integrity (Episcopalians), Lutherans Concerned, Presbyterians for Lesbian and Gay Concerns, Affirmation (Mormon), and Axios (Orthodox Eastern Christians). There is the international World Congress of Gay and Lesbian Jewish Organizations. Within Judaism, widespread organizing even includes loose affiliations of gay men in the Orthodox world. In Conservative Judaism, individual synagogues invite groups such as Response that promote gay-straight dialogue and tolerance within congregations. There are over thirty-five lesbian and gay groups within the Reform branch of Judaism; nearly twenty have their own synagogue or a sizable congregation in cities such as Pittsburgh, Seattle, Atlanta, and Phoenix.

We've been unbound from convention. Remember, pride *was* one of the seven deadly sins, and we've reconstituted it into the very foundation of our freedom movement. Our spiritual work is not limited to organized religion. Less orthodox forms of spiritual expression have emerged at the margins of our communities over the past two and a half decades. With feminism came a rebirth of nature-worshipping "Wiccan" neo-pagan faiths practiced in growing numbers by lesbians. One lesbian organizer tells the story of the opening of the new lesbian women's center in her town: "I don't know who they were or where they came from, but the morning we opened the center, a group of seven self-identified lesbian witches showed up to purify our offices. It was really quite wonderful. They swirled through our office space, saying blessings and smudging the place, cleansing away the old energies by burning sage and other herbs. Then, a half hour later, they were gone. We never saw them again, but even the skeptics had to admit that the space definitely felt lighter, brighter, and warmer."

The gay men's version of neo-pagan rites include woodsy gatherings of Radical Faeries, who celebrate the relationship between spirituality and sexuality.

We are, of course, not alone in searching for new ways to seek and celebrate the sacred. Many Americans are searching along with us. There has been a recent proliferation of new, often experimental forms of spiritual practice and ritual such as shamanic healing journeys; organized vision quests; drumming, meditation, and chanting circles; and more. Faiths coexist as well. I have a Catholic lay nun friend who regularly visits an ashram. I know several religious Jewish women who integrate elements of earth-worshipping pagan rituals into their spiritual practice. I recently served on a panel at a Summit on Ethics and Meaning organized by *Tikkun*. Discussing "how reality would be deepened with a politics that features a soul-sensitive understanding of the world" were New Age guru Marianne

Williamson, African-American Christian intellectual Cornel West, psychoanalyst Michael Bader, feminist writer Naomi Wolf, and Christian progressive thinker Jim Wallis, along with myself and others. Now there's a gang who had never been in one place at one time before! Not only was the mix of folks historic, but it was no coincidence that a lesbian was at that table. This evolving conversation on spirituality and politics will feature more and more of us as it unfolds in the future—I guarantee it.

Of course, there are plenty of gays and lesbians who don't favor the term "spirituality" and don't identify as religious, but whose own lives display highly ethical qualities of caring, compassion, and community concern. One Latina woman said to me, "I'll never identify as spiritual after what I've seen done to people in the name of religion. My faith is in freedom. My belief is in the human drive to strive for justice. That is the powerful driving force in my life."

Current gay and lesbian spirituality is often scorched by the ever-present reality of AIDS and the inevitable collective attempt to find meaning in seemingly meaningless, daily, and overwhelming death. AIDS has deepened the significance of the gay community's collective spiritual awakening. This does not seem like a "phase," a trivial or short-term phenomenon. The quest for spirit is broadening every day. With the inherently politicizing influence of feminism and of AIDS activism, the new queer spirituality has a decidedly social-change bent.

New approaches are marked by innovativeness and creativity, rather than rigid prescriptions. Developing personal relationships with our God rules the day. AIDS activist Bob Hattoy told me, "I had a very New Age-y gay AIDS doc. When he told me a few years ago I had lymphoma, he looked me right in the eyes and said, 'There's nothing you can do about this. You must accept this and seek out the Light. You must move toward the Light.' I said, 'Screw you and your Light! I'm going to seek a new doctor, and then I'm fighting back.' You see, I'm very spiritual but I envision my Higher Power to be like Fran Lebowitz in ACT UP drag—my angel has a vicious wit and fights back."

Many activists, in fact, described as intensely spiritual the sense of purpose and solidarity they experienced at die-ins and other direct action and civil disobedience protests engaged in by ACT UP in its heyday. Funerals and memorial services mingle religious rites and political activism. The AIDS quilt is a contemporary religious icon. It is also a mystical, passionate calling for volunteers in chapters all across the country who organize quilt-making in local communities and bring pieces of the quilt to over a thousand towns every year. The ancient ritual of calling out names of the dead has become commonplace at AIDS conferences and more and more lesbian and gay events. One AIDS educator, who opens every meeting with a moment of silence followed by a group "calling out of names" terms the ritual an "act of resistance." For me, our refusal to forget is a uniting moral force that fuels our collective political determination.

In all its glorious diversity, spiritual practice is burgeoning. Every gay and lesbian religious group is growing in members, and new groups are sprouting. A few years ago, an African-American former MCC minister, the Reverend Carl Bean, formed the Unity Fellowship Church in order to serve the increasingly visible black gay and lesbian community. Services, rooted in black traditional worship, are energetic, inspiring, musical. UFC churches have grown up in ten cities, and more are on the way.

Spirituality is pluriform.

For two decades or more, Twelve-Step programs based on the spiritual model of Alcoholics Anonymous have played a life-saving and life-changing role in the lives of a significant number of lesbians and gay men. Although nobody knows for sure how many are involved, there are certainly thousands who participate regularly. Any major city features upwards of a hundred different weekly meetings targeting the gay community. Says Marie: "I got sober sixteen years ago. For years my Higher Power was my lesbian 'home meeting' of my Twelve-Step group. The program got me clean, and then it gave me spirituality. I would have called you crazy if you had told me when I was twenty that down the line I would pray every night and every morning, make a 'list of gratitudes' at the end of almost every day, and apologize and 'make amends' to those I've harmed. I'm a successful businesswoman with a lover, a beloved partner of over ten years, and I wouldn't have any of it without the spiritual program of the Twelve Steps that keeps me sober and in touch with my Higher Power."

The California AIDS Ride, a 400-mile, thousand-rider bicycle trip from San Francisco to Los Angeles to raise funds for the L.A. Center and the San Francisco AIDS Foundation, is described by many participants as a mystical experience. In 1994, the first year of the ride, many pinned a picture of one or more "angels" to their shirts. On a nightly basis, people talked openly of communicating with their "angels"—the spirits of those dead from AIDS—during their long, solitary days of riding. As Alan, an L.A. newspaper editor, put it: "I signed up for a physical experience and ended up having a magical and mystical one that transformed my life. I proved I could succeed at an intensely rigorous physical challenge, and at the same time I communed with my friends who had died of AIDS. It was partly a way to grieve, partly to remember. I felt I was changing and challenging myself in their names, infused with their energies. It was really quite extraordinary. The ride knitted together a beautiful community and gave me a sense of awe I've never had."

"After we lost our second friend to breast cancer the same year we lost our fourth friend to AIDS, we went through a kind of existential crisis and decided we needed a directly spiritual aspect in our lives," says Anne of her and her lover Carrie's decision to join their local Episcopal church. She says nearly half the congregation is gay or lesbian, and all are fully welcome at the church. "It's a grounding and comforting thing," adds Carrie. "I hadn't been to church in thirty years, but with all the death and dying, we needed to heal our hearts and lives. Having a spiritual awakening has enlivened us enormously—and we find more and more of our friends are going through the same thing. There's a mass migration going on—out of the closets and back to church."

A new Jewish congregant of a gay temple told me that until last year she hadn't been to services since childhood. "I decided to go to Yom Kippur services at the last minute. There were over five hundred people there, and it was amazing. It turned into a communal cathartic ritual of grieving. An AIDS quilt panel was there. The rabbi talked openly about her own grief about her father's death, as well as so much AIDS grief. We all wept and wept. I had no idea how much I needed to be with other people and discharge some of that infinite well of grieving inside. I signed up as a member right afterward, and worship has really added richness to my life."

There are now twenty-nine annual gay rodeos in the United States and Canada, a whole circuit involving hundreds of lesbian and gay cowboys. Every one begins with a procession led by a riderless horse, representing those dead of AIDS.

Shana was a Seventh-Day Adventist minister who left the church, and her husband, when she found feminism and fell in love with a woman. She now teaches "generic spiritual principles from a feminist perspective" to women in group and individual sessions, combining feminist therapy with a variety of New Age and eastern religious forms. She sees it as a way to combine feminist empowerment of women while increasing their appreciation of the sacred in their lives.

Tim Sweeney recalls his family's private ceremony to honor his brother Mark, who died of AIDS in 1994. The Sweeney clan gathered together near their mountain cabin in East Rosebud Lake, Montana, to scatter Mark's ashes and hold a "family healing circle." "Remember, this is my big, conservative, Irish, very Catholic family—eight kids and Hugh and Mary. This ceremony for Mark bonded us in a startling and liberating way. At first, everyone fanned out to remember Mark in her or his own way—my mother prayed in a more traditionally Catholic way; my lesbian sister went off in the woods to do her more Zen-and-nature-based ritual. Then everyone convened for the circle. At first it was awkward, we wanted so much to cover up the grieving—we're a loud family that talks to push away our feelings. But the awkwardness just melted away as we stood there together in that circle, next to the water, feeling the sun, listening to the wind, letting the moment just be. Then we began to share our Mark stories, crying and laughing and talking together in a whole new way. My experience with AIDS—brought home to me powerfully with my own brother's death and my own family—is, gay and lesbian liberation has got to include faith and family or it won't have much staying power. We can't run away from faith, but we just have to reinterpret it so it fits our belief system and includes everybody. If my family could come together the way we did, anything is possible."

An emotional-support group for gay and bisexual PWAs in St. Louis has grown more and more spiritual in content and format over the years. "It's been a natural progression, frankly, as people have died, and we've had to go deeper to search for the meaning of all this," says Lonnie, who has been living with HIV and AIDS for over ten years. "We used to be more of an informal drop-in rap group. Now, we pray together, meditate together, bring in healers and spiritual teachers to work with us. It's been an evolution toward more and more honest discussion of God, life after death, and how to make our lives more meaningful."

There are a host of new groups exploring the connection between the erotic and the spiritual, reinforcing gay and lesbian pride in sexuality. Some teach adaptive Tantric breathing and meditative methods to enhance physical pleasure and integrate spiritual energies into sex. Organized religions have always attempted to control the powerful life-affirming drives of sexuality, largely by repressing them; we are counteracting by exploring some creative, sex-positive new spiritual paths.

———

Gay and lesbian spirituality, in all its forms, refuses to be confined in the repressive vehicles of old-style religion. Less bound by convention, or righteously rebellious against its strictures, gay men and lesbians are nevertheless affirming the human need for awe, for the sacred, in the midst of this alienated, atomized modern existence. At the same time, we are deeply engaged in a passionate and creative conversation about spirituality's relation to political and social vision that will add to a broader, liberating national dialogue as it develops over the coming years.

Here are some general principles that I believe align with a democratic and pluralist vision of spirituality true to America's finest soul. Many of us affirm a transcendent life force (or Higher Power or God or Goddess) greater than each of us. For some, it may take a traditional patriarchal form. For most, it does not. It is not "some storage-battery far away in the sky," as one gay churchgoer put it. Rather, most gay men and lesbians of all faiths and spiritual practices affirm a divine force that is omnipresent, that is personal and accessible to every human, immanent as well as transcendent. In addition, this sacred force does not deny the body but rather affirms sexuality and sexual diversity. It is more likely to be able to be both androgynous or both feminine and masculine in nature. A friend prays nightly to "Mother/Father God."

Within the gay and lesbian world, there is also a burgeoning interfaith movement. We see growing collaboration and dialogue across religious traditions that once again demonstrates the queer affinity for collaboration, community-building, and connectedness across difference. As one lesbian put it, "We take that spiritual link and vibrate it even higher." For example, the predominantly gay Spiritual Advisory Committee to a major urban AIDS organization includes a Catholic nun and a Franciscan monk, two rabbis (one lesbian, one straight), a Buddhist, two MCC ministers, an Episcopal priest, and a Wiccan priestess. This diverse clergy provides spiritual counseling and on-site chaplaincy for people living with AIDS.

In opening up new spiritual possibilities and practices and insisting on participating openly in every existing religious group, lesbians and gay men are engaged—whether consciously or not—in a broad-based and growing cutting-edge movement in this country. From this movement will be gleaned, I believe, key messages—unifying alternatives to the repressive radical right—to promote greater democracy and tolerance and to help heal America. As Rabbi Denise Eger of Kol Ami congregation says: "We can't achieve political healing of this wounded America without integrating spirituality into our social vision. Political vision needs the moral force of faith behind it. Ethics and morals flow from faith. We are going to have to craft some kind of communal agreement, not on *what* we believe, but *that* we believe, in order to repair this broken country."

7. OTHER GIFTS LESBIANS AND GAY MEN BRING HOME TO AMERICA

"Dancing on the Cusp of Yin/Yang": Beyond the Male/Female Split

A split between male and female gender roles is deeply embedded in American culture. As feminists and psychologists have pointed out for many years, rigid and prescriptive gender roles are damaging, particularly to women. The strict male/female split denies the truth that everyone has both masculine and feminine traits. Human beings are complex.

In many ways, society uses homophobia to maintain rigid sex-role stereotypes. Homophobia is sexism's best weapon for maintaining a strict male/female split: if society punishes men for feminine traits and women for masculine traits, then it reinforces gender inequality. A strong woman is automatically accused of being a dyke. A nonmacho man must be gay.

Despite suffering homophobic taunts and harassment, gay men and lesbians upend this attempt at rigid societal consensus on gender roles. As one student in a class I taught put it: "As a lesbian, I feel I'm dancing on the cusp of yin and yang all the time. Sometimes I feel feminine, and sometimes I feel more masculine. It's walking at the edge between gender roles that makes my life interesting."

We defy gender roles and stereotypes, as well as create some new integrative icons. Sexism has dictated straight men's deep dislike and fear of nonfeminine women. "Butchphobia" is rampant, so that, for example, positive portrayals of butch women (whether gay or straight) have been absent from television and film, except in an occasional horror or cult film (such as Sigourney Weaver's *Alien* movies). But the butch woman, the Amazon warrior, in our parlance the dyke, is alive and well in day-to-day life in the gay community. She is a powerful symbol of a woman freed from the constraints of socially imposed feminine behavior. I can't wait until the strong dyke figure populates TV and film to the same extent she exists in real life.

Gender-bending and gender-blending are the everyday stuff of gay and lesbian life. On a regular basis, we "mix it all up." Take Lawrence and Andrew, and Trisha and Kate.

————

Lawrence and Andrew appear to be an archetypal "assimilated" Republican suburban gay male couple. They pride themselves on their "normal, conservative, next-door-neighbor style." They consider themselves married, attend the local Presbyterian church on Sundays, and could pass for straight at their jobs as a realtor and a legal secretary. They are politically moderate, give money to AIDS charities, and attend the local annual black-tie gay gala, but they strongly dislike "in your face" gay activism. After attending their first national gay event, the April 1993 March on Washington, they both came out at work and now bring each other to their respective workplace holiday parties.

But as they came out more and more to family and friends at work, they encountered another unexpected closet. In the privacy of their own gay life and home, they are not in fact exactly what they project to straight acquaintances: they both occasionally like to dress up and visit local leather bars on the weekend. They also spend hours putting on drag makeup and women's clothes on Halloween, and both love to camp it up in the kitchen nightly, dressed in aprons, dancing around and singing along with show tunes while they cook. For a few years, their own internalized homophobia inhibited them from showing their real selves to straight neighbors and friends, in the interest of "breaking down stereotypes we thought were harmful." One day, when a straight neighbor couple stopped by the back door unannounced and caught them in their frilly aprons singing "I Enjoy Being a Girl" to each other, things changed. Although a bit embarrassed that they had clearly interrupted a normally private moment, their neighbors were utterly delighted with this new side of Lawrence and Andrew. Far from promoting a negative stereotype, the men's behavior was clearly so natural to them, and they were having so much fun, it brought them closer to their neighbors. From then on, Andrew and Lawrence began to loosen up, to camp it up more often, to hide their gender-bending less and less. "We even played fairies at our neighbors' daughter's birthday party and sprinkled fairy dust on everyone—it was natural childlike campy play for us—and they loved it. We even got the parents loosened up—they were laughing like kids."

Trisha and Kate look like a clearly defined "butch-femme" couple, and they happily identify as such. Kate drives a UPS truck and is studying at night for a master's degree in geology, a lifelong dream. Trisha, the femme, is a social worker who works with abused children. They live in a house in suburban Detroit. But behind the façade of apparently recognizable gender roles is a more complicated reality: Trisha is a first-rate carpenter and handyperson who wields a mean Skil saw, can build or fix anything, and regularly repairs their cars. With a twinkle in her eye, she self-identifies as a "macha femme." Kate loves decorating the house, does most of the cooking, and knits in the evenings as a hobby. Her lover calls her "the sweetest soft-butch on the planet." "We love it when straight people get to know us a little bit. We just blow their minds—they decide who we are by Trisha's clothes and makeup, and my short hair and more butch job. But we mix it all up, and they find us endlessly fascinating. They do get a bit confused—straight people try too hard to pigeonhole everyone. We think we're educational for them."

As gay men and lesbians come out more and more, the complex truth of our lives does too. Even the most conservative gay men and lesbians don't live exactly the way straight people do. Yes, we have lots more in common with straight folk than they—or we—ever thought in the past. But our differences are wonderful too. In daily life, we model immense creativity and variety in human expression and relationships. We bridge or transgress assumed gender roles in myriad ways: "Dykes on Bikes," a contingent of leather-clad lesbians on motorcycles, is a well-known and beloved fixture in major urban Gay Pride parades. In San Francisco, the Sisters of Perpetual Indulgence, who campily spoof nun drag, have gained notoriety. Every town, big and small, has its own queer gender-blending cultural examples, maybe hidden just under the surface. I was recently presented with a gorgeous black-and-red quilted comforter sewn for me by the Salt Lake City Stitch-and-Bitch Club. They are a gay rodeo cowboys' HIV-positive social circle that gathers together to make quilts in traditional Mormon styles. I kid you not.

Transgendered persons are also increasingly visible and vocal within the gay—and nongay—worlds and, finally, bisexuals are finding and exercising their own voices, adding to the rich multicultural mix. "We trannies and bis are here to stay. Get used to it, girls!" says Connie Norman at every opportunity, laughing.

As straight people get to know us and our relationships, they are unexpectedly exposed to healthy models of intimate relationships. Often, our relationships are based on a peer-based model of egalitarian partnership. Roles are more flexible and likely to be interchangeable; there is more reciprocity and less power difference within our personal relationships. As we emerge from the shadows and interact with nongay people more and more, we may increasingly provide positive role models for them as well as ourselves.

———

Lesbian professor and psychologist Linda Garnets, who has been with her life partner, Barrie Levy, for over fifteen years, told me:

"My stepdaughter—my lover's daughter from her former marriage—was married recently. She told me that she had sought out, and finally found, a relationship with a man that was like her mother's and mine. I had tears in my eyes as she told us she wanted 'the same kind of deep equality, reciprocity, and mutual friendship' that she had observed between my life partner and me. She wished to avoid the power inequity and role restrictions that she observed in many heterosexual relationships. I'll tell you, I was surprised—and very proud—that we were a model of a healthy, happy relationship for her."

———

Celebrating Sexuality

We live in a very puritanical culture, extremely uncomfortable with the entire issue of sex and sexuality. Despite AIDS and marginalization, despite the repression of women's sexuality that affects lesbians, gay people have steadily evolved a culture far more comfortable with sexuality, more respectful of it, and less fearful of it. Our very identities live in our bodies. Our sexual desire, along with our affectional orientation or preference, defines who we are. As a consequence, we explore or examine our sexual natures more openly than most heterosexual people. Our community norms are more accepting of sexual openness, experimentation, and playfulness. We are, quite simply, just not as terrified of the libido as so many straight people seem to be. Our basic struggle has been about overcoming shame about our bodies and our desires, and freeing our erotic energies, something that would considerably liberate the larger society as well. As feminism has established, the ability to separate procreation from sexuality is a positive and freeing development in human evolution for over half of the world's population. Gay men and lesbians help continue this evolution.

Fear of anything is restrictive. Fear of something as basic as our sexual natures is powerfully restrictive. But the issue of sexuality is no longer simply a quality-of-life issue; it's become a matter of life and death. Current right-wing attacks on sex education in the schools are not abstract ideological debate. They endanger the lives of young people—both gay and bisexual young people, who deserve to learn about homosexuality without shame or denial, and straight kids, as well as those who are still sorting it out. Access to the truth about sexuality and its variety, as well as open-minded, full discussion about sexual responsibility, saves lives and much pain. The epidemic of teen pregnancy and sexually transmitted diseases will not stop unless America overcomes its absurd phobia about sex. In addition, growing teen violence, date rape, and sexual harassment require open discussion about dating, power and gender issues, and self-esteem, as well as sexuality. The blood of too many youths infected with HIV is already on the hands of those who moralistically preach heterosexual supremacy and abstinence to the most sexually active group of people in this society. It's murderous hypocrisy. When will America wake up?

———————

Gary, who works with youth in Pittsburgh, is adamant about the need for comprehensive sex and AIDS education in the schools: "By the time these kids graduate from high school, sixty percent have had sexual intercourse. One study, however, showed that only thirty percent of their parents thought their kid might have had intercourse. 'Not *my* kid,' they say. But those kids aren't abstaining. In that gap between reality and parents' hopeful delusion lies a big, fat problem. It's called denial, and, with AIDS, that denial could mean death."

A high school principal told me recently, "I've noticed that the gay and lesbian teachers—mostly still closeted, I'm afraid—tend to be able to teach sex education and AIDS education with real insight, and a light touch. It's obvious they care deeply about the subjects and are less uptight."

One heterosexual labor lawyer friend told me: "As my wife and I have more openly gay friends, we've found our own conversations about sex to be more open. Gay people model frank sex talk. There should be more of it around."

We're Here; We're Queer; We're Funny—Get Used to It!

California Assemblymember Sheila Kuehl tells this story:

"One afternoon during the very first week I was up in Sacramento, I was sitting in my office when a rather large shadow suddenly darkened my desk. I looked up, and there was the big-old-boy conservative Republican leader, standing in my doorway with a slightly quizzical look on his face. 'Um, Kuehl, I got a question for you,' he said. 'If you're gay, how come all my guys like you so much?' Without skipping a beat, I said: 'Well, Jim, that's what discrimination is for—it demonizes the truly fabulous!' I must say I still grin, two years later, when I remember how speechless that guy was. If you ask me, our humor gives us the advantage every time!"

In the face of life's bleakest pain, gay men and lesbians—particularly gay men—never, ever lose our sense of humor. Perhaps it is indelibly emblazoned somewhere on our collective queer DNA.

We turn anything into a party. We have even learned to laugh out loud in the face of death. When his lover, Philip, died of AIDS, Michael put his cremated ashes into Baggies and gave them out to friends to spread in their rose garden. "We called them party favors. I know it's macabre, but what the hell else is there left but humor about this goddamn disease? Philip was roaring with laughter from above, I just know it." The satirical San Francisco–based *Diseased Pariah News* takes AIDS-inspired gallows humor to its ultimate extreme, recently running this blurb: "First there was AIDS Barbie with her new Malibu Dream Hospice. Now all AIDS Barbie needs to finish life's long voyage is Ken. . . . Introducing KS Ken, with press-on KS lesions and stunning, lifelike needle tracks."

Humor and camp are staples of gay art and literature and drama, and daily life. One of my favorite examples of our humorous sensibility is how we've lightened and brightened up the world of street-demonstration chants. When we demonstrated and protested in the sixties and seventies our chants were straight(!)forward and of tedious meter: "One, two, three, four, we don't want your fucking war" was one particularly popular—and eloquent—example from the anti–Vietnam War movement. Gay people, however, in our irreverence and disdain for the mundane, have changed the meter and added in some campy intonation: "We're here; we're queer; we're fabulous! Get used to it!" was the chant of choice of the late 1980s—just as militant, but far more creative. Often performed with a fairy jump or mock cheerleader motion, it tweaks a laugh out of you while being in-your-face. We even satirize the traditional chant, not to mention people's worst homophobic fears, with "Two, four, six, eight, how do you know your kid is straight?"

When demonstrators over the past decade have faced police wearing the inevitable rubber gloves—worn because of AIDS-phobia and homophobia—our uniquely gay response has been, "The gloves don't match the shoes; the gloves don't match the shoes"—sung in the cadence of a child's slightly nasty teasing chant. I've even seen grim-looking police crack up at that one.

EPILOGUE

In these troubled, tumultuous times, the world badly needs us. America could do well to learn from our creativity, our inclusive approach to problem-solving, our skills in building unity out of diversity and in forging alliances and political coalitions. Our families of choice are vibrant, loving examples of how private life is being remade in this complex world in wonderfully democratic ways. Our community ethic of caring is an outstanding model of the kind of values shift that will be necessary to feed America's hungry heart. Our voices will not be ignored in the search for moral and ethical meaning and for definitions of spirituality that will best do justice to this great multicultural and multireligious country. Our passionate spirit enlivens life and fights for social justice. Our gender-bending liberates new possibilities for human wholeness.

Along with our creativity, our leadership in coalition-building and creating community, America's newest minority sings out an important message: if we have found and maintained hope, you can. We know—and you can too—that in the face of pain and horror, there can always be joy.

A few years ago, I had an extraordinary personal experience. I was honored as "Woman of the Year" in the annual Lesbian and Gay Pride Parade in Los Angeles. Ordinarily I would march with one or another contingent, dancing or maybe throwing condoms into the crowd, just one celebrant among the several hundred thousand enjoying the event. This particular year, however, my role as honoree forced me to be on the receiving end of the experience, to observe and soak up the crowd's energy. As a result, I had a totally different experience.

I was seated on the back of an open convertible (a fabulously tacky gold '57 Cadillac), moving slowly along the several-mile-long parade route. Block after block was lined with lesbians in pairs and groups, gay men, their friends and family, shimmering and plumed drag artists, tourists perched on roofs and balconies, parents and kids—a colorful, happy host of watchers who came out with picnics and coolers to view the festive scene. The front row along much of the line of parade was wheelchairs, primarily for persons with AIDS.

I watched—and felt—wave after wave of exuberance, joyful huzzahing, fiercely shouted pride, as I passed each section of the crowd. It was amazing. Gay people—so deeply hated by so many—themselves radiated nothing but love. Tens of thousands of people, many of them doubtless struggling with pain and grief and even despair, reveled in an almost ecstatic ebullience. A surging swell of happiness poured out of the crowd—a powerful, palpable, uplifting feeling of hopefulness. People danced and shouted and jumped and laughed and chanted and waved and blew kisses and sang. An irresistible life force soared skyward from the roaring crowd.

I remember one person in particular. He was young, an Asian man sitting in a wheelchair at a street corner. His face was sad, skinny, tightened in pain. I saw him grimace as a racking cough overtook his frail body for a few moments. Then, at the instant our contingent approached him, a huge, broad, beautiful grin broke out on his face and wreathed it in radiance.

There it is, I thought, as my eyes met his for a flicker of an instant; there's the force that will win in the end: *joy*. Irrepressible, shining joy. Joy in the face of it all, a joy that each of us recognizes and shares as we come home at last.

America, we're coming home.